Enjoy the Edge

Wayne Burke

WIDE-ANGLE VISION

Beat your competition

by focusing on fringe competitors,

lost customers, and rogue employees

WAYNE C. BURKAN

John Wiley & Sons, Inc.

New York • Chichester • Brisbane • Toronto • Singapore

To Martha, who every day helps me to strive to my potential, and to my children, Sharon and Jonathan, whose exciting lives are all potential.

Copyright © 1996 by Wayne Burkan
Published by John Wiley & Sons, Inc.

Library of Congress Cataloging-in-Publication Data

Burkan, Wayne C.
    Wide-angle vision : beat your competition by focusing on fringe
  competitors, lost customers, and rogue employees / Wayne Burkan.
      p.   cm.
    Includes bibliographical references.
    ISBN 0-471-13416-3 (cloth : alk. paper)
    1. Consumer satisfaction. 2. Competition. 3. Employee selection.
  I. Title.
  HF5415.335.B87   1996
  658.8—dc20
                                      96-10239

Foreword

I have known Wayne Burkan for almost ten years. We met on the West Coast when I was doing a speech for a meeting he had organized. The next time we got together, he made me a proposition: If I ever needed help in my business, he would be very interested in supplying it.

By that time my consulting work had grown so fast that I spent more time turning down requests than accepting them, so I took Wayne seriously. I gave him a list of two dozen books and told him to call me when he had finished them. Two months later, he called.

Since that time Wayne has become a colleague, a friend, and an intellectual companion. He and I have talked many hours about the many implications of Thomas Kuhn's concept of the paradigm shift. Kuhn brought the idea to science. I brought the idea to the business company.

Now it is Wayne's turn to bring something to the party. This book, *Wide-Angle Vision*, does that. He has taken the concept of the outsider and focused intensely on all that means for finding the future. What I like best about the book is the large number of examples from which you, the reader, can draw your own conclusions. Again and again, I find myself nodding my head as I read Wayne's work. This is useful. This is significant. From Wayne's recommendations you can take action to improve your future.

In particular, I think Wayne has homed in on an underutilized resource that is available to all of us. But he is right. We ignore those at the margin rather than look at them as bringing unusual and oftentimes powerful new perceptions of our world as it unfolds in theirs.

Wayne has described the details of how to turn what most organizations treat as a liability into a profound and ongoing asset. That is worth a lot in these turbulent times.

I'm glad Wayne wrote this book. It adds significant value to the understanding of paradigm change and how to deal with it. I'm glad you are taking the time to read it.

Joel A. Barker
Author of *Future Edge* and
Paradigm: The Business of Discovering the Future

Acknowledgments

The success of this book is the result of many people's efforts. Any failings are my sole responsibility.

I would like to thank Joel Barker for his years of support, encouragement, and friendship. Joel is the one person to whom this book owes the single most important intellectual debt. He never once complained when our work together forced him to miss a day of golf and, more amazing still, never complained when he was forced to play a round of golf with me. It may not have always been easy, but I'd like to think it was always fun.

My brother Barry was invaluable in his editorial input on this book. Under incredible pressure he helped transform my rantings into comprehensible form and pushed me to dig deeper for what he suspected was there all along.

Finally, I would like to thank Ruth Mills, my editor at John Wiley & Sons, for her faith, understanding, and support.

Contents

1

Diamonds Beneath Your Feet

A powerful force is looming before you. This force has built entire industries and then torn them down again. Companies such as Schwinn and Hayes Microcomputer Products have fallen prey to its influence. It has hobbled such giants as IBM and Boeing. It has helped spawn an international monetary crisis and is the primary reason that companies' most promising business plans go awry. This force is called the *edge*.

Enormous sums of money are invested in a laudable attempt to reduce cycle time, improve quality, reengineer, streamline production, and optimize services. Like sand running through a sieve, much of this money and energy is simply wasted, showing few tangible results. This waste is due to companies' inability to develop wide-angle vision and tap into one of their most valuable resources: the power of the *edge*.

For more than a decade I have worked with more than 1,000 organizations frustrated by their inability to change. Most of these firms were staffed by intelligent and motivated people and were led by insightful executives determined to see that change occur. These companies were less challenged by what they failed to do than by what they failed to see. Like people who lack peripheral vision, the events that matched their line of sight were clear and well understood, while those at the margins were fuzzy if visible at all.

The cure for this blindness is found in wide-angle vision. The ideas found in this book have evolved by practicing my company's (Alternative Visions, Inc.) mission: "Helping organizations discover today's options so they may forge a more powerful tomorrow." For example, if you are frustrated by your inability to dramatically improve customer service, this does not mean that you lack options . . . there are always options. What you may lack is the ability to see those options beyond your peripheral limitations. This dark and shadowy area that borders your visible world is what I call the *edge*.

The *edge* consists of people who are extremely dissatisfied with today's solutions. They firmly reject the popular wisdom for a very practical reason: It does not work for them. The *edge* reveals a unique perspective about our most cherished practices. Not only does it highlight the hidden challenges we face, it also shows how to deal with these challenges in a way that leaves us stronger than ever. Further, because people on the *edge* reject the status quo, they are the first to point out the most exciting opportunities for growth.

People and organizations on the *edge* of your business have enormous impact on your ability to survive. If corporate vision is centered only around a mainstream view of the world, however, the customers, employees, and competitors on the *edge* of our attention remain invisible. The solutions sought by corporations are within their reach but beyond their grasp.

In the early 1980s, people who were interested in personal computing were relegated to the "lunatic fringe." They were the impossible customers, the insignificant competitors, and the troublemaking employees. In short, they were all card-carrying members of the *edge*. Most companies, lacking wide-angle vision, had ignored this elite group and have ceased to exist altogether.

Corporate consciousness is predictably centered around the mainstream. The best customers, biggest competitors, and model employees are almost exclusively the focus of attention. This would seem to be sensible. And yet, although the mainstream has extraordinary value in meeting the challenges of today, it is terribly inadequate at addressing the challenges yet to come. Companies using the power of the *edge*, however, have an enormous advantage in establishing a secure and profitable future.

A FORCE WITHIN REACH

A South African farmer was thrilled to find out that he had just inherited a vast expanse of land. He sold his house, furniture, and a few other possessions to finance the move. With high hopes for a bright future, he and his family set off to find their fortune. When they arrived at their new home, they surveyed the landscape and saw some of the worst farmland imaginable. The soil seemed to be composed of more rocks than dirt. After years of futile efforts trying to make his "rock garden" bloom, he finally gave up and sold the farm at a huge discount. "Let someone else have this headache property," grumbled the farmer. The new owner, shortly after his purchase, picked up one of the rocks that littered the landscape and couldn't believe his eyes: diamonds! This site in Angola is now one of the most valuable diamond mines in the world.

Each day you are stepping over diamonds. Every report you read, every meeting you attend, and every team initiative you launch may be another lost opportunity. Every business has its field of diamonds. These gems come from the *edge*, composed of complaining and lost customers, troublemaking employees, and insignificant competitors. Like the original farmer, most companies either ignore them or curse them, while bemoaning the dearth of solutions to their business woes. The more turbulent our times, the more important it becomes that we expand our narrow view of the world beyond the mainstream.

Wide-angle vision is necessary during times of instability. Products, services, and business practices that once worked superbly no longer match shifting needs. Remember when the operations of every major corporation revolved around a hub of mainframe computing? Soon an increased need for speed and flexibility became glaringly apparent. The first people to recognize this need were a very small but vocal minority of disgruntled customers. They were diamonds in the rough, just waiting to be discovered. For Apple Computer, they heralded a new industry. For much of IBM, they were invisible.[1]

The *edge* always looks at our business practices and products from a radically different perspective than the groups we regularly deal with. Although the majority of customers may be quite satisfied with our service today, this stubborn 1 percent remain critical. For companies trying to reengineer themselves, that critical perspective is invaluable. The *edge* can easily see things that the mainstream cannot see at all.

A powerful benefit that comes from developing wide-angle vision is the ability to reduce the element of surprise. When the Soviet Union fell, most political analysts were stunned. With the inherent wisdom that comes from hindsight, however, pundits have pieced together the signals that should have alerted us to the inevitability of this staggering event. Ultimately, the Soviet Union was like a building with major structural flaws. A little internal stress produced a spiderweb of cracks that spread through its core. It was actually a certainty that it would come crashing down.

Understanding why the world could not see the internal stresses of the Soviet Union will help us to avoid repeating similar mistakes in our businesses and corporations. Apple Computer, IBM, People Express, Xerox, and the worldwide investment community are just a few of the groups that suffered tremendous losses because of their inability to recognize the tides of change before it was too late.

By helping you to develop your wide-angle vision, this book will dramatically improve your ability to be proactive, to see changes early and act before there is a compelling need to act. You will learn how to:

- Avoid crises.
- Solve problems that you have not been able to conquer before.
- Reduce resistance to change.
- Delight your customers.
- Change your organization faster, cheaper, and more efficiently.
- Understand how change can constructively impact your business.
- Identify and overcome your restrictive boundaries.
- Recognize the advent of change sooner than your competition.

This book contains specific recommendations that really work in the marketplace. They are based on my experiences working with hundreds of organizations, each of which was striving to achieve the benefits of wide-angle vision. Some of these companies are among the largest and most successful in the world. Others are small firms you likely have not heard of . . . yet.

INTRODUCING THE EDGE

Every organization contains both a mainstream and an *edge*. The mainstream consists of your established customers, most significant competitors, and best employees. Your barometer for success is obvious. If your established base of customers increases, you know you are making progress. Likewise, when competitors copy your moves, you must be doing something right. The mainstream reaffirms that the rules you are practicing today are *the* right rules.

The mainstream is critically important. It provides your profits, generates cash flow, and funds investment . . . *today*. No one should abandon the mainstream. It's just bad business. But to surround yourself with those in the mainstream while ignoring those on the *edge* is to bet against change. In these turbulent times, that is a sucker's bet.

FORKLIFTS FALL FLAT

Clark Equipment Company, producer of forklifts, learned the value of the *edge* the hard way. Clark had a significant presence in the worldwide market for forklifts and a North American market share of 27 percent by the end of the 1970s. Its forklifts were sophisticated (complicated) and expensive. As one manager recalled, "There were a few of us who campaigned for a more basic and higher-quality product, but customer surveys said they liked the products as they were. I was told that our customers wanted more, not less."[2] These few rogue employees who tried to buck the prevalent view knew that there were disgruntled customers who were not representative of the marketing studies. These employees and customers of the *edge* were out of Clark's field of vision.

The Japanese started to make serious inroads into the North American forklift market by 1978. Their product was low-tech (simple) and inexpensive. Although they had participated in the market for years, these fringe competitors were effectively invisible to Clark. "We hardly paid attention to them," sighed Cary D. Bello, president of Clark's forklift group.[3]

When the Japanese actually grabbed the lion's share of the market, Clark finally began to take notice. Too little, too late. Unable to break out of its downward spiral, by 1991 Clark had reported $30 million in operating losses. Finally, in 1992 Clark was sold to the Terex Corporation. The forklift truck division ceased to exist.

Catching the next wave can truly mean the difference between success and Chapter 11. History shows us that those who are late rarely get a second chance. Once we lose our opportunities, we do not get them back. Those of us who bask in the glow of growth and success actually are the most likely to lose our momentum. Not because we don't want to succeed, but because we lose the ability to succeed.

Now for the good news. With these challenges come incredible opportunities. If you can learn to see these changes early enough, and learn to change fast enough, you will enjoy a sustained life at the top. And you can. You are going to learn how to spot those changes before your competition does and how to actually take advantage of turbulence. The answers to many of your most difficult problems are found by learning wide-angle vision and discovering the force of the *edge*.

The *edge* is a group that is dissatisfied with today's solutions. For very good reasons, those on the *edge* see the world through different eyes. This is not because they are better or smarter or more intuitive. They just have different needs. These unique needs cause them to view the world differently than most of us.

Edge members typically are not interested in creating change or producing turbulence, and they are not trying to be radical. They are only interested in solving their own problems. What makes them useful is not that they have unique solutions but that they have unique problems. These problems prompt them to see the world through a different filter.

People on the *edge* face problems that are effectively invisible to the rest of us. They are on the periphery, pointing to storm clouds that most people cannot see. The closer the clouds, the greater the passion with which they yell. We look up at blue skies and dismiss these troublemakers as though they were Chicken Little—always screaming about some supposed looming disaster. Finally frustrated by our "unwillingness" to see, those on the *edge* drop out, sometimes succeeding very nicely because of their insight.

The irony is that people on the *edge* rarely want to go it alone. They want us to change, to see. They figuratively (and sometimes literally) grab us by the lapels and say, "Don't you get it?!" We look them straight in the eye and say "No!"

What causes us to miss the challenges and opportunities so easily spotted by the *edge*? People and organizations on the *edge* look for changes, because for them, the present set of solutions does not work well. It is this failure of the status quo that allows the *edge* its insight. Like thirsty travelers in a desert, *edge* members are constantly watching for any sign of water.

THE CURSE OF SUCCESS

Most of us are quite successful. That is, the rules we are practicing today have solved problems for us in the past and promise to continue solving problems. Once a pattern of success is established, our filters become fixed. For example, Boeing, despite input from dissatisfied customers and maverick employees, continued using its archaic manufacturing system for many years after it ceased to be productive. Explained CEO Frank Shrontz, "We had 75 years of history, and we were very successful. There was a strong feeling of 'Why change?' "[4]

When we say success, we are not necessarily speaking of market share, profitability, or stock price. Boeing certainly enjoyed that kind of success. But more than that, success means that your solutions have withstood the test of time. Years, sometimes decades, have gone by without fundamentally challenging your rules. This pattern of success ultimately limits your ability to see objectively.

The value of achieving wide-angle vision is that it can help change your cognitive filters and awaken you to challenges and opportunities that you would not have seen until much, much later. It can show what is coming, where to look, and equally important, how to apply that knowledge.

Those who are not members of the *edge* belong to what is called the mainstream. The mainstream consists of the majority. It is the biggest group and contains the longest-term practitioners of the existing rules. The mainstream is the lifeblood of "business as usual."

This does not mean that the mainstream is a fixed group. It is common, in fact, for a member of the mainstream in one area to be a member of the *edge* in another. Likewise, it is very rare for an individual or organization to represent the *edge* in all areas of business and life. Representing the *edge* is a transitory role; that is, when members of the *edge* become successful by applying new rules, they actually become the new mainstream. This is precisely what happened to Apple Computer.

There is little doubt that Apple Computer grew out of the *edge*. The company was invisible to every major computer manufacturer and played by its own unique set of rules. Due to the overwhelming success of those rules, Apple grew to be a force on par with the very companies that had earlier ignored it. Apple became the mainstream.

PROTECTING THE CROWN JEWELS

Apple had a strict policy of not licensing its coveted operating system. This was, after all, recognized as the key to its success since 1977. Few, if any, doubted the wisdom of protecting the company's crown jewels.

Then the market became turbulent, even by PC (personal computer) standards. The price of PCs dropped steadily, putting pressure on the premium price Apple charged for its systems. Compounding that pressure, Microsoft introduced the Windows operating system, and suddenly Apple was not the only game in town for the user-friendly market.

Although events had changed dramatically, Apple had not. The company held fast to its policy concerning the licensing of its operating system. Apple's decision to stay exclusive and continue its premium pricing gave Microsoft the opportunity to refine Windows. Finally, when Windows achieved significant acceptance, Apple decided it was time to act.

Apple approached at least three PC makers in 1993 offering to license its operating system, but there was little interest.[5] It was generally believed that the offer came three years too late— a classic case of experience blinding an excellent organization to clear signals about the future.

More than a year after its licensing attempts, Apple had not signed a single licensing contract. A former Apple executive observed: "Apple had an ice cube in the desert and everyone wanted it. They could have licensed it to everybody. Now all they've got is wet sand."[6]

The mainstream does not just follow the existing rules—it typically helps create those rules. The mainstream has both ownership and investment, in terms of money, time, and reputation. Given the high stake that members of the mainstream have in the status quo, it is easy to understand why they protect the structure that has sustained them throughout the years. They follow established procedures because they have worked in the past, and because they have every reason to believe they will continue to work in the future.

Mainstream members believe, in fact, that they not only are following rules but also are actually conforming to "reality." They would no more consider abandoning their practices than they would consider jumping from a ten-story building. Since everyone "knows" how things should be done, why waste time trying to reinvent the wheel? Yet reality is just a set of rules that we know and practice well. Learn to challenge and change those rules, using the techniques described in this book, and you can transform your reality.

FINDING YOUR ACHILLES' HEEL

Every organization, as well as every profession, has at least one area that it finds very difficult to change. This becomes its Achilles' heel. Regardless of what organizations think they know about competition, technology, the economy, or demographics, there are some things that they consider sacred. This is called their *dominant paradigm.*

Their dominant paradigm is the very last thing that companies are willing to give up when their back is against the wall. For IBM it was the mainframe computer. For People Express it was a bare-bones cost structure. For Kmart it was discount retail. In every case, the rules surrounding these paradigms produced such success that the companies could not conceive of any other approach. And this provides the competition an opportunity to launch a crushing blow.

Entire industries can get caught in their dominant paradigms. Banking is hopelessly wedded to its branch-based distribution system, despite mounting evidence that people are willing and often eager to bank by wire. The steel industry laughed at the minimills, even while it began to lose some of its most profitable business.

What makes a dominant paradigm both powerful and dangerous is that it extends into the very fabric of an organization. It becomes an integral part of the culture and becomes closely associated with the company's identity. When under attack, the dominant paradigm is defended with an almost religious fervor. And like a religious preference, it is typically the last thing a company would consider changing, regardless of how difficult things become. It honestly just never gets considered.

Because of the success of their dominant paradigms, mainstream organizations make wonderfully profitable customers. Because of the inflexibility of these same dominant paradigms, however, these organizations are the last to recognize and respond to challenges to their core.

Consider your organization or profession: Over the past years, especially during times of stress, what has remained basically unchanged, or even possibly has been enhanced? This is your dominant paradigm. Is this paradigm your ally or enemy? Think carefully, because your future survival may depend on the answer.

HELP COMES KNOCKING

If the *edge* is ignored, it is rarely for lack of trying. Customers, employees, and even competitors on the *edge* truly want to be heard. In fact, they *need* to be heard. They passionately believe in what they see, and they want that perception validated. As a card-carrying member of the mainstream, you are in the best position to offer that validation.

The *edge*'s need to convince the mainstream goes beyond validation, however. Members of the *edge* often need help in transforming their vision into reality. Since the mainstream has the power and resources, it follows that the *edge* will first come knocking at your door. How do we react to these persistent attempts to widen our tunnel vision? Consider the following classic cases:

- Steve Wozniak first offered his vision of the PC to his employer, Hewlett-Packard (HP). This upstart technician lacked mainstream credentials or credibility. Besides, his ideas flew in the face of what HP was all about (dominant paradigm).
- Many thousands of women died following childbirth in the mid–nineteenth century. Dr. Ignaz Philipp Semmelweis, a "radical" of the time, worked for decades to gain acceptance for the strange notion of disinfecting hands before assisting in delivery. He was ignored by the mainstream medical community for 20 years. It was not until the later work of Lister and Pasteur that the world recognized his efforts.
- W. Edwards Deming, the father of the quality movement, tried in vain to get mainstream companies in the United States interested in total quality. It is well known that he was rejected time and again. Reluctantly, he took his ideas to the Japanese, who embraced this concept with enthusiasm.

If people on the *edge* merely wanted validation, they could simply submit their premise to the heads of a university or an academic journal. But they want much more. They want to see their ideas acted upon, to turn them into reality. That takes power. This is why the *edge* typically tries to present a case to those with the most power and visibility in the organization. Clearly, this group has the greatest chance of actually implementing the *edge*'s vision. The *edge*'s mistake is confusing potential with probability.

The catch-22 faced by members of the *edge* is that people who are in a position to act on its ideas are the same people who are responsible for the development of their organization's dominant paradigm. When *edge* members present new concepts, they are assaulting the value of these older concepts. This is why an innovation from the *edge* rarely gets a fair hearing.

The only time the *edge* is likely to be heard with an open mind is when a company faces a crisis. During these times of extreme stress, the dominant paradigm is recognized as bankrupt. Without direction, the organization begins to frantically search for a new dominant paradigm—the next great idea. This opens a small window of opportunity for the *edge*.

Unfortunately, crisis also brings with it a sense of impatience. Very real concern for today's problems tends to crowd out ideas with any future potential. Desperation causes the range of our vision to be limited. A magnificent plan for tomorrow is usually discarded in favor of one that offers even minimal short-term promise. I discovered this early in my career as supervisor of financial planning at American Motors Corporation (AMC).

AMC had reported its third consecutive year of losses. Since part of my job was to help uncover areas of potential cost reduction, I had proposed purchasing a mainframe-based Decision Support System. This sophisticated software would enhance our ability to analyze our own performance and create models that would help streamline our operations. I took my case directly to Paul Tippett, who was then president of AMC. After making what I felt was a persuasive pitch to invest in software that would help us improve decision making, Tippett groaned: "Improved decision making? My God, Wayne, we may not be able to make payroll by next year!" Crisis provides the *edge* an opening, but often nothing more.

One thing that makes the *edge* difficult to embrace is the abrasive way that it often presents itself. Members of the *edge* are typically frustrated. They may have been trying for months, or even years, to get someone to listen to their ideas. Each new rejection increases their frustration. What may have begun as a reasoned, temperate observation often degrades into an "in-your-face" approach to presenting new concepts.

Naturally, all members of the *edge* are not hot tempered. Many are perfectly calm and reasonable people. But this sense of calm is severely tested after repeated rejections. Ridicule and disbelief force many innovators to wonder whether their efforts are worth the disdain and embarrassment that they must endure. After a while, most tire and give up. A groundbreaking group rarely has the tenacity to continue after a multitude of slaps to its ego. The result is that, through a natural process of selection, only the most determined survive.

How many people and groups have been turned away by your organization? How many will you turn away today? Despite the fact that they can help you to achieve a long-term competitive advantage, are you unable to even recognize their existence? Before you can reap the benefits of wide-angle vision, you need to understand that there are vital segments of your business and personal life that are as invisible as chameleons in the forest. The reasons for our persistent inability to see the *edge* will be explored in Chapter 2.

2

Why Those on Top Don't Stay There

Surprise ... What events come to mind when you think of that word? The bankruptcy of Schwinn? The fall of the Berlin Wall? The Mexican peso devaluation? Each of these events seemed to arise out of nowhere, totally unpredictable. Even the top experts in their field did not foresee them. Every one of these crises should have been predicted and prepared for. Yet they were invisible until it was too late.

Why are we surprised at things that could be predicted? Basically, we fail to see some events coming our way for the same reason that we easily see others: because people are excellent at spotting patterns. There is little doubt this skill has evolutionary roots. Think about it. Those who were best at identifying patterns could learn where the best fishing was to be found, where the herds would likely migrate, and what herbs produced the best cures. Our ability to see patterns has helped us survive, but it can also wreak havoc.

Look at Figure 2-1. How many triangles do you see? Most people see two triangles: one with a black outline, the other all white. In reality there is only one triangle in this picture—the white one is an illusion.

Look at the picture again. Has the white triangle disappeared? Probably not. There is nothing anyone can say that will prevent you from seeing an all white triangle, even though you know that it does not exist. We are so good at recognizing patterns that even when we intellectually know a pattern is wrong, we are physiologically wired to react to it.

Figure 2-1. How many triangles?

As with the triangle, we often see "truths" even when these truths are based on transient illusions. That members of the *edge* see realities vastly different from what the rest of us see is not because they are smarter but because their past experience has caused them to recognize different patterns. This does not mean we are wrong and the *edge* is right. It does mean, however, that the *edge* is capable of seeing things the rest of us cannot.

Clearly, there are times when we rely on our past experiences to free our conscious minds of immediate concerns. For example, we don't have to wonder each morning whether night will follow the day—we simply *know* that it will because it always has before. This same pattern-recognition system, however, causes disorientation among even seasoned travelers who venture into the Land of the Midnight Sun. In the business world, the pattern recognition that helped us cope previously can become harmful to our well-being. It can cause us either to see things that are not there (like the white triangle or the permanence of the Soviet Union), or to miss things that are there.

As the mainstream, our experience reinforces tunnel vision. But long after our experiences have changed, most of us continue to see within a highly restricted range. Our continued blindness to the *edge* is caused by one of three dangerous conditions:[1]

1. Invisibility.

2. Impossibility.

3. Transferability.

INVISIBILITY

When we are first faced with a dramatic challenge to our underlying beliefs, the most common reaction is literally no reaction at all—we simply don't even see it. For example, the day mobs stormed the Bastille, King Louis XVI of France summed up the events of the day in his diary: "Nothing."[2] As another example, on December 7, 1941, the duty officer was informed that a radar signal indicated at least 50 planes streaking toward Oahu. His response: "Don't worry about it . . . it's nothing."[3] Wide-angle vision is vital, because what you don't see can most certainly hurt you.

Sometimes this inability to see challenges and opportunities lasts just weeks or months, but often we find it lasting years. This experience-based filter can make even enormously important events totally invisible.

Still not convinced? Think about the countries that come to mind when you hear the phrase "high-quality manufacturing." Chances are, the countries that you thought of included Japan, Korea, Germany, Switzerland, the United States, and Sweden. No one ever mentions Mexico. Northern Mexico in particular has been doing some extraordinary work in high-quality manufacturing and assembly for years, but it has gone virtually unnoticed by most of the world. Incredibly, even when I conduct a speaking engagement in Mexico and ask the same question, audience participants from Mexico will include their own country no more than 50 percent of the time.

In 1993 a *Business Week* cover read "High Quality Manufacturing in Mexico." I was certain that this would end my use of the quality manufacturing question. The week that issue hit the newsstands I thought I would try the question anyway. How many people mentioned the invisible country this time? Zip. Even with several members of the audience having copies of the *Business Week* issue on the table in front of them, they reverted back to the old tried and true list of countries.

Even the best of companies can be afflicted with this total inability to see. Invisibility, in fact, sometimes strikes specifically because they are the best. Rubbermaid, for example, which enjoyed double-digit growth for many years, is a model for many businesses. It was selected as the most-admired company by *Fortune* in both 1993, 1994, and 1995. Therefore, many people were shocked when Rubbermaid's second quarter earnings for 1995 plummeted to half of its previous year's level, and its 1995 third quarter net earnings dropped by 25 percent. A significant cause of Rubbermaid's troubles was its inability to see the competitors snapping at its heels.

Rubbermaid has always had competitors, but they historically produced cheap, inferior products. The very substantial price premium over Rubbermaid's pretenders was viewed by its customers (such as Wal-Mart) and its consumers as worth every penny. As far as Rubbermaid was concerned, it had no competition.

In recent years, however, competitors such as Sterilite have substantially improved product quality. How has Rubbermaid reacted? "We let the premium gap get too big in the early nineties,"[4] admitted CEO Wolfgang Schmitt. What was obvious to much of the rest of the world was invisible to the management at Rubbermaid.

Walter Laqueur, a scholar of modern European history and author of *The Dream That Failed*, noted a similar case of invisibility.[5] In a book that he edited called *Soviet Union 2000*, he said it was possible, but not likely, that the Soviet Union would disintegrate. A reviewer of the book wrote that he was far too pessimistic—nine months *after* the Soviet Union fell!

IMPOSSIBILITY

Another form of blindness, often following invisibility, is impossibility. Unlike invisibility, we see the challenge, but the effect is the same—we fail to react. We are shown "proof" of the occurrence but find it easier to reject the proof rather than reject our own closely held beliefs. As Dean Phypers, an IBM management committee member observed, "There were lots of analyses about what would happen if the growth rates [of mainframe computer sales] didn't last, but no one believed them."[6]

IBM seemed to have a singular (but hardly unique) problem with the impossibility syndrome. The company had pioneered the RISC (reduced instruction set computing) chip design. This breakthrough technology could support processing that was 20 to 80 times faster than anything else IBM had on the market. Yet many within IBM's mainframe business rejected the RISC technology, convinced that it was "impossible" to achieve that level of performance.

Back to School

You may be familiar with Jaime Escalante, the calculus teacher made famous by the movie *Stand and Deliver.* The film detailed the extraordinary success of Escalante in teaching "uneducable" south central Los Angeles barrio students advanced calculus. When his students not only passed but excelled at the Advanced Placement exams, they were forced to take the tests again—they must have been cheating. They took the exams a second time, under strict scrutiny and repeated their spectacular performance. Years later, Escalante continued to prepare more students for the AP tests than all but a few of the top schools in the United States.

Several years ago I had the privilege of meeting Escalante at an education conference at which we both spoke. I asked him how it felt to finally be recognized for his contribution. He responded, "What recognition? Every year I have to fight for my political survival." You should never underestimate the power of the impossible.

Foodservice Certainty

Walls of impossibility seem to crop up the fastest whenever new competitors threaten the equilibrium established by existing rules. Minimills threatened the core of what many considered the fundamentals of the steel business. On-line banking is another emerging threat. In both these cases the mainstream has dismissed the *edge* as impossible.

This drama of impossibility is being played out today within the foodservice industry. Traditionally, large broadline distributors have provided food ordering and delivery services to large foodservice companies. Many small- and medium-sized firms, such as restaurants, are unwilling to pay the higher prices for such services and have therefore bought at supermarkets.

Warehouse clubs, such as Sam's, are making inroads into that market. They are offering off-hours so customers can avoid crowds, have expanded their product offerings, and are beginning to create fax ordering systems. Warehouse club sales in total have risen 30 to 40 percent in recent years, much of which has been generated by foodservice providers. "Because we also sell a wide range of other items," observes Ray Hatch, national foodservice sales manager for Sam's, "many on the foodservice side don't recognize us."[7] In other words, although warehouse clubs are visible, the restricted vision of their competitors renders them unrecognized as a force worthy of attention.

As happens so often, the impossibility phase of nonrecognition delays timely action on the part of the competition. This goes beyond a wait-and-see approach—most of the competitors will not even track Sam's progress into their market until it is too late. Acting as spokesperson for the Victims of Impossibility Society, William C. Eacho III, president of Atlantic Food Services declared, "Sam's isn't going to be doing it any better than those of us who have been in this business for a long time. They can't do it as efficiently as we can. It's a different business."[8]

Want to bet?

Technology Transgressions

During the mid-1980s, several companies were investing their research and development (R&D) dollars in the development of PC laser printers. IBM produced very expensive high-speed printers at Lexington, the location of its mainframe laser-printer facility. A number of companies began investigating these printers for PC applications, but IBM, an expert in laser-print technology, knew that the costs would be prohibitive. An affordable laser printer for the PC market was just impossible.

Not one penny of IBM's research money went into this fanciful market. Soon after this, Canon created an inexpensive laser-printer engine that became available to anyone who saw its potential. IBM passed, while Hewlett-Packard bought the engines and captured more than 60 percent of the market. IBM's view of the impossible cost the company billions of dollars.[9]

Impossibility can also result in some pretty funny moments. In 1960, when Haloid (soon to be the Xerox Corporation) ran its first commercial, it showed a businessman seated at his desk. He turns to his young daughter, Debbie, and asks her to make a copy. She skips back from the machine, copies in hand, and goes back to make a copy of her doll. "An angry competitor demanded proof that Debbie was not a midget; how could a child operate a machine like that?"[10]

Almost Winners

The previously mentioned companies were taken by surprise when unforeseen events shook their very foundations. Each event could have been anticipated, but the companies were incapable of acting until the evidence overwhelmed them. A situation may become history before we feel that the volume of evidence supporting its case is credible.

The reverse, of course, is also true. If an event matches our sense of what is reasonable, we require less evidence before we make a move. We are then likely to act on assumptions about a future that we agree with, even though we possess far too little evidence. This prevents us from correctly recognizing future events that others see as irrefutable, only because they conflict with our sense of likelihood.

People like to win in virtually all activities, especially when money is at stake. Because of this, horse racing is a thriving enterprise in many states. Hundreds of millions of dollars are spent by horse players every year who hope to hold the winning ticket in the next race. Fortunately for "stoopers," there is a major difference between hope and expectation.

Stoopers are a small group of people who frequent racetracks. They make a very decent living by bending down (stooping) and retrieving other people's discarded winning tickets. The would-be winners toss the tickets because they expected that their horse would lose the race. Perhaps they didn't wait for the outcome of a photo finish, or perhaps they didn't wait to find that another horse was to be disqualified. They were so sure that they lost that they let someone else benefit from their efforts. This is the same reason that people miss the future. Their expectation is so strong that they require virtually no evidence to support their premise.

A good example of the "impossibility filter" can be found on the floor of the New York Stock Exchange. For years people have made millions on Wall Street by taking advantage of a concept known as "anchoring." This phenomenon is based on the observation that people, especially experts, have trouble abandoning their declared positions, which causes a delay in the increase in the price of a stock whose company shows earnings significantly above the estimates of the stock analysts. Russell Fuller, a money manager in San Mateo, California, is well known for taking full advantage of this lag. "The analysts' first reaction is 'The earnings are wrong and my estimate is right,'" Fuller observes.[11] His deftness allows him to find solid stocks at bargain prices.

TRANSFERABILITY

When we declare that an event is "impossible," we may see it but don't react to it. The third, and most pervasive, of the three forms of blindness is called transferability. This fascinating form of myopia allows us to see the *new* reality but forces us to react as if it were our *old* reality. This is what prompted Ken Olsen, president of Digital Equipment Corporation to declare, "There is no reason for any individual to have a computer in their home."[12] Because events are interpreted through archaic filters, we react, but always inappropriately.

I came across a good example of transferability when I was writing this chapter while staying at a hotel in San Diego. I ordered the "Good for You Omelette" from room service (made with egg substitute). I was more than a little surprised to find my "healthy" omelette filled with hash brown potatoes. Clearly the chef transferred prior cooking rules into this newer form of cooking. Despite the fact that the hotel changed the menu, it was unable to achieve its desired result.

IBM (It's Been Missed)

A classic tale: During the sixties, the Western world quite literally could not recognize Japan's achievements in manufacturing high-quality goods. This was the invisibility phase. Eventually Japan's performance could no longer be ignored, so many moved into the impossibility phase. That is, we saw the quality products that were being produced but could not believe that it could be significant to our marketplace. Finally, no longer able to avoid reacting, we moved to the transferability phase. Since we always "knew" that manufacturing costs were primarily a function of labor, we simply transferred that experience into the new reality: Japan's manufacturing success could only be due to lower wages. American workers were clearly not going to settle for lower pay, so manufacturers in the United States blindly decided that there was nothing to be done at all. The tragic result was that we missed the quality movement by years.

Even after we moved from the "low wages" filter, many organizations merely replaced one filter with another—the automation filter. This was especially true of IBM.

As we've seen, experience is a double-edged sword. IBM had developed a vast well of experience when it came to designing and manufacturing mainframe printers. They were certain that this background would serve them well in the personal printer market, too, and began production at their Lexington facility.

John Opel, then CEO, attempted to analyze the growing Japanese prominence in manufacturing. Like many others, he believed their success was due to their huge automated factories that could manufacture cheap products. So he had IBM fully automate its plant at Lexington to the tune of $350 million. What he couldn't see was that the true Japanese advantage wasn't cheap products, it was innovative and quality products that cost less. IBM never established itself in the personal printer market.

Japan's TV Transferability

The U.S. manufacturers did not see Japan's advantage as quality but, rather, saw it as labor rates and new plant and equipment. The United States does not hold a monopoly on this kind of blindness, however. In Japan the common wisdom holds that

U.S. manufacturers are forging ahead because Americans will tolerate layoffs in order for a company to stay profitable. The Japanese, historically resistant to downsizing, interpret the U.S. advances based on those old beliefs.

Many in Japan share a tendency to dismiss U.S. progress as at the expense of the workers. They have transferred their experience with U.S. manufacturing and therefore missed the real strategic advantage.

The truth is that the United States does not depend on a dwindling labor force for success. Instead, it has cultivated an innovative flow of technology, especially in select fields. This flow allows American companies to respond quickly and efficiently. In Japan this is referred to as the "virtuous circle." One result is that the latest battle over high-definition television (HDTV) has been all but won by the United States. A battle, of course, is hardly the war. But considering that by 1990 most observers were willing to lay odds that the Japanese analog HDTV system would be the industry standard, America's "sudden" emergence of a quality, new digital system is nothing less than amazing.

The Forklift Flop—Continued

You may recall from Chapter 1 the previous example of Clark forklifts. This company's product was sophisticated (complicated) and expensive. The Japanese forklifts were low-tech (simple) and inexpensive and began to erode Clark's market share. As mentioned, Clark responded too late, losing valuable time while it passed through both the invisibility and impossibility phases.

The story finishes with a sad ending, because Clark next moved into the transferability phase. In 1982 the company designed a new forklift with the express purpose of crushing the competition. The savior product that hit the market was actually *higher* tech, *more* complicated, and *more* expensive! Within two years the Japanese had tripled their share of gas-powered lifts.

Although the Clark management team is composed of intelligent, creative, and motivated people, transferability is immune to intelligence, creativity, or motivation. Clark saw the future, represented by the Japanese, and interpreted it based on the company's old patterns.

Hallucinating Hospitals

During the late eighties, hospitals could no longer ignore the fact that the public's utilization of their in-house clinics was sharply declining. Many recognized that they now had to compete with independent, freestanding clinics. Necessity forced their hand, and hospitals began to act in the face of this new challenge to their supremacy.

Some hospitals tried increasing available parking, redecorating, adding TVs, and even placing video games in their waiting lounges. These changes had little impact. The hospitals were looking at a new paradigm of community-based, flexible, and responsive clinics. The hospitals' reactions, however, were based on their old paradigms—leverage overhead by making everything hospital centered.

Today many hospitals have come to recognize that health care is not about buildings—they now understand that health care is a service. Rather than merely sprucing up existing facilities, forward-looking hospitals are opening community-based clinics and are even providing house-call services. Those that make this shift early will clearly have the advantage, but to make a shift, you need to recognize the new reality.

We have seen that we inadvertently blind ourselves in three ways:

1. Invisibility—we don't see the change.

2. Impossibility—we don't react to what we see.

3. Transferability—we react based on our prior experience.

Invisibility, impossibility, and transferability are the enemies of wide-angle vision. The *edge* provides one of the best ways imaginable to avoid the many examples of tunnel vision we've reviewed in this chapter. The following three chapters will reveal the three members of the *edge* and share some techniques on how to leverage their power.

3

Disgruntled Customers

*"Damn! I just can't find it," muttered a man as he franti-
cally searched beneath a streetlight. "What are you looking
for?" asked a passerby. "My wallet—I dropped my wallet," he responded while he scoured the area. "Are you sure
you dropped it here?" inquired the stranger. "No, I think I
may have dropped it up the road," he said, "but the light is
much better here."*

Dilemma: The people and organizations that are vital to your
future are often the least visible. How do you find them?
Most organizations look for answers only where they are used
to looking, but the *edge* is never found in comfortable locations.
The key to tapping wide-angle vision is to learn how to find your
edge.

THE FIVE PERCENT WINNER'S CIRCLE

Even though the *edge* is hard to see, people do recognize it. Sometimes it is sought preemptively, other times circumstances will
force us to face the *edge*. How does anyone find it? There are
three ways the *edge* is identified: crisis, frequent rejection, and
anticipation.

One of the most frequent ways the *edge* is identified is due to a crisis, or acute need. Organizations that find the *edge* are often in such a deep state of crisis that they are willing, sometimes eager, to cast away their old philosophy, because there is little doubt it has ceased being functional. If they do not act fast, they will find that they have discovered the *edge* too late to be able to capitalize on it.

A second way the *edge* is identified is by frequent rejection. Salespeople are excellent examples of a group that regularly faces rejections from those on the *edge*. When sales representatives sell, they are not just selling product or service. They are selling a philosophy. For example, Tropicana sells a philosophy of fresh, not frozen. Nordstrom department stores sell top-notch service. 7Up sells a philosophy of breaking away from the cola crowd.

Many of the rejections salespeople face are, in fact, rejections of a company's philosophy. The rejection of what we sell is the *edge* stating that it sees another truth.

Certainly every rejection is not confirmation of the *edge*. Every rejection is, however, *potential* confirmation.

Change without Crisis

Each of the first two avenues for discovering the *edge* can be painful or costly to your company's growth. A third way that the *edge* can be uncovered, however, is rarely accomplished in corporate America because it is so deceptively simple: Question any and every premise on which your critical business practices are based—*before* external market conditions demand that you address these issues. This means of discovery—anticipation—is painless, inexpensive, and highly productive.

This is the rarest means of discovering the *edge*. It consists of companies anticipating, or even initiating, the challenge to their established positions. For example, companies such as Raytheon and Hewlett-Packard regularly introduce products that deliver superior value to their products already on the market. These actions are repeatedly taken before there is a competitive need to do so. Neither company is particularly concerned with cannibalizing its own products. They both recognize that today's turbulence virtually ensures that if they don't obsolete themselves, it will most likely be done for them.

Probably 80 percent of all organizations react to the *edge* only because they are facing a crisis situation or see a crisis as imminent. Fifteen percent of America's corporations have detected an established pattern of frequent rejection and see that they are in trouble, but they feel that the problem has not yet escalated to crisis proportions. Only 5 percent of companies actively search for the *edge* before they find themselves in a troubled situation.

This book can help you move into that 5 percent. The rewards are tremendous. You can become more innovative, increase customer satisfaction, reduce surprise, and get a major jump on your competitors. None of this is possible, however, until you learn how to identify your *edge*.

THE NATURE OF THE EDGE

Think about the job interview process. Take a few moments and write down some of the rules you practice when meeting a prospective employee. Executives who attended one of my workshops said that:

> "I always sit behind the desk, the interviewee is in front."
> "I take the customary minute to describe the organization."
> "I usually ask some questions to throw the interviewee off base."

People who have recently been on a job interview have no problem verbalizing the interviewer's rules from their side of the desk. Some of the more popular answers are:

> "Never let the interviewee know the answers you are looking for."
> "Pitch the hard questions only after five minutes of fluff."
> "Retain control at all times."

It is usually easy to identify the rules of others, especially those rules with which we take issue. But it is very difficult to list our own rules. For anyone to be successful in the interview process, he or she must understand how the game is played. That does not, however, mean the person has to agree with those rules. The *edge* is defined by the rules with which it disagrees. The greater the disagreement, the more visible the rules. The more visible the rules, the greater the potential to anticipate and trigger change.

MEET YOUR CUSTOMERS ON THE EDGE

Name three of your customers—any three customers. The chances are very good that they all share the following characteristics: large, long term, and usually profitable. It is natural that those particular customers are the ones that come to mind, because they are such an important part of your business . . . today.

Does your organization practice partnering with the customer? If so, it is also likely that those same customers (or customers with similar characteristics) are the ones with whom you partner. Of course, there is absolutely nothing wrong with a close association with your best customers. Pareto's principle reminds us that 80 percent of our business will come from 20 percent of our customers. It makes sense, then, to concentrate on that 20 percent.

Retaining existing customers is critical. Numerous studies have confirmed the extraordinary cost of lost customers. It often takes three or more new customers to equal the value of one existing customer.

OK. Partnering with your best customers is important. With their input you can keep a finger on the pulse of what is important to them at that time. Just as partnering with these customers locks you into their business, however, it also has the reverse effect of locking the customers into your business as well. At first blush, this may seem like a desirable side effect, but think again. As Harold Sperlich, "father of the minivan," can attest, your best customers are often the least capable of helping you to understand what will be important to them tomorrow.

Most people know there was no demand for the minivan. No focus groups requested it, no marketing study disclosed this need. Through their silence, the established customers had spoken. Ford listened to its customers and soundly rejected Harold Sperlich's minivan proposal.

Lee Iacocca, however, gave Sperlich's idea a warm reception. Iacocca, creator of the Mustang, had an instinct for tapping into the pulse of the *edge*. He knew that the established customer base was an excellent source of enhancement ideas but rarely generated ideas for major innovation. The *edge*, complaining that the station wagon was too small, inconvenient, and downright ugly, was an excellent place to look for the big innovations. The minivan was instrumental in turning Chrysler around.

Your best customers (mainstream customers) buy from you fundamentally because they agree with how you do business. They find that the rules you apply to your business complement their own rules. The mainstream customers *today* want incremental improvements. These safeguard their investments.

It's been said that if Thomas Edison had conducted focus groups, he would have developed a larger candle rather than the lightbulb. Looking at mainstream customers tends to result in incremental improvements, reinforcing the wisdom of your business philosophy.

Naturally, it is rare for any customer to completely agree with your practices. Most customers have some preferences that may go unsatisfied. In a competitive environment, however, major disagreements will cause customers to leave. It is no surprise that your biggest and best customers agree with your basic philosophy of doing business.

INVISIBLE CUSTOMERS

Toys are big business. The major toy companies are among the most customer-driven of all businesses. Few industries spend as much money as the toy industry does trying to discover what their customers truly want. In a nation as multiculturally diverse as the United States, you would expect toys to reflect this diversity—but you would be wrong.

Prior to 1994, dolls came in one color: white. In the cockpit of virtually every toy plane, a white pilot was behind the console. A naive observer would conclude that the number of African Americans, Hispanics, or Japanese living in the United States must be insignificant. Despite the industry's best efforts to take an honest measure of its customers, major portions of the population were conspicuously absent. How could this have happened?

According to Jacob Miles III,[1] CEO of Cultural Toys:

The problem was that they [the toy companies] were listening to the wrong thing. It has been determined that Columbus, Ohio, represents the overall buying patterns of the United States. So the toy companies (and many other consumer goods companies) travel to Columbus to conduct focus groups. They often don't even oversee the mix of the groups (women, men, Afro-Americans, etc.), they just assume that the focus groups will reflect the U.S.

Further compounding the invisibility of these other groups is the mainstream orientation of most focus-group testing. The groups are usually drawn from shopping malls and other population segments that are aligned with those that the toy companies are most comfortable with. Notes Miles: "Even if they have some Afro-American representatives, they will not be from the mean of the Afro-American population, but from the mean of the general American population instead. I could have brought in 100 Afro-American moms and their daughters, and they would have had a much different result."

The toy companies were making an honest effort to understand their market. After all, their profitability depends on that knowledge. Their mainstream orientation, however, caused them to look with great care at a severely limited view of their world. Competitors who can expand their vision can profit from that oversight. This was the case with Jacob Miles, who founded Cultural Toys with those invisible customers in mind. As Miles can attest, it requires far more than just motivation and effort to create wide-angle vision.

Hewlett-Packard Falters

Hewlett-Packard is an excellent company, but even the best can trip up on occasion. For HP, this occasion was painfully recent.

Hewlett-Packard has traditionally provided highly personal customer service. This naturally resulted in very favorable customer satisfaction. During the late 1980s, however, prices and margins were falling dramatically. The company could no longer afford the same level of service and remain profitable.

Toward the end of 1989 HP made a tough decision. It chose to maintain the high-level personal support for only its best (mainstream) customers. For an ever-increasing number of smaller customers, HP centralized resources, committing a large number of technical representatives and sales reps to phone support. Each rep was now expected to service, not 5, but more than 50 accounts. In 1993 the number of customer complaints reached such a height they could no longer be ignored. The CSD (Commercial Systems Division) launched *HP Advisor,* a newsletter that was mailed to more than 60,000 of its 3,000 business server customers; the intent was to bridge the now daunting communication gap that had developed. HP later introduced audio conferencing, allowing customers to access important recent developments.

It is not clear to what extent HP's unintended snub had hurt the CSD's business. Newsletters and audio conferencing are quite popular among HP's customers in today's market. In fact, these programs are viewed by HP as a success. The question is, Could the company have improved communications sooner?

According to a manager within CSD, "We began receiving complaints from customers right out of the box, back in 1989. . . . These were the customers who most relied on a close connection with us. We didn't ignore their complaints. We explained why we were forced to do what we did, and said we hoped they'd understand. Some did, some didn't. I know for a fact that a year later, we were losing those customers that felt the greatest loss. But as long as the majority of the customers remained silent, we assumed we were OK."[2]

The first to leave were those who felt that their needs were not being addressed. These disgruntled customers were the *edge.* If HP had tracked that group, and extended its peripheral vision, the company would have seen much earlier that it needed to substantially improve communications. Instead, it listened to the mainstream and suffered three years of customer dissatisfaction unnecessarily.

Many may take issue with listening closely to the *edge.* After all, most organizations have found mainstream customers to be an exceptional source of fresh ideas and innovation merely by carefully listening to their requests for change. In fact, this makes great sense. Although most customers have *some* needs not satisfied by your company today, most of the needs that you meet for your mainstream customers outweigh those that remain unfulfilled.

There is one notable exception to the loss of dissatisfied *edge* customers: When competition is absent, they lack any alternative. This point was driven home recently when I was talking about customer satisfaction to the head of a high-tech products company. The general manager informed me: "We don't have to worry about customer satisfaction. Fact is, most of our customers hate doing business with us. They just don't have anywhere else to go."

Remember that the mainstream should not be confused with the majority (although often the mainstream is the majority voice). The mainstream is made up of those who are most closely aligned with the pulse of your business today. A vice president of sales of a large retail chain remarked, "Fifteen percent of our customers determine what the rest of our market will receive when the dust settles. That's what we call being customer-driven. . . . When five out of ten agree, we listen. That's what we call market research." Such a business philosophy leaves little room for the dissident voice. Nevertheless, the *edge* will find a way.

There are two types of *edge* customers: those who complain and those who have left.

COMPLAINING CUSTOMERS

Complaining customers perceive their needs as quite different from the mainstream. Both the mainstream and the *edge* want to solve their problems and satisfy their needs. When you substantially satisfy those needs, the customer is in the ranks of the mainstream. When the needs go unmet, the customer becomes a member of the *edge*.

There Should Be a Law

I used to regularly get hate mail from my financial lawyer, Jeff— he would send the mail, I would hate it. Every letter was an invoice for "services rendered." It was never a lot, just enough to annoy me. His invoices were always accompanied by a detailed explanation, of course: 10 minutes for reviewing . . . 20 minutes for checking status. . . . I always meant to call him and discuss these charges, but with a hectic travel schedule, I never quite got around to it.

Then it came. The proverbial straw that broke the camel's back. This invoice included 40 minutes for meeting with my insurance agent, whose name is also Jeff (hey, I don't name them, I just pay them). "What meeting?" I thought. I didn't remember asking for a meeting. I called my agent, ready to take months of frustration out on him. I probably should have called my lawyer, but he charges by the hour. I wasn't *that* frustrated. "Jeff, what's this about a meeting between you and Jeff?"

"Slow down, Wayne," he said, "I don't know what you are talking about. Jeff and I never had a meeting." That took me back. I asked him to check the date. "Oh," he laughed, "I had to drop some papers off at his office that day. I remember because he was telling me about the golf clinic he just attended." Golf clinic? "You didn't discuss my insurance?" I asked. "Your name might have come up, but we weren't talking about you. You don't play golf—at least not well enough that we'd include you in a golf conversation."

Ignoring that well-deserved slight at my golf skills, I thanked him and next called my lawyer. After a ten-minute conversation (it is amazing how brief lawyers become when the financial clock is not ticking), I recognized that I was the *edge* banging on the mainstream's door.

Let me make a few observations:

- My financial lawyer and his firm prided themselves on client service. They believed they were the best, delivered the best, and people were happy to pay for that advice.
- Historically, their office serviced large estates and very wealthy individuals. These groups had contributed to their growth over the past 12 years.
- Over the past two years, their growth had slowed. The law office decided that it had to go slumming (my word) and work with those who have more aspirations than money.

This firm had an excellent working relationship with its traditional clientele but was not even close to serving the needs of the *edge*. The funny thing was, I never once considered myself as a member of the *edge*. To me, I was mainstream, and my requests were perfectly reasonable. I wanted to be quoted, in advance, one specific fee for the job the firm did. I did not want to constantly watch the clock every time I called my lawyer, and be penalized financially for establishing a relationship with him. Most important, I did not want to receive an invoice every time he copied a piece of paper, filed a contract, or mentioned my name over coffee.

At first, my requests were not exactly embraced. But when I asked about the firm's success in migrating into this new market (meaning people like me), my lawyer admitted it was slow. To his credit, his office agreed to change its rules, and we established a very different relationship. Having adopted this new set of rules, he informed me that a year later, the firm is on the track to high growth with this new market.

How long complaining customers will remain a customer varies for different industries. As competition increases and the barriers to switching decrease, customer complaining begins to disappear. A dissatisfied AT&T customer, for example, gets bombarded with phone calls and advertisements on television, radio, and print media, all promoting the competition. Switching is simply a matter of saying yes. Long-distance phone companies will not find many complaining customers.

Toyota Motor Sales USA Inc. does an extraordinary job in making it easy for customers to complain, and more importantly, in taking action on those complaints. Toyota has created a measurement system, called the blue-card process, that enables the company to track shifting complaint patterns and mark unusual problems.

Ninety-six percent of calls and complaints are recorded on a database so the company can easily and quickly identify common problems. If employees spot an unusual complaint, they write the data on the designated blue cards. During the weekly customer service meeting, the blue cards are reviewed to track early changes in patterns.

Sometimes you have a customer who wants more than you are prepared to deliver. Most companies ignore these demands, instead tracking only those requests that they view as "reasonable." But what is unreasonable today may well become expected tomorrow. *Track all customer demands, even the unreasonable ones.*

This is the practice of Eigen, Inc., a medical equipment manufacturer. In 1995 a handful of Eigen's customers complained that some of the features on its medical equipment were too complex to use. Some companies would have ignored the minority voice. Others might have elected to educate this group of "slower" customers. Eigen concluded that if this minority was having problems, then others might be having problems, too. The company elected to redesign the equipment with simpler features.

LOST CUSTOMERS

The second type of *edge* customer is the lost customer. Like complaining customers, lost customers perceive needs that are quite different from the mainstream. While complaining customers still hope to influence your products and services, lost customers have abandoned such hopes. They have moved to another company that promises to meet their needs.

By the time complaining customers become lost customers, they have usually shifted completely to the new company's philosophy. This is why it is especially difficult to win them back. The longer they complained, the more passionate the separation upon leaving.

Edge *Insurance*

For automobile insurers, the customer on the *edge* was easy to spot. If you had a poor driving record, or even just an accident, you became persona non grata. Only "perfect" drivers escaped being relegated to the status of hot potato. As far as the established insurance companies were concerned, anyone with less than a perfect driving record need not apply. During the 1970s I was one of those unfortunate drivers. I asked companies why they would not cover me and was told, "We lose money on 'high risk' drivers."

I was an *edge* customer in the extreme, and so were the over one million other drivers like me. Beyond complaining, beyond leaving, we were customers no "sane" member of the mainstream wanted. We were lost customers in the extreme—we were severed! In the health care industry, these customers are represented by the Medicare patients. The policy of capped fee reimbursement means that they are usually taken only grudgingly.

The Silent Minority

The more a customer disagrees with your business practices, the greater their value as a member of the *edge*. How well do you know your customers on the *edge*? The CEO of a medical insurance provider invited me to see his executive information system (EIS), which provides computer-based delivery of the information deemed most critical to executives. He was especially proud of the screens that dealt with customer service, the core of the company's mission statement.

The EIS reported that 89 percent of the provider's surveyed customers rated its performance as better than 4.0 (on a scale of 1–5). I asked about the other 11 percent. "That number is down from 14 percent last year," the CEO boasted. I persisted, asking him what he could tell me about the customers the 11 percent represented. "I don't know much about them," he said, "except that they represent a fairly low percentage of our business. Our largest customers give us some of the best ratings."

Like many executives, this CEO was receiving extraordinary amounts of information about the mainstream but knew virtually nothing about his *edge* customers. Although the *edge* represents an organization's greatest threat and provides the greatest opportunities for growth, even seasoned executives are blind when it comes to understanding this critical component of the business environment.

LISTENING TO YOUR EDGE CUSTOMERS

Living on the *edge* does things to people. Maybe it is all those years of knocking on doors and being rejected. Perhaps the air is just thinner out on the *edge*. Whatever the reason, many people on the *edge* are not exactly easy to work with—that is, if you are a member in good standing of the mainstream.

During a conversation with John Saxon, a maverick mathematics textbook publisher, I suggested that he might want to speak to someone I knew who was working on innovations in education. Without hesitating for an instant he shot back, "That's the last thing we need, another damn theory of education."[3] OK, so you wouldn't exactly call Saxon open-minded. But he and others like him have been fighting for so long, they often don't know how to stop.

People on the *edge* are not used to encountering openness from the mainstream. They often become suspicious, hostile, and bitter. In short, once having created the *edge*, it is very difficult for the mainstream to welcome it back with open arms.

Cutthroat Customers

My airport meeting with the president of a medium-sized construction supply company was not going well. After 30 minutes, he was still complaining that his partnering sessions with key customers had not told him what he needed to improve customer service.

I suggested that he was talking to the wrong customers. Certainly his key customers had done business with him for years specifically because they liked how his company operated. We discussed how the best customers usually request small, superficial changes because they essentially share the same perspective on how to transact business.

I steered the conversation to my favorite topic and told him about the value of getting to know customers on the *edge*. After I described the two types of *edge* customers (complaining and lost), he leaned back, then suddenly sat up straight and slammed down his fist on the table. "That's it! It was the wrong damn customers!" He assured me that, as soon as possible, he would speak with lost customers from each of his three business units.

Two weeks later he asked to meet with me again. I asked him how his session went. "It didn't," he lamented. "We sent out ten invitations, expecting six to RSVP. They RSVPd, all right. Two expressed obscenities, four just said, 'No,' and one said, 'You've got to be kidding.'" The remaining three simply did not reply. The invitation he had drafted, inviting lost customers to help improve his company, clearly had not worked. We spent the day planning a new approach.

The new invitation was not on the company letterhead but was a formal invitation. It offered a gourmet lunch (menu enclosed) and a $300 honorarium if the former customers would do him the kindness of telling him just how screwed up he really was. On each invitation, before signing his name, he wrote "Where else do you get wined, dined, and paid to tell me why I'm an ass?" Five lost customers indicated that yes, they most certainly would attend. Following the meeting he said, "That was the hardest, and the most informative day of my career!" He told me that he doubted a full year of input from a consultant could have told him as much about his business. Yes, the value is definitely there, but first we must understand how to work with the customers on the *edge*.

No Escape

Edge customers by definition do not like doing business with you, at least in some major respects. If they continue to do so, it is usually because they either have no other choice or they are prisoners of habit.

When customers have limited freedom to leave, you can expect them to complain loud and long. Don't be too quick to dismiss this concept of limited freedom. One company I worked with never thought of its customers as having limited freedom. However, because the company's products were very expensive and were usually accompanied by long-term maintenance agreements, a great deal of financial inertia was keeping its customers in place.

Other products or services do not necessarily represent a major financial investment but, rather, a training investment. Regardless of the kind of commitment, businesses with high entry costs have a higher percentage of complaining customers. Naturally, this also follows for any organization that enjoys a monopoly status.

The U.S. Postal Service (USPS) has long been a severely restricted market, so a relatively high percentage of customers have been complaining customers—there was simply nowhere else to go. Liberated now by such diverse competitors as the Internet, on-line services such as CompuServe and America Online, Federal Express, fax and E-mail, business has been lost across the board. Since 1987 its global market share has dropped 13 points. In the last four years alone, the USPS correspondence market share has dropped almost 9 percent.[4]

To his credit, Postmaster General Marvin T. Runyon has begun a serious overhaul. He is improving technology, hiring part-time workers to eliminate delivery delays, and modifying postal stores to make them more consumer friendly. How many decades earlier could these changes have been initiated, had the USPS only widened its field of vision to accommodate the *edge*.

Almost Customers

Along with the complaining and lost customer is the "almost customer." Strictly speaking, this customer, who came close but never actually purchased from you, is also a customer on the *edge*. The almost customer has never used your service or product or dealt much with your organization. I rarely speak of these customers because they are often so far out on the *edge* that they are unreliable. This kind of *edge* customer is a valuable barometer when trying to gain insight about new directions in your market but less useful for actually learning about your company. There are exceptions.

I had the honor of playing "almost customer" for a company in the early 1980s, when I worked for American Motors in the area of finance and planning. I was a big promoter of end user computing, as opposed to the data processing professionals having sole access. In that capacity I often spoke on behalf of a company whose software I used and believed in.

I received an invitation from another software company that was new in the market. It asked me to evaluate its product concept and give my feedback. I had no particular interest in participating, since AMC was already committed to a product that

I felt was the best. I had no need to "tell them off" nor any other motivation to help. The company called me back and offered me $50 plus lunch. This was hardly a fortune, but with a new family on a tight budget, it was enough—I said yes.

The company that "rented" me for $50 and a plate of chicken showed a lot of courage, given my vocal stand in support of its largest competitor. I said the traditional approach was fine, thank you. There is absolutely no need for any "revolutionary approach" to the market. I was so far on the *edge* that I was off the cliff.

That afternoon I was in rare form—abrasive, opinionated, and aggressive in defense of the market leader. Nothing the company's representatives presented made the slightest bit of sense to me, and I let them know it . . . the perfect customer on the *edge*! Two weeks later I heard from the executive vice president of the new software company. He informed me that after viewing my tapes (the session was filmed) he went out and got "roaring drunk." He said that I had completely shot holes in their savior product and that he now recognized there were major challenges that they would have to prepare for, challenges they had not considered. He then thanked me.

Not all people on the *edge* will cost as little as did I, nor will all be as forthright. But I can assure you that nothing can match the insights per dollar that you will gain. Anything you can do to attract *edge* people is well worth the effort and price.

CASE STUDY: CUSTOMERS ON THE EDGE

Kranton and Company (the name is fictitious, the company is real)[5] is an insurance underwriter specializing in engineering and architectural professional liability insurance. If you design a building that burns down or collapses in an earthquake, for example, Kranton funds your liability exposure. It is ironic that the company took so long to recognize its own exposure to a disaster of its own making.

First, Kranton ignored its rogue employees. It saw itself as successful because the company was secure, conservative, and had strict standards. Some of its employees, especially those with regular contact with customers, argued that Kranton had become arrogant and inflexible. These employees were never given much attention, but following the 1985 insurance crisis that developed, they were resoundingly put down. "With so many insurance companies folding, how can you consider questioning our approach?" The better Kranton's business became relative to its competition, the less tolerance was shown the *edge* employees.

Second, Kranton ignored its disgruntled customers. The company had created a process that many customers found difficult to work with. Kranton's high standards, to which it attributed much of its success, were applied without exception, to every engineering and architectural firm, regardless of size or need:

- Every firm, regardless of size, had to fill out a seven-page detailed and burdensome application.
- Applications required several weeks to be processed to determine coverage and price.
- Every firm was underwritten as though its needs represented a unique risk.
- Kranton measured its performance based on profitability, quality of product, analysis, and comprehensiveness. Customer satisfaction was never considered an issue.

Kranton considered its customers to be the insurance carriers and the Oversight Committee. When it did have contact with its insured professional firms (its true customers), the company worked only with the largest (the mainstream). This group was the least affected by Kranton's rigid and uncompromising practices.

The 1985 insurance crisis forced many of the low-premium underwriters to fold. Companies that previously had refused to do business with Kranton now had no other choice. In 1985 these companies began transferring their business.

The volume of customer complaints grew quite loud at this point. The new customers constantly criticized Kranton for having high premiums and being very hard to work with. Kranton's attitude was quite different. As one manager remarked: "They were complaining about our rigid standards, cumbersome procedures, and high price. These were the very things we congratulated ourselves on, believing that they were the secrets to our success."

Rather than listen to customers on the *edge*, Kranton took their complaints as a "badge of honor." With other underwriters failing and Kranton's success growing, the Kranton code was celebrated all the more.

Third, the competitor on the *edge* entered the scene. One of the many small, invisible underwriters that almost went bankrupt in 1985 received new investment and reorganized. It started to deliver the true customer service that the architects and engineers had craved. This company grew quickly and by 1987 had already made a noticeable impact in Kranton's market. Both profitability and renewal rates began to drop.

Notice that, as is typical, the *edge* customer foretold of the *edge* competitor. Had Kranton paid closer attention to its *edge* customers, the new competitor would not have made much impact.

How Kranton Responded to Its Edge Groups

In 1987 Kranton's CEO took a position that the company had to become more customer oriented. The following changes were instituted that year:

- Recognizing that the broker was a critical link to customer satisfaction, Kranton formed a broker advisory committee.
- The company formally recognized that there were differences in firms (small, medium, and large).
- Employees answered the phone with "How can I help you?" rather than "Kranton" as they used to.

The changes Kranton instituted made management feel like they were making progress. They believed the company was now customer oriented. Still, those changes made no noticeable impact on the business. This was not surprising, since we first try to address those things that are easiest (least painful) to change.

By late 1988 the CEO was actively searching for something more substantial that could help the company. The employees on the *edge* again became vocal. At this time they were finally given a "fair" hearing. Careful notes were taken of their suggestions, but management couldn't really believe that the company could remain successful while messing with its most closely held principles of operation. The next two years were marked by committee meetings, hiring consultants, and numerous "pep rallies" to promote customer service. Market share continued to slip.

In 1991 Kranton's management began to recognize the need to dramatically simplify the application process. They knew that their customers, especially their smaller customers desperately wanted this, and that the new breed of competitors were delivering it. Still, they couldn't see how it would work for them. "We were saying things like: 'Of course it would be best to have a simplified application process. We just can't do it because of the unique character of our business.' "

In 1992 Kranton hired a new CEO. He was an outsider to Kranton's line of business. Like his predecessor, he had the enthusiasm to change; but he was not encumbered by the company's established standards and practices.

The value of outsiders is that they do not share the rules so integral to the organization they join. They are able to see what the insider cannot. An outsider is not, however, necessary for change. In the case of Kranton, if the company had simply listened and responded to the *edge*, it could have changed, even without outsider influence.

Wisely, the new CEO chose to tackle Kranton's biggest problem first. The smaller firms with billings under $250,000 were being required to run the same hurdles as the larger, multimillion dollar firms that had much greater exposure. The CEO recognized that by treating the smaller firms with the same rules as larger ones, Kranton was depleting its own resources. Large firms could not get the attention they needed, and the smaller firms were being buried in a blizzard of unnecessary paperwork and red tape.

Kranton honestly believed that it was giving every customer individual attention—indeed, it was. What the company was not providing was *customized* attention. The new CEO understood that this was the crux of the problem.

After a very difficult and painful year, Kranton finally accomplished the goal established by the new CEO. The following chart (Figure 3-1) summarizes Kranton's results.

Old Application Process	New Application Process
• Complex, seven-page questionnaire	• Simple two-page, nine-point questionnaire
• Several days to complete application	• 5–7 minutes to apply, even over the phone
• 2–3 weeks waiting period to receive policy quote	• Receive a quote over the same phone call as application

Figure 3-1. Application process.

The change that Kranton experienced will seem neither profound nor painful for those readers not in its industry. Change seen from the outside often appears trivial, but for those who own the rules being shifted, that change is profound. As one of Kranton's managers noted: "What looked easy, what looked mindless, was extraordinarily difficult."

Kranton instituted many other changes as well. For example, it moved from requiring a new policy every year to issuing three-year policies. This reduced the risk and uncertainty to customers and gave them a three-year predictable price.

As a result of its movements toward the *edge*, Kranton's renewal rates jumped from 72 percent to 97 percent over the course of just two years. Although it has always been an innovative company, these new policy changes bought Kranton a two- to three-month lead over the competition. As a result of these *edge*-inspired innovations, Kranton feels that its lead has grown today to more than a nine-month lead, effectively leaving the competition in the dust.

Kranton regrets not having been more responsive to its employees and customers on the *edge*. Certainly, the company could have avoided several years of pain and lost business. By responding to a competitor on the *edge*, however, Kranton transformed disaster into success.

EXPANDING MARKET SHARE THROUGH DISGRUNTLED CUSTOMERS

A mainstream orientation reduces market share. This is the paradoxical message behind a recent study published in the *Sloan*

Management Review.[6] The authors closely tracked four firms with excellent customer service performance and found that they produced results superior to the industry average in every category except market share. The reduction in market share was attributed by the authors to the niche product strategies embraced by all four firms.

Adopting a niche strategy is the ultimate in mainstream orientation. Companies that go after these narrowly defined market segments choose to do so by aligning themselves with those who value their strengths. Their high marks for customer service should not be surprising; you would expect overall service ratings to improve once you cast off the bothersome detractors.

The study also found that all the firms collected data exclusively from customers who liked their products enough to purchase them initially and were current customers. They did not poll the ex-customers or those who never purchased anything in the first place. Therefore, the firms were measuring the satisfaction of those who already liked the products to a minimum degree. They were measuring "the mainstream of the mainstream."

The upside of going after a smaller, niche market is that you can expect excellent retention and relationships with your customers, all other things being equal. The downside is that you become increasingly isolated from the changes in the market, since the mainstream is the last to know. This was the plight of companies that marketed the now-proverbial buggy whips at the turn of the century.

If single-minded dedication to the mainstream results in smaller market share, does it follow that attention to the disgruntled customers increases market share? Bruce Grench, CEO of HDIS, a mail-order firm in Olivette, Missouri, agrees enthusiastically.

HDIS, a provider of personal-care products, has a long history of contacting almost customers, discontented customers, and even lost customers.[7] "It's tough to do," said Grench, "but we find we are able to learn things we're not doing right. At the very least, we gain an opportunity to improve. Often, we end up capturing business we would have lost, and sometimes, we get entirely new business."

What were some of their lessons from the *edge?*

- "We're a catalog company," said Lisa Messmer, the HDIS customer service manager. "We found our customers didn't like finding out about all the standard hidden costs, such as shipping and handling. And they certainly didn't like looking through charts to find the S&H costs for their states. Based on that feedback, we now incorporate S&H into the unit price of everything we sell."
- HDIS found that some of its older customers would not do business with the company because HDIS, like all its competitors, would not ship without first requiring either prepayment (check or credit card) or a credit check. "These customers were not comfortable using credit cards over the phone," explained Messmer. "We changed our policy, and will now ship their first and every subsequent order with the invoice enclosed. They only give us their names and address, and we ship it 14 days payable."
- "Some of our customers liked our service and appreciated our trust," explained Grench, "but stopped giving us their business because our prices on name brands were high compared to a Wal-Mart brand item. We introduced our own brands at very reasonable prices. We found their trust in us carried over to their trust in our brands, and we regained their business."
- HDIS shipped in the manufacturer's original boxes, as was the industry norm. For some products this didn't matter, but for incontinence-related products, these boxes on the doorstep were embarrassing. People didn't complain, they just stopped buying. HDIS started shipping most products in unmarked boxes. "This actually turned a problem into an advantage," noted Grench. "We not only regained our lost customers, but picked up new customers who wanted anonymity when purchasing these products."

What makes HDIS stand out among most is not just its excellent customer service. Too many companies first decide what is "reasonable" and then work to deliver excellent service within those boundaries. The four companies cited in the *Sloan Management Review* article, for example, would easily have missed every one of the lessons just cited. Their line of sight is targeted to only the current users of their products. HDIS stands out because, using wide-angle vision, the company has been exposed to new insights and challenges to its most closely held beliefs.

Remember also that lost and highly disgruntled customers are usually the best means of extending your line of sight. To appreciate why, remember that the primary reason the *edge* is invisible to the rest of us is our proximity and ownership of the rules. The greater the distance and rejection of the rules, the more likely you will see things missed by the mainstream.

4

Fringe Competitors

Who are your competitors? Probably the ones who come to mind are the ones who are similar to you: They go after the same customers, offer similar products and services, and practice business in much the same way. They may even share the same employees, who often participate in a grand game of musical chairs, moving from one competitor to another. Add to this the inevitable similarity of their investment, and the result is a collusion of ideas.

In Chapter 3 we introduced Jacob Miles, CEO of Cultural Toys, a company that created the multicultural toy category. Although Cultural Toys' first full year in business was as recent as 1994, its products are already being sold by Wal-Mart, Target, and Toys 'R' Us. Cultural Toys has strategic alliances with Hallmark and is projected to grow at a rate of 300 to 400% by 1998, in a market that is considered already overcrowded. Pretty impressive, considering the market the company pursues was absolutely nonexistent just a few years ago.

Given the success of Cultural Toys, you would expect that mainstream toy companies would be diving in with both feet. Acuity of vision does not quickly replace *edge* blindness, however. With a slight smile, Miles observes: "We don't even show up on their radar screens . . . yet! Because of their history, they missed this market, and because of that history, they have greater risk in jumping in. They don't understand this market at all." That's the competitive advantage that comes with wide-angle vision.

Your mainstream competitors do not necessarily look like you. They may have different histories and cultures. But if you want exposure to those who are most likely to challenge your industry's fundamental beliefs, would you look to the mainstream? If history is any gauge, you had better not ignore the *edge.*

LOOKING AT THE WRONG COMPETITORS

Many companies define themselves, not by the customers they serve, but by the competitors against whom they battle. Coke versus Pepsi, General Mills versus Kellogg, Ford versus Chrysler—each of these companies keeps a very close eye on its competitors, matching them move for move. When new competition emerges, however, these same companies often cannot shift their field of vision.

Disgruntled customers are not the only members of the *edge* who can redefine your business. Fringe competitors, appearing as if out of nowhere, can fundamentally alter the rules of the game. Ultimately, your organization needs to learn from them, but first, it must learn to see them.

Typecast: Smith Corona Stumbles

In July 1995 Smith Corona (SC) filed for bankruptcy after more than a century as king of its hill. Inexpensive personal computers had destroyed the market for typewriters and hobbled the word processor business. Despite its 1995 introduction of a new series of notebook personal word processors, Smith Corona found the market too anemic to support it any longer.

As recently as three years before closing its doors, the company was unable to recognize both its real enemy and real problem. "Smith Corona is a victim," lamented Lee Thompson, Smith Corona CEO, "not of better foreign workmanship or a better foreign product—but of foreign competitors' routinely ignoring American trade laws and exploiting the U.S. government's political unwillingness to enforce those laws."[1]

Thompson was referring to Smith Corona's 14-year battle with Brother Industries, its nemesis in the typewriter and word processing markets. While personal computers continued to grow and dominate, Smith Corona persisted in its singular struggle against its old competitor. The company continued to seek antidumping duties on typewriters and word processors imported from Japan, spending millions in this futile trade battle.

Throughout the 1980s and into the 1990s, Smith Corona repeatedly lost its suits against Brother. Finally, in 1992 Smith Corona closed the last of its manufacturing operations and moved them to Mexico, while Brother opened manufacturing facilities in the United States. In an ironic twist of fate, the International Trade Commission in 1993 ruled that Brother was more representative of the U.S. portable electric typewriter industry than SC. To add insult to injury, the Commerce Department's International Trade Administration also ruled that Smith Corona was dumping typewriters from its Singapore plant.

For 14 years Smith Corona fought a battle against the wrong competitor. CEO Thompson was correct in his assertion that the company was a victim, but it was not a victim of "competitors openly thumbing their noses at our trade laws."[2] Smith Corona was so focused on its mainstream competitor that it became totally blind to the real threats surrounding the organization. As Ben Franklin admonished, "Folly is wisdom spun too fine."

RISCy Business

Most people know that IBM pioneered the breakthrough RISC (reduced instruction set computing) design. The RISC chip could support processing that was 20 to 80 times faster than anything else IBM had on the market. The RISC chip was considered ideal for typewriters and minicomputers. It was also perfect for workstation design, since high-speed performance was critical to serving the computing needs of multiple connected systems.

What is not well understood is that IBM lost a valuable opportunity to leverage the RISC technology because it was looking in the wrong direction. IBM was keeping its attention on its mainstream competitors—Fujitsu, Hitachi, and NEC—and never saw the *edge* competitors (Apple and the then-small Sun Microsystems), who virtually took over this lucrative market.

The Japanese computer industry also had been significantly hobbled because it concentrated on its largest mainstream competitor, IBM. Hitachi, NEC, and Fujitsu all set out to beat IBM at its own game. So intent were they on the mainstream, *edge* companies such as Apple and Sun Microsystems were all but invisible.

CREATING YOUR COMPETITION

As was demonstrated earlier, *edge* competitors are often created from the customers that you cast off. As the size of your *edge* increases, so also does the attraction to new competitors increase. When the mainstream competitors agreed that "high-risk" drivers were not good business, Progressive Corporation, in Mayfield Heights, Ohio, somehow missed that lesson.

Progressive reasoned that where there is a demand, there is a way. By specializing in "high-risk" drivers, it projects $10 billion in revenue by the year 2000. The company grew from relative obscurity to tremendous success in less than ten years. Like hundreds of other specialty insurers around today, it owes its success to the big-name insurers' inability to listen to their *edge* customers.

Case Study: Math Maverick

John Saxon, an ex-test pilot turned algebra teacher, found teaching at a junior college very frustrating. "I was a singular failure," he says, with passion. "So many of the kids failed the exam, something wasn't working. I knew I was a good lecturer, but that didn't make a difference."[3]

Saxon evaluated all the available textbooks and found that each one echoed the same message. This would have been fine, except that their approach didn't work. Rather than lecture on the concepts, John tried to simply teach students how to solve the problems. He discovered this fundamentally different approach worked well with his kids. Like so many other *edge* customers, he experienced a critical moment of doubt: "If something this simple works so well, why didn't all the experts think of it?"

Infused with his student's enthusiasm, he went door-to-door asking schools to try his method. The success of those few who tried his technique led him to seek a publisher for a book on his practical approach. Publisher after publisher dismissed him.

Typical of the attitudes he faced, Zalman Usiskin of the University of Chicago wrote of Saxon: "Compared to recommendations in reports emanating from NCTM, NCSM, CBMS, and the MAA [four authoritative groups] in recent years, Saxon's solution represents a perpetuation of the status quo if not a step backward."[4]

It is ironic that the very groups that allow a problem to exist are often the same ones we turn to for a fix. It is not surprising that these groups are highly vested in the current paradigms and, predictably, resist all challenges to those rules.

Based on his personal success (and the cold shoulder he received from mainstream publishers), Saxon began self-publishing his own style of math textbooks. "I never wanted to be in the publishing business," he noted, "I just wanted the kids to learn." Finding himself with little choice, the mainstream publishing world gave rise to a new competitor.

The Saxon paradigm is that the easiest way to learn math is by practicing problems. His method employs just ten minutes of lecture, and the remaining time is dedicated to exercises. Most of the class time reviews previous lessons, which reinforces skills and keeps them fresh. He encourages students to help other students when practicing their problems. His technique violates the established paradigm for math instruction (Figure 4-1) but produces spectacular results.

Since 1981 this maverick publisher has sold more than 2.5 million books. He clearly has garnered a significant number of supporters. At North Dallas High School, the percentage of the student body passing the state math skills test went from just 10 percent to 91 percent in three years. Although plenty of testimonials confirm the success of his method, Saxon's ideas remain controversial. Reportedly due to this controversy, North Dallas replaced the Saxon books with traditional texts and saw the percent of passing students drop back to below 20 percent.[5]

COMPETITORS AT THE GATES

John Saxon started out as an involved customer, and the publishing industry turned him into one very determined competitor. Had any publisher actually listened to his "radical" ideas,

Contemporary Scott, Foresman Method	Saxon Method
• Teacher-centric; teacher decides allocation of time between lecture and exercises • Teacher helps students with problem exercises • Main emphasis is conceptual learning • Regularly introduce new material, new concepts • Books are colorful, many pictures, and center around long explanations	• Teacher lecture limited to ten minutes, remaining time for exercises • Students help other students who need help with exercises • Emphasis is problem solving • Regularly repeat prior material, gradually introducing the new material with prior • Books are plain, lack pictures, and keep explanations short

Figure 4-1. Paradigm shifting: Math education.

the industry would have been minus a painful thorn in its side.

Sometimes, however, competitors are not made, they are born. They arise simply because they have a better idea, not in response to someone's action or inaction. The more an idea challenges the status quo, the greater the likelihood that it will begin and remain for some time on the fringe.

Gaining Competitive Advantage

If you wanted to create a new model for providing training to management, how would you go about it? You might suggest focus groups and customer surveys, but we've seen the limitations of those approaches. Because mainstream customers have largely embraced the status quo, the best you could hope for would be incremental improvements:

- Provide better food.
- Find a more attractive locale.
- Hire better presenters.

- Make the sessions more interactive.

Each of these suggestions would improve the value of your training delivery, but none of them would result in a significant competitive advantage. Company A, improving its food and presenters, for example, might find its market share improved. Several months later, Company B recognizes what is happening and also improves its food and presenters. The result is that although overall value to the customer is increased, the effect is just to have raised the bar—everyone moves to the new standard.

This is why quality, although critical, rarely provides a clear competitive advantage. Sound strange? Consider this: As long as there are no barriers to both the transfer of information and the willingness of your competition to change, every improvement by one company will be quickly followed by improvements across the industry. Improvements in quality and service can quickly become a zero-sum game.

This is why competing with the mainstream is so difficult— progress is too often measured in inches, not yards. For every one company like 3M or Motorola, a thousand others are slugging it out for a few points of market share. The easiest way to gain and retain a sizable competitive advantage is to learn to attack where they can't see . . . on the *edge*.

Case Study: A Different Train of Thought

Gordon Peters, who has developed corporate training programs for companies such as Del Monte, understands that strong training practices can have a dramatic impact on management decision making. He has been frustrated, however, because too few managers receive the appropriate training.

Peters thought about surveying those who attended training classes, to learn why more managers didn't attend, but decided against it. "I knew that was the wrong group," he explained.[6] "I wanted to understand why the right people don't attend available training opportunities. If anything, I wanted to speak to managers who don't receive training."

Armed with only insight, he drafted a list of reasons that managers do not attend training sessions. His list included the following:

- Sessions are only for policymakers (such as many of the university programs).
- Topics are limited to planning, rather than action.
- Too much time commitment.
- Too costly.
- Travel restrictions.
- Too little influence over selection of topics.

Based on this *edge* perspective, Peters created the San Francisco–based Institute for Management Studies (IMS). "Universities primarily use their own faculty, and therefore end up making decisions as to what the market needs based on inside-out approaches," he notes. "Developmental organizations, run by any number of gurus, are primarily interested in selling their own products, not in education in the purest sense. IMS is based upon a fundamentally different model."

To appreciate the competitive advantage provided by Gordon Peters's *edge* perspective, let's briefly review some of IMS's policies:

- Anyone in management can attend, although programs do carry a "target" level.
- Sessions are provided monthly in 25 cities, including several in Europe and Canada. This greatly reduces the need for travel.
- Each session lasts only one day, minimizing time away from the office.
- Every city has at least 12 monthly sessions.
- Topics are largely determined by an advisory board, consisting of member company representatives and the coordinating city chairpeople.
- For a single annual membership fee, a company can send attendees to any of the 25 cities.
- Only top presenters are retained.

Compare the IMS model with those of most training organizations and the potential advantages are clear. Most important from a competitive perspective, however, is that the traditional providers would have a very difficult time emulating IMS's success formula. Their historic investment in experience, faculty, and facilities become powerful barriers to emulation.

"We really have no competition," remarks Peters. "We've been in business and growing for years, yet surprisingly have never faced a serious challenger." Coming from the *edge*, that's not really so surprising at all.

Case Study: Health Care Heretics

It is widely believed that when organizations or professions enter times of crisis, they willingly abandon their old rules and embrace a new world order. This is false. There is a big difference between others believing that you are in crisis, and *you* believing that you are in crisis. This distinction has a major influence on how you relate to new competitors.

Health care is in crisis. In recent years it has been assaulted legislatively, economically, legally, and technologically. Most health care publications regularly use the term *crisis.* Yet observe the actions of the health care community, and you strongly suspect it is still in denial.

The word *crisis* is from the Greek root *krinein,* which means to separate. When you enter a time of crisis, current and future events become separated from their historical path. In other words, the rules of the game have changed.

When you accept that you are in crisis, you also recognize that *your* rules have to change. Recognize crisis, and you circle the wagons; accept crisis, and you search for new answers. Organizations that recognize their state of crisis know they need to learn from the competition. Smart ones know that they can learn the most from competitors on the fringe. One such competitor is Dr. Francis Barnes.

Dr. Barnes, a Columbus, Ohio, physician, is in every sense a product of the *edge.* His mood swings from frustrated and angry to determined and, sometimes, arrogant in the knowledge that he is right, and the rest of the world is wrong. Like most people who fall victim to other people's tunnel vision, he started with what he felt was a simple idea:

> I am an efficient doctor. I have an unbelievable utilization record. Unlike most physicians, I am always within the Medicare DRG guidelines. I know surgical units can be run far more efficiently than they are today. The key is to free yourself from your historical investment.[7]

Although most outpatient surgical centers are owned and run by hospitals, Dr. Barnes proposed that he build one of the first independent centers. His goal was to gather 165 of the best surgeons, each selected based on ability and efficiency. "Today," says Barnes, "HMOs and PPOs select surgeons based primarily upon price." His proposal, called the Northwest Surgical Center, would directly compete with the three major hospitals in the area.

With new procedures, lean administration, and an integrated information system, Barnes believes he can provide top-quality surgical care with costs 10 to 20 percent lower than other centers. With obvious disdain, he points out that on average, "For every 4.3 FTE [full time equivalents], 1 is in administration. Only 28 percent of a nurse's time is spent at the bedside, delivering care. I know we can deliver much better than that!"

At first, Barnes was surprised at just how vigorously his competitors were reacting: "I'm not even big enough to be David," he remarked, "I could hardly lift the sling."[8] Quickly, however, he prepared himself for battle. "They're going to fight us tooth and nail on this one," said Barnes, "It's a direct threat to the way they do business."

At any point the local hospitals could have used Barnes as a possible model for a new type of health care delivery. They could have offered to cooperate, and thereby learn from his efforts. After all, at the time he had registered his plans, none of the hospitals had outpatient care facilities—they had time to change. These were some of the things they could have done; but they didn't. As predicted, they fought.

First they fought Barnes legally, maintaining that there was insufficient proven need for more surgical capacity. Second, they rejected his applications to be part of their Physician Hospital Organization (PHO), ostensibly denying him referral of patients. Finally, they fought him legislatively, insisting that since they were unwilling to accept patients from Northwest Surgical Center, its existence was a violation of public safety.

Barnes successfully defended himself against every tactic the local hospitals could throw at him. With every new assault, he was pushed further from his intent to form a cooperative hospital relationship. In December of 1995 ground was finally broken for his center. What is his attitude today? "Our goal now is

to take two-thirds of all outpatients away from the local hospitals
. . . and we'll do it!"

When *edge* competitors first appear on the horizon, there is
often a window of opportunity to learn from them and gain a
multiyear competitive advantage. There was a time that Microsoft was eager to establish a highly cooperative relationship with
IBM. Unfortunately, IBM couldn't stop treating Microsoft as the
enemy. The pattern of old habits dies slowly.

5

Rogue Employees

How does your organization deal with maverick employees? These are the complaining, bothersome employees who always seem to stir up trouble. If you are like most companies, you suffer them when you must, segregate them when you can, and when they get too vocal, ship them off to someone else. Employees on the *edge* have two things in common: They are vocally opposed to any number of policies, procedures, and plans; and they are never team players.

Consider the example of a company called Surtak (not its real name).[1] It wanted to improve the effectiveness of its sales force. While en route to one of Surtak's offices, I was sitting with the president of Surtak and the vice president of sales. Bob, the president, asked: "You've had a chance to get to know us. Tell me, why do you think we've been so successful?"

This is the kind of a question you learn to dread. I knew that he was expecting me to mention Surtak's advanced R&D and the openness of the management staff. The problem was, neither attribute was true. Taking a deep breath, I gave it to him with both barrels. "Bob, your success isn't due to any open management style. In fact, during the time I have been working with Surtak, I've seen several instances when either you or Andrew (the sales VP) have virtually booted innovators right out the door." The air grew deathly still, but I threw caution to the wind and continued: "Honestly, the only thing that you and Andrew do right is to not kill the innovator. They are endured rather than skewered. Your mavericks know that although they may get chewed out, they can keep on coming back and not damage their careers."

What Surtak did *right* was to intuitively recognize that the employees on the *edge*, although a great deal of trouble, had the potential to contribute. What the company did not get, however, was that it had created a gauntlet through which only the most stubborn and thick-skinned dared pass. Further, Surtak had maintained a filtering mechanism whereby only product-related employees on the *edge* were tolerated. Anyone criticizing the organization was transferred to one of its more unsavory locations.

Not all malcontent employees are mavericks, but virtually every maverick is a malcontent. The word *maverick*, in fact, can be traced back to Samuel Maverick, a western rancher who refused to brand his cattle. He was seen as stubborn and willful— in short, he refused to follow procedure that did not make sense to him.

Most mavericks are purely goal driven. They are apolitical and become frustrated by everything that detracts them from their goal. When faced with resistance, they often are incredulous, thinking that if they can see things so clearly, everyone else must also. They conclude that people reject their ideas because they (a) are stupid, (b) have a hidden agenda, or (c) are out to get them. As a result, mavericks are usually terrible at selling their ideas.

Edge employees usually create disharmony. The more these employees push, however, the harder companies push back. At the risk of understatement, disgruntled employees rarely display good selling techniques.

CASE STUDY: MILES APART FROM THE REST

Employees on the *edge* can become competitors on the *edge*. For example, we saw how Jacob Miles capitalized on disenfranchised customers to form Cultural Toys. The irony is that while employed by the toy manufacturer Kenner, he wanted nothing more than for the company to use his idea.

Miles was a manufacturing engineer at Kenner. As the only African American in management, he was bothered that he saw no images reflecting the world in which he was raised. With an easy smile and a winning way, he was on very friendly terms with his peers but felt increasingly frustrated with this cultural gap in Kenner's products. He began to question why every doll had European features and was white. "Being from engineering, I had very little credibility, possibly even negative credibility in these areas," said Miles.[2]

Like most *edge* employees, Miles had no strategy, no grand plan on how to convince the others. It never occurred to him to have one. He thought the wisdom and importance of multicultural toys was so obvious, he need only repeat the message frequently enough to finally get the decision makers' attention. And repeat the message he did.

"Whenever I was asked to talk about any topic (manufacturing, engineering, or design), I would always first get on my soapbox and talk about the need for multicultural doll representation. Every time they had a meeting and I had to assess the manufacturability, I would say why they should be doing this. Every time!"

It is easy to see why most organizations consider rogue employees to be frustrating. Their view of the world is so obvious to them, so implicitly true, most never think in terms of developing a strategy for selling their idea. In retrospect, Miles agreed that learning the language and tools of marketing would have helped him sway supporters. At the time, however, he saw no need. To convince people the sun is shining, merely point out the window. The rest should be obvious.

How did Kenner executives react to his unrelenting multiyear campaign? "At first they tried to show me why I was wrong. Then it became 'OK, here we go again.' They would allow me to talk through it, and we would get nowhere. Then they would say 'We have already told you our position on this,' and they wouldn't respond. Finally they would roll their eyes, hold their heads in their hands, as if to say 'OK, he's doing it again!' It became the joke around the office."

Kenner accepted Miles's ritual because of his talent and good humor. Miles persisted as long as he did because of his inexhaustible patience. Most mavericks become frustrated and bitter. Working relationships become strained, and they quickly become forced by circumstances to leave. Miles, on the other hand, is on friendly terms with Kenner management to this day.

One night, on the third shift, one of his plant managers ran about 1,000 brown dolls. "He came to me the next morning and said, 'Here, I ran some for you, so you at least have them for your family and friends. What do you want me to do with them?'" Miles went to the marketing head and asked that the brown dolls be mingled with the others on the store shelves "just to see what happens. No one has to know." The marketing department tracked those dolls, which sold at a rate three times faster than the other dolls.

Did Miles ever have any doubt, despite studies to the contrary, that he was right? "There was no question," he responds emphatically. "People buy dolls, and a percentage of that market is not white. They will buy ethnic dolls if given a choice. There is no reason to believe they wouldn't do it. I knew they would buy it. That was never, never the issue."

All employees on the *edge* have the same certainty, the same sense that their position is right and obvious, and the rest of the world is merely slow in seeing reality. That sense of certainty, of course, does not mean they are right. It does, however, contribute to the strain in working relationships I spoke of earlier.

Despite the success of the Miles experiment, Kenner never really changed its policy toward ethnic toys. This was fortunate for Jacob Miles's company, Cultural Toys (see Chapters 3 and 4), because this leaves the entire field to his business.

What words of advice does Miles offer the army of rogue employees out there? "Determine what your agenda is, and operate within that framework. Do your job, but remember that your agenda is more important than your job. My agenda was to get them to do what I knew they should do." Spoken like a true employee on the *edge*.

JAVA—THE ONE THAT ALMOST GOT AWAY

Patrick Naughton, a software engineer, is one of the best minds on the computer scene today. Patrick Naughton will soon develop one of the most important innovations to hit communications since the Internet. Patrick Naughton is walking out your door.

That was the position in which Scott McNealy, president of Sun Microsystems found himself in late 1990. Exhibiting extraordinary wide-angle vision, McNealy was able to leverage Naughton's ideas. Five years later, on May 23, 1995, Sun formally announced the development of a revolutionary software program called Java. Designed to greatly simplify and enliven the Internet experience, Java was an immediate hit. On the same day it was introduced by Sun, Netscape, the Internet powerhouse, declared its intention to license Java for use in its Netscape Browser.

Within six months of its introduction, it seemed everyone was running furiously to embrace this new technology. With its ability to run on virtually any machine, hardware manufacturers as well as software developers have been swept away by a feeding frenzy over the potential applications. McNealy has publicly stated his hope that Java will help Sun to once again differentiate its line of computers, opening markets that have been closed to it for over a decade. Yet five years earlier, this apparent key to Sun's future had very nearly walked out the door.

Patrick Naughton, a brash, 25-year-old engineer at Sun with less than three years with the company, had announced his resignation late in 1990. "Before Sun," he recalled, "I always created my own software, did my own business. At Sun, the only thing that mattered was the large agenda, the big programs—we call them 'big wads of software.' No small projects could get approval . . . all important developments begin as small projects."[3]

Naughton complained about the bigness of Sun, the confused priorities and its lack of customer responsiveness. Above all, however, he complained about the "insane" 175 different configurations of Sun software, all of which had to be supported. Although recognized as talented, like most *edge* employees he was also widely viewed as negative and a troublemaker. "There were 120 of us, full time," said Naughton, "and we still couldn't keep up—and we never would!"

After almost three years Naughton was unable to find a sympathetic reception among Sun's management. Unable to bear the frustration any longer, he informed McNealy of his decision to move to NeXT Computer, Inc., " . . . to work on a software environment that makes sense." Fortunately for Sun, Scott McNealy was able to convince Naughton to stay and design such an environment, which he later called "Stealth Project." (For more insight on how McNealy learned from Naughton, see "Plugging Your Innovation Leak" in Chapter 10).

With Patrick Naughton concentrating on the graphics system and team member James Gosling on the programming language, this project (later dubbed "Green") actually failed to achieve its original objectives. "Out of those ashes," recalls Naughton, "rose Java, as well as other valuable developments."

What made Patrick Naughton (now vice president for technology at multimedia start-up Starwave Corporation) such a tenacious member of the *edge?* "You have to take a stance," he notes, "but it also helps to know that [with somewhere else to go] you don't need the job." For most rogue employees, there is always somewhere else to go.

CASE STUDY: DISSIDENTS WITHIN PROFESSIONAL ORGANIZATIONS

If nothing else can be said of the people on the *edge*, they are persistent. Ignore them, belittle them, even abuse them, and they seem to invariably come back for more. Such was the case with Robin Williams.

Williams was a pathologist for the Royal Perth Hospital in West Australia. In 1979 he discovered bacteria in a biopsy taken from an ulcer patient. This struck him as curious, since it was well known that nothing, not even bacteria, could possibly grow in the highly acidic environment of the stomach. He began to test other ulcer biopsies, only to confirm his original discovery.

Williams brought his discovery to the attention of others. They listened politely, sometimes pointing out that it was obviously an error. Still, he persisted. Day after day he pleaded for someone to help him investigate this perplexing paradox, to no avail.

Robin Williams was clearly a rogue employee. He did not want to cause trouble and certainly did not want to make waves. He felt that his request was innocent enough, and he was genuinely surprised by the resistance that he encountered. Like most rogue employees, though, he could not let go.

In 1981 Barry Marshall, a young gastroenterologist, was searching for a research project. After being offered several dreary possibilities, he was told that if he was really desperate, there was this fellow in pathology who "never shuts up" about this bacteria he found. Marshall thought it was worth investigating.

Marshall confirmed Williams's findings. Together they discovered that 90 percent of all cases of ulcers had the h. pylori bacteria present as well. By 1982 Marshall was convinced that bacteria was causing the ulcers. He began to present his findings at medical conferences and was routinely roasted after every presentation.

We typically think of employees as those who receive wages. Robin Williams was clearly an employee on the *edge*. In a broader sense, however, those who deliver a service to a larger group can also be said to be employees. Within that context, Barry Marshall was an employee of the medical profession to which he belonged. In no uncertain terms that profession was telling Marshall that he was certifiably nuts.

Finally, out of desperation, Barry Marshall drank fluid containing the h. pylori bacteria and came down with a raging case of gastritis. Ten days later he was given an endoscopic exam, and sure enough, his stomach was shown to be badly infected by a bacteria that had no right existing at all. Fourteen days after his fateful cocktail, he took antibiotics, and his condition cleared up.

Shortly after that Marshall decided to take his case to the United States. He received the same hostile reception everywhere he went. In an attempt to disprove his theory, doctors conducted a new study. Much to Marshall's delight, they discovered that the body tries to kill the bacteria by increasing acid secretion sixfold. Gradually, he began to win converts. Finally, in February of 1994, the National Institutes of Health endorsed the treatment of ulcers with antibiotics.

People like Barry Marshall are mavericks, but they do not fight the establishment because they want to be different. These rogue employees are rebels *with* a cause. Barry Marshall continued his campaign for 12 years without letting up. He experimented on himself, and literally moved to the other side of the world in search of acceptance. In the end, that is all any of these employees on the *edge* desire: an open mind and, ultimately, acceptance.

CASE STUDY: THE WIZ THAT WOZ

Steve Wozniak was a technician at Hewlett-Packard. He was reported to have been persistent and stubborn as he repeatedly insisted HP management listen to his idea for a personal computer. That would not happen. Wozniak committed two cardinal sins against mainstream HP: He was a lowly engineer (he had no Ph.D.—can you imagine?), and he made waves.

The conclusion of this story has become almost a legend. Wozniak teamed with Steven Jobs and formed what was to become Apple Computer. The moral of the story, however, seems to have been lost: Employees on the *edge* often lack mainstream credibility and are the worst team players.

Edge employees provide valuable perspectives often because they lack the mainstream certification, the seal of approval. When they present their unique view of the world, the mainstream rationally responds: "Who the hell are you?" Membership in the employees on the *edge* club virtually demands a lack of credibility.

Sometimes worse than their lack of credibility is *edge* employees' almost total ignorance of procedure and decorum. They see with great vividness not because they lack preconceptions but because they have very different preconceptions than the mainstream. The clarity of their worldview, combined with the frustrations that come from being ignored, turns hardy *edge* employees into abrasive, nonteam players. Less-resilient employees on the *edge* give up, either developing low morale and cynicism or exiting the company.

Not all *edge* employees have words of wisdom. Many, in fact, may just be what they seem—complainers with an ax to grind. In the realm of the *edge*, however, it is difficult to tell the difference early on. This is one time when it pays to suffer fools gladly.

SUPPLIERS ON THE EDGE

Much less common than *edge* competitors, employees, and customers are suppliers on the *edge*. Popular purchasing wisdom, for instance, is to designate preferred suppliers, establish extremely close working relationships with them, and give them all of your business in exchange for price and quality concessions. It is difficult to fault the bottom-line wisdom of this arrangement. Companies are saving tens of millions of dollars by establishing strategic supplier relationships (SSRs).

Nevertheless, there is an ominous downside to strategic supplier relationships. We have seen that an organization's potential to "see you with new eyes" diminishes with its proximity to you. An SSR supplier is not likely to function as any more than a mirror to your organization. The very nature of SSRs, in fact, is that they *must* closely align to your business practices. Fringe suppliers that offer innovative business approaches need not apply.

I am not suggesting that any organization abandon strategic supplier relationships—the advantages are just too compelling. Most purchasing executives will admit, however, that they could be more flexible when it comes to applying these relationships. Instead, consider sole or dual sourcing 90 percent of your purchasing budget. This would still leave 10 percent to provide incentives for the suppliers on the *edge*. If you ignore this option, you risk turning the SSR into a Faustian contract: short-term gain, long-term pain.

KNOWING WHO TO LISTEN TO

The downside to developing wide-angle vision is that you begin to cast a very wide net. As someone once remarked: "There's an incredible number of nuts out there! How do you know which ones to listen to?"

There is no pat formula that I have discovered that can unerringly direct you to those who have *the* right answers. You can take several steps, however, to greatly reduce the likelihood of overlooking those people most likely to influence your business.

First, let's quickly identify some guidelines that can be used to identify true customers, competitors, and employees on the *edge*:

1. *Never rely on intuition.* I am a great believer in the power of intuition, but it has limitations. For most of us, intuition is based on our past experience. Because the *edge* breaks the patterns of the past, it often seems counterintuitive. It is certainly counterintuitive to ship to customers based on a verbal handshake, but for HDIS it works.

2. *Never rely solely on experts.* There is a great difference between expertise and being considered an expert. Expertise is a body of knowledge, and we have seen that past knowledge is one of the least reliable ways of judging the *edge*. Experts, however, have been "certified" by their profession as holding the correct body of knowledge. This investment in prestige is one of the root causes of organizational tunnel vision.

3. *Never let past investments influence your views.* We typically see most clearly that which enhances our prior investments. The *edge* arises because those investments have ceased to produce returns for a particular group or individual. An entire industry had developed around the belief that stress caused ulcers. This investment on the part of pharmaceutical companies, hospitals, and the entire medical community diminished the quality of life for literally millions of people.

How then do you know who to listen to? The single most important thing that you can do is to explicitly understand your areas of strategic vulnerability. Not just your critical success factors (those things most important to your success), but your critical failure factors as well (things whose existence or lack of existence can most cause you to fail).

Determining your strategic vulnerability does not tell you who to listen to, but it does provide you with valuable guidelines as to who not to listen to. It is not possible to listen to every fringe individual or to investigate every wild idea. Strategic vulnerability tells you that unless an idea *might* significantly affect your organization, don't pursue it. Using this filter will most certainly result in the dismissal of some great ideas. It will just as certainly guarantee that you will not dismiss those ideas most important to you.

Once you've developed a strategic vulnerability filter, you need to evaluate, investigate, and then invest in everything that passes through that filter.

1. *Check out every idea that could potentially influence your strategic vulnerability.* This is not the same as trying to dispute a new idea. Your goal should never be to confirm that an idea is bad. Let others squander their resources in search of the abstract. Your goal should be only to determine a new idea's impact on your organization, assuming it is valid. You might ask yourself:

- If we were to adopt this idea, what would it do for our customers, our competitors, and ourselves? (Recognize that with this question, you are evaluating the impact of the idea on the mainstream.)
- If we do not adopt this idea, and it turns out to be valid, what would it do to our mainstream customers, our competitors, and ourselves?
- Under what conditions would we accept the validity of this idea?

You might decide, after discussing these questions, that your best choice is to simply track the changing conditions that would signal that this idea can no longer be ignored. In fact, this approach should be your minimum reaction to every idea from the *edge*. You can sometimes determine during evaluation that an idea is worth pursuing, but you can never be certain early on that an idea should be ignored.

2. *Investigate every idea from the* edge *that can influence your strategic vulnerability.* Evaluation tells you how important the idea might be, but there is no way to know whether it is viable without expending some effort up front. For example, common wisdom dictated that inexpensive doctors were lower cost than high-quality, efficient doctors. If you ran a Columbus hospital, could you have tested this? You could have researched whether anyone (not just mainstream hospitals) were lowering costs the Dr. Francis Barnes way. You could even comb through your own data to determine the performance of the quality, efficient doctors on your staff.

3. *Invest in ideas that seem to have merit.* This does not mean that you should necessarily implement those ideas. You can easily evaluate *edge* concepts without necessarily investing much time or money.

For example, Smith Corona could have evaluated the personal computer and determined that it very much influenced the company's strategic vulnerability. If management had investigated it, they would have concluded that (a) it made more sense for the business to become a keyboard manufacturer for the computer companies, (b) they could have created a joint venture with a word processing software manufacturer, (c) they might sell their business to Brother, or (d) they could move into still another niche that has been unfilled by the marketplace. Investigation tells you what you want to do; investment tells you whether you can do it.

You cannot possibly explore every idea that your wide-angle vision will light upon. You can and must explore all fringe ideas that might possibly affect your future. Otherwise, you are seeing with new eyes but acting based on old habits.

6

Avoiding Crisis, Reducing Surprise

"The 21st century belongs to those managers that learn to anticipate."

Bob Galvin, ex-chairman of Motorola

Imagine you are driving down a residential street. Your eyes are intent on the road ahead. Out of nowhere, a child leaps out from behind a parked car, directly in front of you. Your foot slams on the brake. As the car screeches to a halt, you pray your response was fast enough.

That is the value of quick response time. When your reactions are fast, you avoid the negative surprises and enjoy greater benefits from the positive surprises. Quick response provides an edge when facing the unexpected twists and turns that pave the way to our future.

To survive and thrive in an ever-changing world, it is vital to anticipate the future. Our objective is not to *forecast* the future but to foresee *aspects* of the future. "Forecasting" limits our options and fences us in. "Anticipating" increases our options and contributes to our freedom.

Now you're back driving on that street. Your eyes are not fixed on the road before you but are constantly glancing from left to right, looking for signs of the unexpected. You notice that children are playing near the road, so you slow down. You are anticipating.

71

Suddenly you see a ball roll by the side of the road. Now you have choices. You can slowly stop your car well in advance of the scene, avoiding the sudden stop and possible loss of control. As another option, you can steer clear of that side and slow your speed. A disaster is averted, not because you forecast the child in the road but because you anticipated that a child *may* be in the road.

At its best, anticipation makes quick response irrelevant. In the late 1980s IBM interviewed scores of customers to determine their computing needs. As a direct result of those interviews, IBM released its award-winning portable . . . just when the market was moving to laptop (much lighter) computers. Although the company felt it had moved fast, it was too late. Had IBM anticipated the shift to laptops, it undoubtedly would have owned the new market. Quick response, which is required when forecasts, projections, budgets, and plans are faced with change, is ultimately reactive. Anticipation prepares us for multiple *possible* futures, so that we might act before the change is detected. It is proactive.

There is one more very important reason to anticipate. Anticipated crisis is an infinitely healthier motivation to change than real crisis. As you will see as you read further in this book, people often resist change because they either don't see or vaguely see the same vision of the future that highly motivates the person promoting change. All too often we don't react until the crisis is at our door. For example, a salesperson doesn't see why he or she should begin selling products that produce only a fraction of the commission of his or her standard line. Or your organization is resisting merging with a prior competitor: "After all, we've done OK up to now."

TO SEE, OR NOT TO SEE . . .

It is amazing to think about it, but most companies see their challenges long before they become crises. We usually think of crisis as something that comes upon us suddenly. My review of crisis situations, however, reveals that in almost every case, the events uncover themselves well before the situation becomes critical.

Because of the overwhelming influence of prior experience, we see the signs but don't recognize them. Today's bankers acknowledge that over 50 percent of all banking transactions are conducted using ATMs, telephones, or computers; customers need not even walk in the door. Yet paradoxically the industry is frantically involved in expanding its retail branch network through megamergers. In 1995 alone, slightly under 400 mergers have been announced, more than twice the previous record set in 1991. An interesting response to an increasingly remote consumer.

IBM's legendary PC crisis offers another excellent example:

> IBM's executives actually saw most of their problems coming both in PCs and in the rest of the business. They commissioned months-long task forces with loads of smart people and forecasted the changes in the market that would cripple IBM, but IBMers couldn't quite bring themselves to do anything about those cataclysmic changes. . . . IBM was the most profitable, the most admired, the best company in the world, maybe in the history of the world. Why change?[1]

I mentioned earlier that forecasting creates boundaries. Those boundaries take the form of historic patterns. For IBM, decades of success created the patterns. The Mexican peso, which created a worldwide financial crisis, was bolstered by enthusiasm and blindness formed by years of profitable transactions in Mexico. Although no one may have been able to foresee the breathtaking collapse of Mexico's economy in 1995, the crisis should not have been a surprise.

First came the guerrilla fighting in Mexico's Chiapas. That was quickly followed by the shooting of President Carlos Salinas's likely successor. At this point, investors pulled $25 billion of the Mexico government's peso bonds. Most investment experts I spoke to recognized this as indicating a fundamental lack of support for the peso. A typical assessment was: "We all knew the peso was overvalued. Moody's and Standard & Poor's [the bond-rating agencies] both considered Mexico a high-risk credit. But we had experienced such a ride of success, we just never thought it would happen." Success is often the nemesis of wide-angle vision.

Near Airforce Plant 42, where the Challenger space shuttle was built, a sequence of signs reads: "The time spent now"... "to build it right".... "will keep them safe".... "on every flight." The signs went up following the 1986 Challenger disaster. But the crisis that killed all seven crew members cannot be simply attributed to time pressure. Authorities, although clearly feeling pressured by time, could just not conceive of failure. There had been so many successes, the pattern was established—this despite the fact that the disaster was predicted by those familiar with the infamous O-ring design.

The Denver International Airport delays occurred under eerily similar circumstances. Those in charge were alerted to the problems, caused by a disastrous baggage handling system, by some experts as well as some contractors. As far back as October 1990 city officials knew that there could be problems with their computerized system. A consultant's report on the luggage handling system was received and read. Believing the problems could be handled, officials took no action.

Time and time again we discover that the signs were there all along—we just didn't recognize them until it was too late. How can we avoid surprise and crisis?

THE END OF FORECASTING

It has been said that history repeats itself. I'm convinced that one of the reasons for this is not that we fail to learn from history but that we learn too well. There is no reason to believe that historical patterns will repeat themselves. In fact, the more turbulent our times, the less likely it will be that we can depend on those patterns.

Forecasting is impossible. Sometimes we are lucky and a complex of events all conspire to support that forecast, but long term, we fool ourselves into thinking we can forecast. I know that is a very uncomfortable position to take, but the riskiest position on the future is the one based on certainty.

According to quantum mechanics, it is not possible, *even in principle*, to know enough about the present to make an accurate prediction about the future. There are just too many events that are governed by chaos.

John Paulos—a Temple University professor, author of *A Mathematician Reads the Newspaper,* and columnist for *The Economist*—pokes fun at the Wall Street forecasters. He maintains that stock price forecasting, like so many other things we think we can forecast, is a fiction: " . . . much of what's written about stocks is worthless. . . . It's not so much that the [market] forces play a small role. It's just that their role is so impossible to fathom."[2]

Particularly fascinating is Paulos's assessment as to why we continue to believe we can forecast the market. He attributes it to the experts' convenient analysis when things inevitably go wrong: "Well, it's because of profit-taking . . . price-to-earnings ratios . . . 'head and shoulders' patterns . . . Yeltsin's been drinking too much." "Almost all these analyses are nonsensical attempts to impose order whether it's there or not. . . . It's surprising to me how seldom analysts just say, 'I don't know what the hell happened.' "

In every case, the experts are applying their prior market experience to the changes they see. I referred to this tendency earlier in Chapter 2 as transferability. Our experience gives us confidence in our ability to forecast. As events move faster, the half-life of our forecasts diminishes at alarming speed.

For evidence of the frailty of forecasting, we need look no further than the Federal Reserve's FOMC (Federal Open Market Committee), which prepares forecasts concerning the future of the economy. According to *The New England Economic Review* from the Federal Reserve Bank of Boston, the FOMC's annual projections for real gross domestic product were within projected ranges only one-third of the time, from 1980 to 1994.

Despite the best technology employed by top dedicated economists, the *Review* also noted that *not once* did the real gross domestic product end up within the central tendency range. And remember, the FOMC is only preparing forecasts ten months out.

Beyond the folly of the numbers, remember that forecasting creates boundaries. When we forecast we make a commitment to a set of beliefs, and in that commitment, we limit options, we limit perspective, and we sow the seeds of crisis. Anticipation breaks boundaries. It does not tell us how to act but, rather, prepares us for action.

SELECTING YOUR TARGET

This book shares techniques on how to anticipate, create breakthrough ideas, and master various aspects of organizational change. To more effectively learn to use these techniques, you should apply them to an objective that is meaningful to you.

Because the term *objective* has several connotations, we'll be using the term *target* instead. A target is a place in the future for which you are aiming; it represents a major change you would like to achieve. For some organizations, that might be the doubling of revenue in five years. Others strive for an increase in market share by 15 percent. A school system can have a target of improving SAT scores by 15 points.

Give this some thought, then record your selected target. Remember to make it specific, in the future (give it a date, if possible), and have it represent a significant stretch.

BREAKING THE PATTERN

How do you break from the tyranny of past patterns? A simple and powerful way to begin this process is to identify and test your strategic vulnerability (introduced in Chapter 5). Strategic vulnerability consists of those things that, by virtue of their existence or lack of existence, contribute to your success or failure.

For example, a bank might list its large number of local branches as a strategic vulnerability. For a grocery retailer, it might be its state-of-the-art inventory ordering system. Sometimes a specific strategic vulnerability can contribute to success for one organization and failure for another. A small midwestern college listed its rural location as helping it to attract the kinds of students the college wanted. Yet a 300-bed hospital on the West Coast listed its rural location as a strategic vulnerability contributing to its failure.

Remember that strategic vulnerability is not the same as a critical success factor (CSF). CSFs tend to attract your attention to those things that can contribute to your success but distract you from those factors that can contribute to your failure. Surprise can come at you from both sides. Strategic vulnerability should direct your attention to anything that might have a significant effect on your business.

Naturally, being able to anticipate applies to any scale organization. I've helped departments, professional organizations, schools, and multibillion dollar corporations to use these concepts. Just follow the suggestions as they apply to your organization.

It is important to explicitly know your strategic vulnerability, because no single firm can anticipate on all fronts. Organizations need to have a finite number of critical things to watch. Therefore, as you begin to think of your strategic vulnerabilities, remember to be specific. Clearly, customers are critical to your success, but what kind of customers? Children, married women, diabetics, and men over 60 all fall under the category of customers, but they are quite different in their surprise potential.

If money is a strategic vulnerability, also try to be specific. Do you need access to funds at reasonable interest rates? A steady flow of capital? For one client, strategic vulnerability meant privately held stock. Please give the identification of your strategic vulnerabilities serious thought. Not only will you be using that information throughout this book but also as you begin to develop your *edge* action program. Take a few minutes now to think about your strategic vulnerability.

If you can detect early a major development that could negatively affect your strategic vulnerability, you will likely avoid crisis. If you can anticipate something that would positively influence your strategic vulnerability, however, you can create a competitive advantage that may remain for years.

Of course, knowing what to look for is only half the battle in coming up with an *edge* action plan. Understanding how and where to look is also vital.

LEARNING FROM THE FUTURE

Ignorance kills. Peter Senge, in *The Fifth Discipline*,[3] entreats the reader to help create a learning organization. But learning is not just about history or the present. Every business and every not-for-profit entity must know how to learn from the future. This is perhaps the most important twenty-first century skill.

FOUR POWERFUL ANTICIPATION SKILLS

Life-and-death decision making is most likely not part of your daily routine. For some professions, however, the ability to anticipate has, quite literally, life-and-death importance. When learning how to anticipate the future, these are the groups to whom we should turn. What professions *demand* that the practitioners anticipate as a regular part of their job?

Three professions whose requirements seem to go beyond mere quick response—where anticipation is a matter of survival—include: fighter pilots, snipers (a legal profession within the U.S. Marine Corps), and the Secret Service. All these groups have four things in common:

1. They have been trained in how to search, using "splatter vision."

2. They have learned how to develop mental models.

3. They have developed specific methods of "reading the signs."

4. They have specific early warning systems.

These are the four anticipation skills discussed in detail in this chapter.

Let me emphasize that anticipation is not just for those in life-and-death situations. It is a critical skill for anyone who cannot pay the price of quick response time. This was the case with People Express (PE) Airlines.

People Express Airlines is now a historic curiosity. Once glorified on the covers of *Fortune, Business Week,* and *Forbes,* People Express went from explosive growth in 1981 to bankruptcy in 1986, an incredibly short life, even by today's volatile standards. Some have blamed the airline's demise on hubris. Others have pointed to competition and technology. What really killed People Express was surprise.

Surprise occurs the moment we realize our view of the world no longer matches reality. For Donald Burr, founder of People Express, this moment of surprise came when he recognized that American Airline's SABRE System was not just another technology. SABRE freed American to introduce yield management, allowing it to meet and sometimes beat PE's low prices.

SABRE itself did not surprise Donald Burr. He knew about it 18 months *before* its introduction. What completely dumbfounded Burr was the realization that American's new technology was important. This is the nature of surprise. Most experts knew about the events leading up to the fall of the Berlin Wall, the Challenger disaster, the Cuban refugee crisis, and the peso crisis in Mexico. But most experts do not know how to read the signals.

When I teach people techniques for anticipating the future, it is always predicated on the ability to learn from *indicator species*. This is a term used by evolutionists and environmentalists to describe those groups that exhibit the results of change before anyone else.

For example, snails and other aquatic life living along the shore of Monterey Bay, California, act as indicator species for global warming. Intertidal systems have begun to show changes tied to rising temperatures. Although there is no sure way of knowing whether this increase in warm-water communities is due to global warming, there is little doubt that aquatic warming is occurring.[4]

If you will pardon the use of one metaphor to describe another, it is like old-time miners who used canaries in the shafts to detect gas before humans could be overcome. Change can easily sneak up on you. If you know your indicator species, crises can be avoided. By the time People Express realized the importance of American's technology, PE was already in crisis, and its only option was quick response.

The company did respond quickly, hiring NEC to immediately create an on-line reservation system for the airline. After one year, however, People Express still was without a working system. Donald Burr blamed NEC for this failure. But as anyone who has ever been involved in "crisis" projects knows, communication and planning all too often go out the window when time is short. NEC's inability to deliver a working system had as much or more to do with People's inability to anticipate.

People Express hired a different firm to create a reservation system, building on NEC's work. One year later, on the day People Express declared bankruptcy, its reservation system was ready to go on-line. The inability to anticipate cost the airline two valuable years. Those two years cost Burr the company.

Dennis Hayes, founder of Hayes Microcomputer Products, did not anticipate the strength of companies such as Boca Research and U.S. Robotics—that cost him his company. Rubbermaid did not anticipate the public growth and strength of its competitors, which cost Rubbermaid its working relationship with Wal-Mart, its single largest customer. Finally aware of the changes around them, both these companies tried to respond quickly. But during turbulent times, quick response is rarely enough. Anyone in a profession where survival depends on speed will tell you that quick response is a necessary, but not sufficient, skill. The four skills described in this chapter are critical to your survival during these turbulent, fast-paced times.

SEARCHING THE FUTURE

You think you've got it tough! The Secret Service, responsible for protecting the President of the United States, as well as other important public figures, must anticipate attacks. Agents cannot afford to respond quickly *after* the event. They must anticipate attacks to prevent the event from occurring.

When protecting the President, for example, Secret Service agents know that an attacker might be a single person in a crowd of thousands. How do they prevent becoming overwhelmed by the sheer number of people? This is very similar to the problem every business faces. Every day you are bombarded with hundreds of signals, concerning every aspect of the business. Computers, E-mail, voice mail, cellular phones, and video conferencing have all increased the number of signals, thereby exacerbating the problem. How do you keep from becoming overwhelmed?

Skill #1: Splatter Vision

An agent for the Secret Service who I interviewed said, "There is one key concept that makes protection viable. Never look through the crowd to find a potential assailant. The sheer number of people [signals] will leave you snow blind."[5] How then, I asked, do you find the security risk?

He told me that it is critical never to stop and look in one spot. The moment you stop scanning, you are vulnerable. Using different words, this is exactly what a fighter pilot told me. He said that he is constantly searching the sky, trying to take it all in as a sweeping motion.

Snipers face a very similar challenge. Professional snipers who move behind enemy lines must simultaneously search for distant targets and avoid becoming a target themselves, both from regular troops and, as was the case in Vietnam, other snipers. "We call this 'splatter vision.' It means taking everything in as a whole, focusing on nothing."

In business, *splatter vision* means never becoming so focused that you expect your challenge to come from a specific direction. As the preceding three survival experts agreed, focusing leads to blindness.

The Maginot Line is a powerful example of the dangers of focus. Named after France's war minister, André Maginot, the Line was an elaborate, permanent fortification—a 200-mile line of defense designed to prevent an assault by the Germans. So focused were the French on a frontal assault along the northeastern border of France, they didn't anticipate the Germans invading France in 1940 by outflanking the Line.

By focusing on an expected future outcome, we create our own Maginot Line. Surprise turns into crisis not because we don't look to the future but because we look to *a single* future. Change usually hits us where we least expect it. As an African proverb reminds us: "It is on the regular path we take that the wild beast attacks."

Earlier in this chapter, you were asked to list your areas of strategic vulnerability. How many did you identify? Many companies create lists of 20 to 30 critical items. How many of your critical items do you regularly scan for? Too many businesses focus on the most obvious, perhaps zeroing in on a few core competencies. They have very thorough plans in place to cover those few critical areas and think that they are protected from surprise.

A West Coast bank was determined to avoid the regular surprise that seemed to be an integral part of its lending operations. Although the bank's executives recognized 17 areas of strategic vulnerability, they tracked only a small handful in depth, including the obvious ones: prime rate and default ratios. The senior vice president of operations put it this way: "I felt like our business was like a dam, with surprise pushing against our walls. We would spring a leak, concentrate [all our] attention on that one area of surprise. No sooner would we plug that leak, than another would appear. We finally realized that we could not concentrate all our attention on all areas of vulnerability. This year [1995] we decided to cast a much broader net, and track every potential area of surprise. The funny thing is, we're spending fewer resources and yet feel much better protected from the unknown."

Remember that France's André Maginot was a firm advocate of military preparedness. France fell not because of a lack of defense but because of too much defense of too little. Develop splatter vision, avoid narrow future focus, and you won't get outflanked.

Skill #2: Develop a Mental Model

What would you expect to see, given your current assessment of the situation? For most organizations, this is "off-the-shelf" material. Your sales forecast, for example, is a mental model of the quantity, rate, and mix of product or service you expect to sell. Your strategic plan consists of assumptions regarding the future business environment. Again, this is part of your mental model.

Back in the 1970s, General Motors made the following planning assumptions:

- Energy will always be cheap and abundant.
- The American car market is isolated from the rest of the world. Foreign competitors are limited to 15 percent of the market.
- Cars are primarily symbols. Styling is more important than quality to buyers who are going to trade up every other year.

- The consumer movement does not represent the concerns of a significant portion of the American public.

Everyone has a good laugh at these outmoded perspectives, but at least General Motors had the wisdom to explicitly record them . . . do you? These assumptions become part of the mental model.

We all have mental models. If the model is implicit, as it is for most of us, then it filters our vision and blinds us to the future's signals. If the model is explicit, however, then we can use it as does the Secret Service, to notice those signals and anticipate the future.

Even if you make your assumptions explicit, it is no guarantee you will actually use your mental model. The U.S. automotive companies watched as foreign competition exceeded 30 percent and yet still did not act on this critical signal. At the beginning of the oil crisis, *The Wall Street Journal* reported that although virtually every business polled acknowledged that oil prices were going to skyrocket, they were not adjusting their business plans.

How do you use the concept of mental models to improve anticipation? To be effective, use the following when developing your model:

1. **Be explicit.** What are your assumptions regarding customers and competitors (both mainstream and on the *edge*)? What about suppliers and regulators? Remember not to include only assumptions that reflect changes. If you are assuming there will be no significant new regulations, then express that as well.

It is ironic that most organizations that do explicitly state their assumptions only record those that are beyond their sphere of influence. Inflation rates or raw material pricing certainly have a direct financial impact on your plan, but there is little most organizations can do in response to those variables. Leading indicators usually have a more fundamental and systemic impact on your organization, but because their influence is less direct, they are omitted from your filter.

2. **Be detailed.** As you build your model, have *every* part of your organization explicitly state its assumptions. Accounting,

for example, may be assuming that there will be no new regulations regarding transfer pricing (the price at which one division sells to another). Sales may be assuming that Apple Computer's Macintosh will grow 5 percent in corporate acceptance. Every one of these assumptions becomes a lead indicator. A challenge to one assumption is indicative of a possible change to your future.

By insisting on detail, you not only make your model more useful but also develop anticipation skills within your organization.

3. **Be consistent.** This can be applied in different ways. For some organizations, this means that every group must apply the same assumptions in both kind and amount. Everyone would therefore use the same inflation numbers. While this makes it more convenient for the corporate staff, it does diminish the autonomy of the organization as a whole.

Consistency does mean that everyone use the same assumptions in kind but that each group can decide the amount. In this scenario, corporate acts as a clearinghouse. It can communicate its specific view of the future and also report on discrepancies between divisions. Each group ultimately has the power to decide which numbers it wants to use.

4. **Be monitored.** Usually this task is shared by both corporate and its component groups. The important thing is that everyone understand early when variations occur.

Remember that the sensitivity of your monitoring should vary, depending on whether you are tracking the mainstream or margin. For this reason it is preferable to track rate of change. For example, it is important to understand that sales are up over 6 percent as well as that the rate of growth is increasing. The rate of change holds the most valuable information.

Prior to monitoring for variations to your mental model, it is very helpful to assess what deviations in your lead indicators might mean. If you are a university, what does it mean if the number of credits per student starts to drop? If you are a manufacturer, what is indicated by a decrease in the lead time of orders?

You want to explore the significance of deviations *before* they occur. This provides two benefits. First, you can look at the changes more objectively if you do not have daily performance pressures. Before the deviation there is the time to explore the meaning, whereas after, there is the push to explain it away.

The second benefit of previewing deviations is that it provides time to consider alternatives, which is, after all, the benefit of anticipation. The more lead time you can give yourself, the more reasoned your actions will be.

5. **Be explained.** In the early 1980s Uniroyal Chemical had an agricultural division that was experiencing declining sales.[6] At the monthly performance review the sales manager for the group reported that disappointing performance was due to the eruption of Mount St. Helens. Certainly this was a major setback for agriculture in the Northwest and would reasonably affect the sale of pesticides.

For the next eight months, sales continued to slide, and each review was prefaced with "Our performance continues to be hit by Mount St. Helens." After the first few months, the president of the division questioned how a sales decline in the southeast could be attributed to the eruption in the Northwest. Each time he was given an intricate explanation of the cause and effect factors at play.

Finally the president declared that no one was allowed to mention, or even allude to Mount St. Helens. Suddenly a litany of other factors, not before disclosed, became the center of the review. The more cynical among us felt that the agricultural sales manager was deliberately hiding problems. I believe that he honestly believed the volcano was the root of his difficulties (remember transferability).

Whether the deception was deliberate or unintentional, had Uniroyal Chemical management employed anticipation techniques to review their explanations of variations to their assumptions, the other problems would have most likely surfaced earlier.

Skill #3: Reading the Signs

What do you look for when you don't focus? How do you spot the threat in a crowd of 10,000? "We are taught to develop a mental map of the situation," the Secret Service agent said. "For example, at a rally you would expect happy, cheering, expectant faces. You would expect people to be standing relatively still, applauding. You expect a certain type of clothing appropriate to the weather, and specific locations where you would not expect people to be standing."

He explained that an agent must keep that mental model in the foreground and scan the area looking only for the *deviations* from that map. This may surprise you. You might expect just the opposite, that they look specifically for the suspect. The more you think about it, though, the more sense it makes. This is one way corporations can keep from becoming overwhelmed by the sheer volume of signals from the future. It is still possible that by looking for the deviations you still may miss a vital signal, but no one can concentrate on all the data all the time.

Skill #4: Early Warning Systems

The Secret Service agent remarked that it was very easy to let your guard down. Day after day, event after event, nothing happens. Eventually, he said, even the most vigilant of agents can get careless. This is the challenge when we personally scan the future for trouble.

Scanning for business risks can also be very monotonous. Most of the factors you track will barely move, especially over the short term. This can lead to "being blinded by the crowd," as the agent called it. What is the solution?

One of the nice things about computers is that they are never bored. Give a computer a repetitive task and it will execute that task day in, day out, for weeks, months, or years. (Information and technology issues are discussed further later in the book.) By creating systems that regularly audit your leading indicators, the computer will do the job of scanning the environment. When a variation occurs, your computer can notify you of what has changed.

Could an early warning system have averted the February 1995 Mexican peso crisis? Unlikely. But there is little doubt its impact could have been significantly lessened had the warning signs caught the attention of the International Monetary Fund (IMF).

The IMF keeps close tabs on the 60 countries with outstanding credit. The remaining 119 nations undergo what is generally recognized as lax scrutiny. In other words, the IMF carefully tracks the actions of the mainstream while treating the *edge* countries as an afterthought. This is especially unwise, considering which of the two groups are most likely to produce surprise.

As reported in *Business Week*, "On February 7, Camdessus [IMF managing director] vowed to increase surveillance of economies in 'convalescence' to avert future panics. . . ."[7] This change of policy comes none too soon, given the recent disclosure that the IMF now has identified ten other currencies that might be moving toward crises this year.

WHY DON'T YOU HEAR ABOUT ANTICIPATION?

You may wonder why information on the *edge* and anticipation have never received much press. Why is it so few organizations can answer even 30 percent yes on the quiz presented in Figure 6-1? The answer is that you have never been taught how to anticipate . . . never.

Think back to all your years of school. Have you ever had one course on anticipating the future? One class? I have yet to have one member of my various audiences respond in the affirmative. Even those few who have had a class on "the future" tell me that the message was focused on what the future may bring rather than how to think about the future.

We have all had many years of education on history. We are told that we can learn from history, and we can. But with all your years of education, the implication has been that you cannot learn from the future. You can, and you must learn from the future. Trial and error is a luxury we can no longer afford.

The rate of information transfer has dramatically shortened our response time window. Consider the elapsed time from the discovery of the following technologies until their commercial development:

- Photography took 112 years from discovery to development as a commercial product.

- Telephone, 56 years.
- Radio, 35.
- Radar, 15.
- TV, 12.
- Transistor, 5.

Today, the time line for a new technology or a new product can be one year from conception to obsolescence.

Many have heard the argument that change was just as much a factor 100 years ago as it is today, and that might be true. Speed is relative. What may have seemed like a rapid-fire pace of change at the turn of the twentieth century seems like a snail's pace today. That doesn't reduce the impact of change as felt by our great-grandparents. They most likely felt much the same mental whiplash we feel today.

One of the major differences today versus even just 20 years ago is that we no longer have the recovery time enjoyed by even our parents. You may not be able to avoid the whiplash, but you can greatly reduce it by learning how to see the future sooner. Anticipation may not have been a critical skill 20 years ago (that is arguable), but it is a survival skill today.

1. Can you identify three *edge* customers?
2. Can you identify three *edge* competitors?
3. Does your organization make an effort to give *edge* employees a hearing?
4. Is anyone in your organization responsible for recording and tracking the *edge*?
5. How many reports in the last year have highlighted the *edge?*
6. Does your organization regularly track early warning signals?
7. If yes, how many areas of your strategic vulnerability are covered by the signals you track?
8. In the past year, have you specifically considered the *edge* perspective in making any decision?
9. Is your organization's future focus limited to its strategic plan?
10. When you partner with customers, suppliers, or distributors, do you ever include the *edge?*

Figure 6-1. Wide-angle quiz.

Can you always avoid crises? No, there will always be some things that seem to come from nowhere and take us completely by surprise. That does not mean that these things cannot be *anticipated*. Everything that occurs is due to cause and effect. If we understand that chain of events, and anticipate, we avoid crises.

A freak tornado touches down and wreaks havoc (creates a crisis). Can that be avoided? Perhaps it can! Tornadoes will always be a part of our climatic patterns, but if we knew how they developed, we might be able to accurately predict their course. Once we understand the cause and effect, we can anticipate and, given enough response time, avoid crises—but therein lies the rub.

Our ability to avoid crises is a function of both our ability to anticipate and our ability to respond quickly. If the knowledge and flexibility are both in sufficient supply, then we can avoid all crises.

Before moving on, take a few minutes to complete the quiz in Figure 6-1. It is designed to help you assess how well your organization is poised to learn from the future.

How did you do on the quiz? Give yourself ten points for each yes answer. Did you do better than 70 percent? If so, your company is doing well in practicing wide-angle vision—you are in an excellent position to apply the four anticipation skills described in this chapter. Compared with the great majority of organizations today, anything better than 30 percent still marks you as one of the rarefied few.

Knowing how to search for signals from the *edge* is important, but without understanding what you will be searching for, this knowledge is not as powerful as it could be. Seeing with splatter vision, developing mental models, reading the signs, and using early warning systems must be combined with an understanding of what those signals are. This is the topic of the next chapter.

7

What You Don't Know Can Hurt You

To eliminate crisis and reduce surprise, you need to understand not just how to look at the future but what specifically to look for. This chapter will share techniques for guiding you to some of the highest potential areas to find information on your future. Rather than deal with these ideas on a purely conceptual basis, apply them to your areas of strategic vulnerability. Before reading on, record three of your most important vulnerabilities on the lines below. Remember that strategic vulnerability can apply to any level of your organization, from departmental on up.

1. _____
2. _____
3. _____

Throughout this chapter you will have the opportunity to apply the techniques you will learn to *your* areas of strategic vulnerability. Please resist the temptation to just read the material and come back to it later on. Its real power is in what it reveals about your knowledge (or lack of knowledge) concerning your most vital interests.

SIGNALS FROM THE FUTURE

Your organization must be alert to six signals to thrive during turbulent times. These six involve:

1. Identifying people working on your hardest problems.

2. Evaluating the rule breakers.

3. Recognizing your diminishing return.

4. Looking for the bandwagon.

5. Learning from the language we use.

6. Tracking historical patterns.

Each of the six has power in its own right, but the more the signals correlate, the greater their significance.

IDENTIFYING PEOPLE WORKING ON YOUR HARDEST PROBLEMS

Each area of your dominant paradigms will be challenged and ultimately replaced—every one. It is hard to imagine that some of your most closely held beliefs, including total quality, empowerment, and globalization are not eternal. While we are successful in the application of our beliefs we see with great clarity and conviction: "This is *the* answer." History has taught us, however, that we invariably look back at those same beliefs after they have been replaced and say, "Weren't we silly back then?" Every answer has a finite life.

Those who are successful are typically the last ones to abandon the beliefs that made them successful. The inevitable result of this inability to see the end coming is to lose out on the next cycle. This is what happened to People Express, Hayes Microcomputer Products, Apple Computer, Clark Forklifts, and very possibly the banking industry as we now know it. This is also a big part of the reason most of the Soviet experts missed the coming collapse. Their success grew as the Soviet Union developed; the more prominent the Soviet Union became, the more the experts were in demand. Because their success became integrally tied to the Soviet Union's viability, they failed to anticipate the most important change of their career.

How can you anticipate the end of a successful process, product, or program? As illustrated in Figure 7-1, a very predictable life cycle governs the kinds of problems we choose to work on.

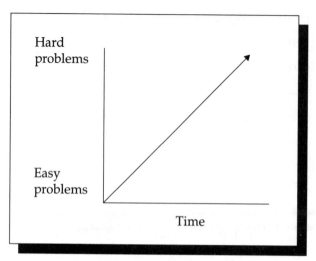

Figure 7-1. Life-cycle problem solving.

When tackling any new challenge, you would first naturally focus on the easier problems. The tougher problems are not necessarily ignored, just placed on the shelf until you have more
time, more money, or better technology. That makes sense: Early
on you are trying to understand all the things the new approach
can do. By drawing on past experience and the experience of
others, you can quickly move along the learning curve.

Over time, as the easier problems are solved, you begin to
concentrate on the more difficult problems sitting on the shelf.
Because your success has increased with the success of the old
approach, and because you are typically quite close to the old
approach, you are rarely able to recognize when the life cycle of
a process, program, or product begins to mature.

Hayes Microcomputer Products made what were arguably
the world's best consumer modems. Most of its competitors'
products were so low quality, people were eager to pay the stiff
premium to own Hayes. That propelled Hayes from a $3,000
start-up to a $150 million company by 1984. If you were the
founder, Dennis Hayes, your list of tough problems might then
have included:

- Wireless modems.
- Triple transmission speed with no increase in errors.

- Error-free transmission.
- Substantially reduced cost without loss of performance.

Notice that not all of these "tough problems" were necessarily desired by Hayes. Reducing the cost of modems was most probably not a goal. It was, however, a very tough problem; that is, solving that problem would make a major difference to the company.

During the 1980s, companies such as Zoom Telephonics, Boca Research, and U.S. Robotics were making impressive progress toward solving one tough problem in particular: achieving lower cost with high quality. Had Hayes treated this as a possible indicator that it might have to change its high-quality/high-cost philosophy, the company might be around still. Rather than change, however, Hayes elected to purchase Practical Peripherals, a low-price competitor, while still pricing Hayes modems far above the competition.

In the end, Hayes was so resistant to change that it began to advertise that anyone buying the lower-priced modems risked losing critical data. The company was later forced to cease these false ads. Hayes was willing to try anything to combat the assault on its established business practice—anything but learn to build low-cost modems.

Every industry and profession has its share of tough problems on the shelf. What are some of your hard problems? Take the time to list them, recruiting others in the effort. Armed with that list, look for an increase in the number of people or organizations trying to solve your hardest problems, which is a sure indication that your old approach will soon be under attack.

One word of caution: Because your old approach is under attack does not necessarily indicate its demise. The steel industry, for example, has repeatedly been able to extend its life cycle through process and product innovation. Early warning enables you to redouble your innovation efforts while there is still time. It also gives you time to search for the next big solution (see Chapter 12, "Breakthroughs for Your Toughest Problems"). In short, early warning allows your organization to change itself, rather than someone changing you instead.

EVALUATING THE RULE BREAKERS

Most people do not want to break rules. As psychologists have confirmed time and time again, most people will tend to follow rules, even when they violate the individuals' sense of morality. This tendency was highlighted in what has become known as the Milgram experiment.

The researcher would select people at random, who were informed they would be part of an experiment. These subjects were placed in a divided room so that they could hear but not see their "companion" in the experiment. They were told that their companion (whom they did not know) was connected to a machine that would transmit electric shocks of varying intensity. The companion was not actually hooked up to any equipment. In front of the experiment subjects was an indicator, reflecting how much shock they were supposed to administer. Each companion was instructed to react as if the indicated dose was actually being delivered. The subjects of the experiment were instructed to deliver increasing doses of electricity and to ignore all screams and pleas coming from the other side of the divider. As they were instructed to turn up the power, they heard moans, groans, screams, and pleas to stop. At 285 volts the companion gave a sharp scream and went silent. Although obviously under great stress, 62 percent of all participating continued to up the power beyond the silence, all the way to the limit of 450 volts. Most of those interviewed later said that they were amazed they had demonstrated such blind adherence.

The Milgram experiment demonstrates that under pressure to conform, most people will fall in line. As organizations increasingly make progress toward empowering employees, I am optimistic that we will learn not only to tolerate but also to celebrate the rule breakers. Empowerment, however, gives people the freedom but neither the encouragement nor training to break rules. For these reasons the rule breakers will be in the minority for some time to come.

Despite what the results of the Milgram experiment say about conformity, some people do break the rules. Typically they take this unpopular step simply because they want to solve problems the established rules prevent them from mastering. Because a rule is under assault does not necessarily mean that the rule, the old approach, is due to be toppled, but it is a pretty good signal that it *may*. Understanding how to identify the rule breakers can be an excellent way to ensure that you master your own fate.

When Employees Break the Rules

No matter how "empowered" an organization believes its employees to be, there are still more than enough rules and procedures to fill a bookcase. A lot has been written about how to handle the rule breakers, but little has addressed the significance of breaking the rules.

Trouble. No matter how Brad thought about it (and he thought about it a lot), a phone appointment with the administrative vice president at 5:30 P.M. was not going to be a congratulatory message. He had heard rumblings that he had upset headquarters. Brad, sales manager for California, had sidestepped the corporate consultancy-relationship (CR) initiative after almost a year had produced no visible results. Worse yet, the West Coast partner of the most prestigious firm was now insisting that he work with Brad rather than the corporate representative.

This company believed that it had to make an example of Brad. After all, several other sales managers were beginning to follow his lead, and this was threatening to undermine the CR project. Senior management believed that the success of the initiative was predicated on it being a centralized, coordinated effort.

This organization was reacting as most do to employees who break the rules: Control them! Without control (so the philosophy goes), anarchy reigns. Often the rules are broken because they interfere with the employees' natural and positive desire to get the job done. This is where the black and white of truth gets a little gray. Sometimes the rules are in place because they protect the interests of the organization from the sometimes conflicting interests of individual factions. This is what Brad would undoubtedly hear in his phone conversation.

Sometimes the rules have either stopped working, or in the case of new rules, may never have worked at all. When this happens, the sooner and more completely the rules are violated, the better off the organization will be. This is the dilemma. No organization creates rules with the deliberate intent of hurting itself. Every rule is honestly believed to be in the best interest of the whole. Since corporate (or divisions, or departments) are the ones who create the rules, they are the least appropriate people to evaluate the rules' effectiveness.

Employees will break rules for a variety of reasons. The reason of particular interest here is that the rule no longer serves the new reality. Under these circumstances, rule breaking should be considered as a leading indicator that the rule(s) *may* need to be changed. There is no way to be certain that rule breaking heralds the demise of an existing rule, but it should always be treated as a warning.

Brad's company had launched its program as a corporate initiative for very valid reasons. Unfortunately, it was discovering that, although compelling, those reasons did not fit with the reality that consulting relationships needed to be local. The program was modified so that corporate became the coordinator rather than initiator and, at last check, was doing quite well.

At Rubbermaid, the rules are clear: price high, and justify that price through quality and innovation. Certainly, it's hard to knock that philosophy in the face of ongoing success. But even in Eden, there are employees who attempt to break the rules. One such employee lamented: "Rubbermaid is a great company, but we have our Achilles' heels. Some of us have been saying *for years* that we need to scale down costs. We knew we had a lot of room to improve. But until the roof collapsed [resin costs almost doubled], you'd shoot yourself in the foot just by saying those things."[1]

In December 1995 Rubbermaid announced that it was dropping 40 percent of its product line, closing nine factories and laying off 9 percent of its worldwide workforce in an effort to lower costs. There is little doubt that this could have been done much sooner and without such dramatic dislocation had Rubbermaid been more attentive to its rule-breaking employees.

Rule adherence can be achieved by either aligning the employees' interests with those of the corporation's, or through control. Control means that the organization is fighting itself, which results in wasted energy, low morale, and lost talent. It also means that the organization is attempting to hold back the tides of time, always a losing proposition. This certainly doesn't mean that you should abandon all controls. But you should consider every violation of a rule as a possible signal that some of your most-cherished rules and paradigms may be under assault from the future.

When Customers Break the Rules

Customers regularly break rules, usually by making "unreasonable" demands. You need to decide how you will react when they try to break *your* rules.

For example, there is an enormous potential market consisting of small and medium-sized restaurants and other foodservice providers. We saw in Chapter 2 that Sam's Club and other warehouse clubs are poised to capitalize on those buyers. What may not have been clear is that this market consists of rule breakers.

The traditional foodservice distributors offer catalog buying, delivery, and credit terms, for which they charge a premium. Small and many medium-sized buyers resist the higher prices and do not order in sufficient quantity to make delivery worthwhile. The established distributors have made it clear that unless you are willing to play by their rules (large orders and higher prices), they don't want your business. No pesky customers are going to make them rethink their policies.

Compare the approach of the mainstream foodservice distributors with HDIS, the distributor of personal products introduced in Chapter 3. When their customers broke the rules and made "unreasonable" demands, HDIS challenged and then changed its established policies. You want your order shipped without offering credit history, credit cards, or other payment? No problem. You don't want your orders shipped in the manufacturer's boxes? Again, no problem; HDIS repacks all merchandise so its contents can't be gleaned from the outside. In the first instance, the mainstream challenges the insurgent customers, in the second instance the customers challenge the mainstream.

Most organizations have isolated examples of not listening to certain customers. But when customers break the implicit rules governing how products and services are used, the offenders are isolated at best or disenfranchised at worst.

The most common form of isolation is education. The attitude is that the customer neither understands nor appreciates how the product or service needs to be used. I have seen this in virtually every industry in which I have worked:

- An appliance manufacturer would purchase boxes, break them down, and reassemble to provide better protection. The paper manufacturer of the boxes said its design was best, so there was no need to change the design.
- A software company would fly out to the client's location and spend hours explaining why the client really didn't need the improved security it was requesting. Kranton and Company, the insurance underwriter, explained to its smaller customers why it was in their best interests to endure the long, involved applications and approval waits.

Training, in fact, is often the first frontier of isolation. It is far easier to educate the customer as to why it is wrong to mess with our rules than to consider changing the rules ourselves.

The ultimate isolation is to treat the customers who screw around with the rules as *edge* customers. They become headache customers or lost customers, but we preserve our rules, at least in the short run.

When employees break our rules, we seek to control them. When customers do it, we try to educate them. In both cases we deny any challenge to the status quo and are in turn surprised by the future.

When Competitors Break the Rules

There are many examples of competitors breaking the rules but few as dramatic as Xerox's rules under attack from its "insignificant" competitor, Savin. Figure 7-2 compares the rules of the two companies.

Xerox	Savin/Ricoh
• Direct sales force.	• Distribute through office equipment dealers.
• Promote service.	• Build and promote machines that break down 1/3 as often.
• Design customized components.	• Use standardized parts.
• Lease machines.	• Sell machines.
• Premium price.	• Discount price.
• Sell copies.	• Sell copiers.

Figure 7-2. Comparing two companies.

When Savin introduced the Savin 750, it broke virtually every rule that had contributed to Xerox's success. The reaction of Xerox was the expected blindness, and the unfortunate result was too little and way too late.

The reality is that virtually every rule you hold will be broken at some point. It is ironic that your customers, your employees, even your competition may be telling you which of your rules are next to fall. You have only to listen.

The Excuse Industry

When employees, customers, and competitors break the rules, it is one of the most potent predictors of change. Unfortunately, many organizations miss their window of opportunity to profit from this early indicator. These companies expend extraordinary effort working to avoid blame rather than learning from the reasons for the rule breaking.

Of all the defense mechanisms organizations develop to protect themselves from the truth of the *edge*, few are more frustrating than the tendency to react as if the problem is "them," not us.

- The U.S. auto industry insisting that Japanese imports be curtailed.
- Some West Germans demanding that East Germany be partitioned once again.

- U.S. educators bemoaning that if only their budgets could rise, the educational system would be fine.
- The husband who complains that his in-laws haven't changed after all these years.

The painful irony is that even if we could get "them" to change, our problems would not stop. Other challenges to our beliefs will arise. With each new challenge our certainty will increase that if only *they* could change, everything would be fine. This has led to what columnist George Will has called the "Excuse Industry."[2]

> The surest path to economic decline, for a nation or a business, is to blame others for your problems. . . . Lee Iacocca is the spiritual leader of the Excuse Industry. In the early 1980s, he claimed that if only the Japanese yen weren't so low, he could easily compete. Well, the yen has risen sharply since 1986, but Iacocca is still loudly complaining about all the special burdens of American industry: heavy taxes, bad trade policy, excessive health costs. . . . His list is a long one.

On the outside looking in, we think the champions of the Excuse Industry are intentionally searching for a scapegoat when they know that they are the problem. My experience confirms that in most cases, the excuse mongers honestly believe the outside influences are to blame.

Smith Corona blamed Brother, unwilling or unable to acknowledge its own blindness when faced with the personal computer revolution. People Express blamed American Airline's SABRE System and NEC for its downfall, not its own inability to act when the need became pressing. In 1975 Xerox blamed both the recession and inflation for its financial troubles. Certainly, these contributed to their woes. As highlighted by Smith and Alexander in *Fumbling the Future*, however, management had far more culpability than they recognized:

> Most of the pressure on Xerox's profits, however, came from the failure of management's layoff and other expense control programs to bring costs in line. The increases in interest, payroll, and materials robbed the company of an extraordinary amount of income. In 1972, the cost of interest, payroll, and materials had accounted

for under 60 percent of revenues. In 1975, those same expenses absorbed close to 70 percent of every dollar Xerox received—a 10 percent difference that reduced the company's bottom line by more than *$400 million.*[3]

Xerox's management concentrated so much on the external reasons (excuses) for the company's financial performance, they were unable to see the central role they played in their own problems. The price we pay for this indulgence is significant:

> The biggest casualty in these crusades is the truth. We lose our sense of proportion. .... What's wrong is the spirit of the Excuse Industry: someone else—or something else—is always to blame. Just the opposite is true. .... Our economic performance depends on how well countless individual enterprises and their workers perform. Sure, they all face larger social and economic forces beyond their immediate power to alter. But that doesn't mean they have no control over their future.[4]

We have enormous control over our future. When our outside boundaries contract, however, we can think of little else. Whether due to regulatory change, economic or competitive conditions, or simply executive dictate, we rail against the shift in the rules. Our trade publications are filled with discussions on that change. We meet for hours on end, exploring every aspect of the new boundaries. Yet the truth is that even if we could influence the external shifts, the potential would be minor compared with that of shifting our own limitations.

We all live in prisons. The bars of those prisons are composed of those self-imposed rules with which we agree. When the *edge* points to those bars, we all too often renounce them. Renounce the excuse industry instead, and you discover options you never realized you had before. Use the *edge* to challenge and expand your own self-imposed boundaries, and your future is virtually limitless.

RECOGNIZING YOUR DIMINISHING RETURN

Your beliefs, procedures, and practices do not stop solving problems. Their existence is testimony to their problem-solving power. They do, however, cease to solve *new* problems with the same effectiveness of the old. Anyone who has ever played a ball sport (golf, tennis, baseball) is familiar with this principle. Up to a point, you can increasingly improve your game by approaching it incrementally—hit the ball harder, larger, tighter, closer—but beyond some point, you get a diminishing return. The more you put in, the less you seem to get out. Beyond the point of diminishing return, you have to fundamentally change your swing or your stance if you expect to improve your game.

This concept of the diminishing return is a powerful indicator of when your most closely held principles will come under attack. If you are reactive, you will actively begin to search for evidence of people working on that shift. If you are proactive, you will begin to work on the shift yourself. Either way, diminishing return is a powerful signal of both where and when your next "surprise" will hit.

If you are beyond the point of diminishing return, then a doubling of input will result in less than a doubling of output. If your budget were to double, could you *more than double* your performance? Certainly your performance would improve, but would it more than double? If your answer is no, then you know that some or perhaps many of the paradigms you practice are ripe for change.

Diminishing return can be applied very specifically. A secretary attended one of my seminars and asked me about her big problem during the break. Due to downsizing, she shared, she was responsible for supporting 70 percent more people, with no increase in resources. What could she do? I asked her whether a second secretary would more than double her productivity? "It would be heavenly," she responded, "but not double." I asked her if she worked twice the number of hours whether that would more than double her output. Again, she said no.

After further discussion, she disclosed that most of the people she supported had electronic calendars but "preferred" to continue using her to keep appointments. "Besides," she said, "I'm too busy to learn how to use their electronic calendars." They also had filing cabinets but "preferred" that she do the filing for them.

Everything the secretary had tried (more hours worked, requesting assistance, flexible work schedule) helped but could not solve her problem. Her traditional approaches had reached the point of diminishing return, a good predictor that things were about to change significantly. She could fundamentally alter her definition of what her job entailed, or she could leave. Either way, it was a safe bet she would not be continuing on the old path for long.

Innovation is another area that is susceptible to diminishing returns. Doubling resources will rarely result in more than doubling the rate of innovation. If either the budget increases without an increase in output, or the budget is unchanged but the rate of innovation declines, diminishing return has been exceeded. This is the time to actively devote yourself to finding the next paradigm.

For example, in research it is standard procedure that the early (predictable) lab work is done by technicians, who then hand off the results of their efforts to the doctoral researchers. Most firms recognize that the standard approaches of adding more bodies or purchasing more technology can rarely be expected to seriously increase innovation. Although they passed the point of diminishing return, however, these firms continue to tweak the established rules of research.

The UOP company had also tried to increase its rate of innovation but recognized that the rules would have to change. Rather than waiting for someone else to shift the rules, this company took a chance based on the understanding that many innovations, from Teflon to Silly Putty, come from unexpected results.

UOP broke the technician rule and now often requires that its scientists conduct the initial lab work. Due to that change, a team under researcher Edith Flanigen discovered a new generation of materials that could dramatically affect the chemical processing industry. All because UOP hit the wall of diminishing returns.

LOOKING FOR THE BANDWAGON

Sir James Goldsmith, the well-known financier once said, "If you see a bandwagon, it is too late." Although not as useful as recognizing a diminishing return, looking for the bandwagon is a valid indicator of potential change.

Kodak watched as the instant camera industry grew by leaps and bounds. Just when it seemed everybody was buying instant cameras, Kodak made the decision to enter the market—just in time to watch it decline. The bandwagon signal also holds true for marketing. When it seems every product has become an "ultra" version of itself, you know the power of that word will decline.

Other examples of bandwagon signals include:

- The popularity of junk bonds and small capitalization stocks.
- Offering corporate credit cards such as AT&T and GM credit cards. By the time General Electric offered theirs, demand was already on the decline.
- The use of "clear" as a marketing tactic (as in clear soap, clear soft drinks, and clear gasoline).
- When everyone was talking about "computer literacy," this tolled the warning bell for ease-of-use computing—Windows.
- The bursting of the Japanese real estate bubble. When everyone in Japan seemed to have invested in real estate, you knew the decline was imminent.

The challenge with the bandwagon effect, of course, is to get the timing right. Naturally, everyone would like to jump in just when the bandwagon begins and exit right before it declines. Unfortunately, I know of no way to do that with any confidence. Those who benefit from applying the bandwagon effect don't push the timing to the edge. When it seems "everyone" is doing it, they recognize that the shift is likely to come soon. They recognize that this is the best time to begin searching for the next bandwagon.

LEARNING FROM THE LANGUAGE WE USE

In 1993 and 1994 General Motors made impressive improvements. Productivity and development, however, still lagged Ford and Chrysler. According to David Bradley, an analyst at J. P. Morgan Securities, "The low-hanging fruit has been picked."[5]

You may be telling people about the future and not even know it. When events are about to fundamentally shift, when the rule changes become imminent, the words we use to describe our problems often signal these changes long before we ourselves are aware of them.

I was asked to address a joint Ford/UAW conference several years ago. The general manager of the casting division spoke before I did. He opened his talk with the words "All the easy problems are behind us, we just have tough problems ahead." He was speaking about Ford's efforts to improve the quality of cast engines. He was also unintentionally telling the audience that the old rules were running out of steam. It was time to expect a whole new set of rules for casting steel.

Diminishing return, as we discussed, is often the precursor to a fundamental shift in the rules. Phrases like "All the easy problems are behind us . . . " and "The low-lying fruit has been picked" are how we announce (often unwittingly) that we are beyond the point of diminishing return. The irony is that the general manager's talk centered around the need for everyone to work much harder on improving the existing rules.

A little uncomfortable, I next told the group that an hour spent, a dollar spent, improving the old rules was well spent. However, the more we feel *"it is all uphill from here,"* the more effort we should probably invest in actively searching for the new rules.

When you get to the point where you seem to putting more in and getting less out, your language will change. Perhaps you'll find yourself saying, *"You can't get blood from a stone."* The phrases all mean essentially the same thing. Treat them as the lead indicators they are.

TRACKING HISTORICAL PATTERNS

The rent-a-car (RAC) market has always been a good business. As recently as seven to ten years ago, a RAC company could expect:

- An unlimited number of vehicles available for purchase.
- Multiple incentives to purchase, such as a free vehicle for every 50 vehicles bought.
- A $1,000 (and up) rebate for every vehicle.
- Any mix of models and options available on request.
- Unrestricted advertising allowance provided by the manufacturers.
- A hospitable, virtually tax-free welcome at every airport.
- Ownership or a controlling interest by one of the car manufacturers.
- The majority of their business to come from the business traveler.
- An unlimited availability of cheap and available labor.

In short, this has been a business marked by growth, profitability, and predictability. How could anyone have anticipated the tumult that would mark this industry? The *edge* competitors, represented by the auto manufacturers' own RAC businesses, seemed too small to consider. The *edge* customers (leisure renters) were generally acknowledged to be opportunistic business, at best. Due largely to shifts in these two groups, this once-placid industry found that in just ten short years it faced:

- Severe limits on the numbers of vehicles available.
- The disappearance of virtually every incentive.
- All rebates revoked.
- Only severely limited availability of models and options.
- Strict limitations on advertising allowances.
- Airports levying ever-increasing usage taxes on car rental firms.
- Car manufacturers' sale or spin-off of their RAC holdings (Budget sold by Ford Lincoln/Mercury, GM selling National and reducing its interest in Alamo and Avis, Chrysler selling Thrifty and Dollar, and Ford reducing its interest in Hertz by taking it public).
- A tenfold growth in the leisure market.
- A shortage of labor in virtually every region.

Crisis and surprise, such as that which has rocked the RAC industry, can be diminished by learning to read the signals from the future. That does not mean that we cannot also learn from the past.

As an example of historically based anticipation, let's assume that your revenue has begun to decrease slightly. Some in management have been speculating that the shortfall indicates that the salesforce needs more training. The sales group, meanwhile, maintains that the services being offered need to be updated.

Is the sales decline temporary, fixed by merely improving your organization's selling skills, or is it a reflection that your market is going to change? The following approach will allow you to build on history and anticipate structural changes in your market:

1. Examine your business activity to determine the historical patterns of both your mainstream and *edge* customers, suppliers, and competitors.

2. Create a time line of that activity.

3. Based on the time line, what are your conclusions?

4. What could happen in the future that would change those conclusions?

5. Track events to see whether the future is confirming or contradicting your expectations.

If you were considering moving into the rent-a-car industry, these five steps could have helped you avoid the dislocating shocks that have rocked it these past years. For example, if this were 1986:

1. You would have easily identified the nonbusiness renter as an *edge* customer.

2. A time line using the past 20, 10, or even 5 years would have recorded the nonbusiness renter as constituting a very minor part of the market.

3. Based on that time line, you reasonably might have concluded that the nonbusiness renter will continue to constitute a minor part of the market.

4. Any significant growth in the nonbusiness rental market would quite possibly indicate that your conclusions (in #3) were mistaken.

5. Tracking the nonbusiness RAC market for just a few years would have confirmed that this market was exploding. It would be time to revise your plans that were based on your prior conclusions.

Notice that even if you had tracked *edge* competitors instead of *edge* customers, your conclusions would have been the same. Enterprise Rent-A-Car, with a meager 6,000 cars in 1980, was reporting 89,000 cars in service ten short years later.

This is not to say that this is an undesirable industry in which to invest. Clearly, however, the rules have changed in a big way. At the very least, knowledge concerning the shifting historical patterns could have influenced the timing and magnitude of your investments.

The use of history in anticipating the future is not new. What is different about this five-step approach is that it directs your attention to the *edge*. It also compels you to think about the things the future can and likely will do to contradict your expectations.

There is no magic to this technique. Certainly, when conditions change, it is time to reevaluate your plans. Yet we have seen instance after instance where companies, from IBM to Apple, from Schwinn to Smith Corona, have missed those very same changes in conditions.

In the case of the RAC industry, the five-step process would have alerted the user to major discontinuities. The same approach can serve as a warning that history is likely to be repeated. Such a warning could have been quite useful to the Clinton administration.

In the fall of 1994, thousands of Cubans risked their lives in a "sudden" exodus from their homeland. This flood of refugees seemed to take President Clinton by surprise. The only real surprise was that he did not anticipate the refugee problem himself.

In 1980, while governor of Arkansas, Clinton fought hard against the hardships imposed on his home state by the mass exodus of Cuban refugees in the Mariel boat lift. His problems culminated in the rioting at Fort Chaffee by the recent Cuban arrivals. He believed this was partly to blame for his defeat for reelection as governor.

Despite those events, President Clinton tightened the restrictions on Cuba. He banned U.S. residents from sending money to relatives in Cuba and stopped the charter flights on which families were visiting those left behind. Yet his administration was unprepared for the "sudden" onslaught of refugees. It was clear he had remembered the events of 1980. If only he had learned from them.

Tracking historical patterns is simple, but it does take some time. I am not suggesting that you use this technique for all activities in your business. For those aspects of your business that you have deemed strategic, however, this is a powerful way of avoiding the nastiest of surprises.

Of course, using the *edge* to minimize surprise and crisis depends on your ability to work with the *edge*. Establishing a relationship with a group you have disenfranchised is not nearly as difficult as it sounds. But working with the *edge* is a far cry from Customer Service 101.

8

Creating Sizzling Teams

THE BENEFITS OF BRAIN DAMAGE

Why are maverick employees able to see things the rest of us are not? Quite simply . . . they are brain damaged! Maybe I'm being a little facetious (just a little), but quite literally, we can be fairly confident their brains are wired differently than the brains of the rest of us.

Researchers at the University of California, in Irvine, have discovered that the brain is an effective energy conservation device.[1] When a test group was given the task of playing a new computer game for the first time, positron-emission tomography (PET) scans showed a very high rate of glucose consumption, indicating significant energy consumption. This made sense, since learning new tasks takes effort.

After a month or two of practice, the researchers found that the average brain metabolism (energy usage) dropped significantly. In fact, the experienced game players were actually using less brain energy than the control group that was merely watching the game. Similar results have been reported by other researchers exploring music as a form of expertise.

These experiments strongly suggest that the intensity of brain activity diminishes as we get better at a task. Richard J. Haier, a neuropsychologist researcher, noted: "It's possible that the brain learns over time what neural circuits *not* to use to perform a task, eventually relying only on certain important circuits."[2] In the interest of conservation, the "normal" brain physically changes to reflect experience. The expert's brain is an efficient brain. This efficiency brings great power. This is why experts can look at a situation for a few seconds and see things that the rest of us couldn't see in hours. Their experience enables them to deal with repeating patterns with ever-increasing sophistication and speed. As long as the conditions that created that expertise are still in play, there is little doubt as to the advantages of experience.

After the test group mastered the computer game (became experts), the researchers altered the rules significantly. The established neural patterns that the test subjects developed had to slow down severely. Thus, they often had more difficulty learning the new rules than when they first started the game. Their brains had become "hardwired" in rigid patterns. This is why experts have a hard time seeing new influences—they contradict the experts' wiring. It is not that experts can't change. They can and do change. But their knowledge makes change more difficult, and more mental effort is required for them to adapt their wiring in response to major change.

What of maverick employees on the *edge*? Despite the fact that they may be experts, their mental patterns are usually not as fixed as the patterns of mainstream employees who *know* the rules. In some fundamental way that we do not yet understand, mavericks don't share the wiring of the rest of us. They quite literally think on a different plane.

So the next time you tell a maverick that he or she is brain damaged, be sure to explain that you mean it only in the most complimentary way.

TEAMS THAT BLAST THROUGH PROBLEMS

Dramatic change is risky, painful, and scary. Just ask any parent watching his or her teenager go out the door on a first date! Fortunately, most of the problems we encounter on a daily basis do not demand radical measures. Probably 95 percent of all problems can be handled with small, safe, incremental change. Tweak a little here, enhance a little there, and the problem is solved.

Still, the other 5 percent remains. These problems constitute your most difficult and persistent challenges. Their longevity stands as testimony to the need for drastically different approaches—if a solution could have been easily accomplished, you would have done it long ago. For these problems, only the most original thinking will do.

How do you guarantee that you will get the most original thinking? First and foremost, do *not* rely on your experts. It's OK to use experts in a limited fashion, but be sure they do not dominate your focus. Recognize that most experts, by definition, are part of the mainstream. They know the rules inside out, but those rules may be the very obstacles that prevent you from finding new solutions. I do not suggest that experts never create breakthrough solutions, only that they are less likely to do so. Experts who do arrive at breakthrough approaches are typically mavericks, members of the select group that has mastered the rules but has not absorbed the rules as part of its filter.

Opposites Attract

One of my clients, a paper products manufacturer, aspired to become a major player in the global marketplace. We created a team to explore what might be done to expand the company's performance worldwide. The team consisted of various cross-functional employees who helped set up their new initiative. I requested that the team also include someone who was a critic of the team's recent efforts.

My suggestion was flatly rejected. "We can't afford the time to bring someone else up to speed," was the response. "OK," I replied, "that sounds reasonable enough, *if* we wanted to bring them up to speed. That is not the point. The idea is not to bring the person up to speed. I just want you to include someone who can look at your efforts with an outsider's perspective." I must have been exceptionally persuasive that day, because they agreed to humor me in this matter. When I added that the person ideally would be a vocal and strident critic, two of the team members groaned and said in unison . . . "You must mean Tony."

Tony did not want to be on the team. He did not go to any of the seminars attended by the rest, insisting that it was a waste of time. Finally, he was just instructed by his boss to show up.

After 40 minutes of silence, Tony became visibly agitated. "Come on," he said, "be honest. We don't even *really believe* in globalization." Talk about hitting a sore point! The team leader (who was also Tony's boss) hit the roof. "Tony," he responded through clenched teeth, "you're dead wrong. Globalization is a key component of our strategic plan. We have doubled our number of overseas trips and have even hired a vice president in charge of global development. I'd say we're walking the talk pretty damn well. Right?" He stared Tony down with an "I dare you to cross this line" expression.

Tony was not to be dissuaded. "Look," he responded, "you insisted that I come here to tell you what I think. And that is exactly what I am gong to do! I'm the guy who's responsible for product support. I am compensated based on how quickly I can respond to requests, as well as the number of requests that I satisfy. A nondomestic product support call takes twice as much time for me to handle as the domestic calls, between all the agency communication, time difference, and special needs. You *say* that you believe in globalization, but I get penalized for every international transaction."

There was silence in the room as Tony's words began to sink in. He made a powerful point that was hard to deny, in spite of his abrasive attitude. All of a sudden it seemed obvious. Of course Tony was right! The company was concentrating so heavily on the "big picture" (globalization), it missed all the organizational inertia associated with its old approach. Tony had always assumed that everyone must know that he was being penalized for global support. He was convinced that they never *really* believed in globalization, that it was window dressing.

I hear so many organizations tell their employees on the *edge* to "get with the program." They assume that anyone who resists "such an obviously good idea" is misguided, misinformed, or just "doesn't like anything." Obviously, sometimes that is the case. Often, however, people resist because they see something that the mainstream cannot.

Innovation occurs when we challenge our assumptions. That is one of the spectacular benefits of wide-angle vision. Rather than trying to control or segregate disagreeable employees, we need to involve them in the very efforts they criticize. What do you think would have happened to Tony had he not been involved in that session? He was feeling frustrated and destined to fail. How could he possibly succeed, he reasoned, when he was penalized for not supporting globalization, and penalized for not concentrating on domestic needs? To make matters worse, he was feeling increasingly disenfranchised by the company. Put it all together and you have the perfect formula for a lost employee.

One word of caution: I am not suggesting that you involve vocal and strident employees in every team activity. This technique is a powerful approach when applied to problem-solving teams of a limited duration. Employees who tend to be mavericks may not be the best material from which to create extended work teams.

Who, then, do you invite to help solve your most difficult problems? A team of people unlike those you have ever used before. First, let's make one thing very clear: Whenever you can pull together a truly perspective-diverse group, you greatly maximize the likelihood that it will identify the rules and assumptions you have been employing. It is these rules and assumptions that make up your filters.

This is the value of cross-functional teams. The sales group needs to know accounting's rules, explicitly because they work with accounting on a regular basis. But because they are not part of accounting, they don't own those rules. For sales, it is an easy matter to list the rules employed by accounting.

The reverse, of course, is also true. The accounting department can identify the rules and assumptions of the sales group, even though they would have great difficulty listing their own. If you want to understand the filter of any group, look to those with whom that group has contact.

This is not always a peaches-and-cream scenario, however. In our example, both accounting and sales are part of the same company. Although they are separate, they still share much the same perspective. This limits their ability to see their own filters.

Let's say your company is Gadgets, Inc. and you want to anticipate the future of training as it relates to your sales organization. Using what we have discussed concerning groups on the *edge*, you have identified the following people and groups that you would like to participate as a team:

Employees

- Nancy—In three years, Nancy has attended only one sales seminar. She registers but does not show.
- Bob—This sales manager is always complaining that training is a waste, an expense of people and time with little value.

Customers

- Acme, Inc.—This company continually gripes that it knows more about how your product is used than your salespeople.

Suppliers

- TrainCo—One of your divisions used this company for a while and swears by their technique of "immersion" learning.
- HyperTrain—You've never considered using this supplier's services before, but it is well regarded in the industry. It doesn't "train" but makes the information easily accessible via sales force laptop computers.

Competitors

- Widgets, Inc.—New in the market, this organization has been hiring its customer's employees sales assistants (SAs). These SAs provide much of the application knowledge.

In addition to this abbreviated group on the *edge*, you can expand your team by asking:

Who has significant influence *on* my target?
Who is significantly influenced *by* my target?

Obviously, these two questions cast a much larger net when creating your teams. Gadgets's list might include:

- Mainstream salespeople.
- Management.
- Training designers.
- Mainstream customers.
- Mainstream competitors.
- The sales trainer who quit last month.

Your own list might also include regulators, union representatives, or even stockholders. The idea is to include a list of people and organizations who *might* help in anticipating your target. Don't worry, we are not suggesting you actually invite competitors to your session. For now, just appreciate that their perspectives could be useful. Take a moment, and create your own list.

HOW DO EDGE TEAMS DIFFER?

If you gave it serious thought, your list should be fairly extensive. Unless you have the remarkable luxury of having unlimited access to team members, you will have to decide which potential participants present the most value. The criteria is important: Whenever possible, select those team members who are outspoken, confrontational, and strident.

This suggestion runs squarely against popular team philosophy, but consider its merits. The *edge* team is a short-term instrument. It is created for the specific, discrete purpose of dramatic problem solving or anticipating future challenges and opportunities. This contrasts with management teams, where managers meet regularly with no calendar limit, and with work teams, where workers associate on a continuous basis.

When a long-term relationship is important, a carefully coordinated grouping of personalities is mandatory. Since management and work teams are unstructured in terms of their day-to-day efforts, this smooth relationship is all the more critical. This is why it is not unusual for organizations to conduct psychological and work style profiles when creating such teams. We try to promote a sense of unity and community around these teams. We absolutely want harmony to reign supreme.

Edge teams are created for very specific and discrete purposes. For this reason alone, the personality mix is much less important. Beyond this, such a mix will actually yield negative results. The desired attributes of unity and community, so important for work teams, will typically result in a uniformity of perspectives. This virtually assures us that the team will get along, but team members will find it exceedingly hard to identify one another's filters.

IBM worked hard to ensure that teams got along: " . . . IBMers began to focus on winning arguments without 'breaking glass'—which meant offending colleagues. Harsh, scratchy people disrupted things and just didn't seem necessary."[3]

It does not matter whether people on the *edge* are actually right. What makes them valuable is their penchant for challenging the mainstream. No one should be expected to create a team that will attack each other—this is not necessary or productive. But *edge* teams must be more concerned with exploring their target than with protecting their sensitivities. A salesperson who wants to avoid making the accountant feel bad is of no value on this kind of team.

There is another, more basic reason to avoid the personality traps of traditional teams: perspective diversity. We've seen how fundamental differences in perspective will lead to increased visibility. This can be viewed as a kind of "spectral analysis." The whole of any situation can be best understood by looking at its individual, composite factions. Teams that share a sense of community (just like a single color of the spectrum) rarely possess the variety that is needed to strip away their blinders. Those blinders are there whether we are aware of them or not.

A wonderful example of the value of *edge* teams was conveyed by a woman who conducted classes about coping with diversity in the workplace. She said:

> My typical class consists of about 25 people: a mix of women, African Americans, Hispanics, Japanese and white men. I begin the class by asking each of them to write down the organization's rules of operating in a white, male-dominated environment.
>
> The women begin to write. The Japanese begin to write. The African Americans and Hispanics begin to write. And then we have the white men . . . staring uncomfortably at the people around them, and unable to think of a single rule.
>
> Often the women are asking for a second sheet of paper, and still the white men cannot come up with one rule![4]

This story is terrific because it perfectly describes the down-side of community, the *blindness* of shared filters. As a group, the white men share a relatively seamless and smooth culture. As long as our interest is in supporting that culture, a single-community team consisting of only white men will be quite effective. If our goal lies in challenging that culture, however, they are clearly the least appropriate group to whom you'd turn.

Often, practical concerns limit just how diverse our teams can be. This will be addressed in the next chapter. For now, let's agree on the following point: The effectiveness of a problem-solving team is in direct proportion to its diversity of perspective.

This is vitally important. If you want to reinvigorate quality as a discipline, do not stack your team with quality experts. If you want to anticipate the future of packaging, do not invite only those who are vested in your packaging paradigm.

THE DISBELIEF OF TEAMS

We have all seen it. Management creates a team to work on a problem and then dismisses the solution the team presents. What could be more frustrating? The team members are indirectly told that they should have just rubber-stamped what management wanted in the first place, and then the proposal would have sailed through. The team assumes (incorrectly) that management never really wanted original thinking. The team members place the blame on management, when they should be blaming themselves.

Work teams are often conducted in total isolation. They meet for days, weeks, sometimes months, considering every aspect of a problem. When a team presents its conclusions, the final report often includes a full explanation of the team's recommendation. What is missing is any discussion of what the group considered but did not recommend.

When the challenge the team tackles is not considered critical, or when the team's suggestions match management's expectations, the lack of full documentation is rarely a problem. When the challenge has significant reach, or when the recommendation is a radical departure from what was expected, however, adequate documentation is invaluable.

Every team should fully document not just its recommendations but every option it considered. For *edge* teams, especially, full documentation is essential. Because *edge* teams are far more likely to generate unexpected results, it is vital that they be able to share all major aspects of their work.

Many modern companies encourage personal empowerment among their employees, but this does not relieve the teams from an obligation to fully explain their work to management. Because an empowered workforce is not a separate entity from the corporation, employees must work with management to stimulate productivity and maximize the assets of the organization. The credo of "never complain, never explain" may work for generals, but it has no place in a corporate environment.

YOUR WORKING TEAM

It's time to create your own *edge* working team. Remember not to restrict yourself while you are creating the team. And take your time! After all, this may very well be the most valuable enhancement that you have ever utilized in your business. When you've listed all the potential candidates, then you can trim your list back to a more useful and manageable size.

Earlier in this chapter we asked questions concerning who has an influence *on* your target, and who is influenced *by* your target. These are the potential candidates for your *edge* team, but the list can become incredibly large. Some of these people will never show up, however, either because you don't want them (competition, regulators, and members of the media, to name a few) or because they don't want you (your lost customers). This will decrease the size of your team but most likely still leave you with a long list of people and organizations to focus on. How do you decide who to include?

First, in creating an *edge* team, remember that small is beautiful. With very few exceptions, there is no such thing as a problem-solving team of 15 people. Such large teams invariably become informal sets of multiple, smaller teams.

When a large group informally branches into smaller groups, you can bet that each offshoot has a great deal in common. They may be from the same division or perform the same function.

Perhaps they share the same geography or the same politics. Regardless of what they hold in common, these informal teams all hold one other thing in common—the same filter.

Large teams, even large diverse teams, inevitably break into their lowest common denominator. This defeats the very reason that we create *edge* teams to begin with. It makes no sense to carefully select those with the greatest disparity in perspective, only to allow them to organize based on common interests.

If you feel that you need a large *edge* team, carefully "shuffle the deck" and break it into a set of smaller teams. Fewer than four to a team makes it difficult to generate the diversity you need. Greater than seven, and you risk creating multiple informal teams. In most cases, an *edge* team of five is ideal.

Remember that the purpose of *edge* teams is to generate a wide variety of viewpoints. One opinionated, vocal team member is worth three of more moderate temperaments. Recruiting "moderate" members is a fatal mistake many make in creating *edge* teams. On paper, it may look like you have a powerful mix of views, only to have those views fade into an atmosphere of "reasonableness." Our aim is not to ferment discord among participants, but without a diverse and *vocal* perspective, we dull the *edge* of our team.

The way to minimize *edge* team antagonism is through structure. Brainstorming has its place, but not with *edge* teams. Because of the necessary mix of personalities, it is crucial that members' attention be focused on the team's purpose and not on the jugulars of their teammates. In Chapter 9 you will learn some simple yet powerful techniques that can be used to get powerful results from *edge* teams.

9

The World at Your Fingertips

Crashes don't occur only while planes are in flight. Sometimes they happen before they leave the drawing board. Unfortunately for Beech Aircraft, it didn't hear the crash until it was too late.

Beech wanted to build the world's first all-composite business airplane, called Starship. Everyone agreed that it had to be special. The company hired Burt Rutan, the world-class designer who built the Voyager, which flew around the world on one tank of gas.

Under Rutan's direction, Beech engineered the plane from the ground up, engaging only top people in the field. An 85 percent scale model was flown to demonstrate its potential to customers in 1983, and orders rolled in. Success seemed assured. Yet in six years, Beech Aircraft sold less than 20 planes. Why? Because the plane's designers did not take into account the rigid mentality of the Federal Aviation Administration (FAA). This mistake cost Beech over $350 million dollars.

Even though composites are more than three times stronger than aluminum, the FAA required that Starship conform to the structural specifications of conventional planes. This meant significantly increasing the thickness of critical components, which increased weight. The result was an all-composite plane that weighed roughly the same as a metal plane.

Consequently, most of the expected performance measures were not met. The FAA's discomfort in regulating this first-of-its-kind aircraft resulted in delayed production and decreased efficiency. The designers projected the plane would go on sale in a record two years, but the first Starship was not available for almost six years.

Was the FAA to blame for Starship's failure? Certainly it could have been more flexible in evaluating a new design, but when it comes to air safety we expect and welcome a cautious approach to flying. The engineers and designers shared no blame. The Starship (pre-FAA) was a testimony to their creativity and skill. And Beech's management demonstrated imagination and daring in backing this innovative concept.

The reason Starship failed was that Beech was unable to *anticipate* the FAA's reaction to the plane's radical design. Beech's management was understandably excited over their pioneering efforts. They correctly perceived that customers would be fascinated and attracted to this visionary product. What their optimism and enthusiasm prevented them from seeing, however, was that innovation and daring can be daunting to a mainstream perspective.

The blindness described in Chapter 2 affects us all. Creating *edge* teams is a powerful method of curing that blindness. *Edge* teams provide perspectives that challenge the inevitable tunnel vision that we all fall prey to. Yet *edge* teams cannot work, no matter how well conceived, if the required members of the *edge* are not present.

Even if Beech had created an *edge* team to consider Starship (it did not), management probably would not have invited a representative of the FAA to participate—regulators are typically avoided, not embraced. And if, under the extraordinary condition that Beech *had* invited the FAA, it is quite unlikely the FAA would have accepted. The accepted sequence places regulators at the end of the process, not the beginning.[1]

VIRTUAL REALITY AT WORK

The *edge* team, by definition, is always an incomplete solution. Perspectives that may be of enormous benefit will always be lacking, no matter how carefully you select your participants. The Ideal Team, however, is a phenomenally effective method for simulating perspectives of the *edge* that you otherwise might miss. This team consists, not of real people, but of virtual, simulated people and organizations that act as representatives from the *edge*.

Just as Beech Aircraft experienced, there are occasions when you don't really want participation from the *edge*, even though that perspective would be very useful. When you roll out a new product, for example, you could certainly benefit from the knowledge of how it might be perceived by your competition. I doubt, however, that anyone would consider such an invitation.

There are also times when a member of the *edge* would not want to participate, in spite of your best efforts. The FAA would most likely decline your invitation, as would most other regulatory bodies. Many *edge* customers also would reject participation, regardless of inducements.

Finally, there are those whose involvement you would welcome but, for any number of reasons, they cannot participate. After all, their world does not necessarily revolve around your schedule. In all these cases you are forced to build your *edge* team around a less-than-perfect set of circumstances. In these cases, the *simulation* of the *edge* perspectives of various members is an astonishingly effective technique that captures the fringe input you would otherwise miss.

When should you use the Ideal Team? Anytime you need a diverse perspective but cannot get it through the use of a real, working *edge* team. My clients use the Ideal Team when trying to move toward a new vision, reengineer a process, or solve a stubbornly difficult problem. They apply it when considering new products or services and even use it informally to gain insights into perspectives otherwise lost during business meetings.

CREATING AN IDEAL TEAM

To create an Ideal Team, simply start by asking the same questions you asked to create your *edge* working team: Who has a significant influence *on* my target? and Who is significantly influenced *by* my target?

Those who do not make it to your real, working team are perfect candidates for your Ideal Team. The first step in creating the Ideal Team is to select those on your list who represent the greatest diversity in perspective. As mentioned earlier, it makes little sense to include members on your Ideal Team who share your outlook.

A West Coast medical center that wanted to improve patient care asked a group of nurses to identify changes that would accomplish this goal. A very commendable task! After a grueling day, a set of recommendations was drafted. The nurses suggested changes for the physicians, administration, engineering (maintenance), and admissions—but not one change they themselves had to make.

I was asked to conduct a second workshop, and the nurses agreed to employ the Ideal Team technique. One nurse said with some hesitation, "I think I know what the complaining patient [customer on the *edge*] would say to us. 'Nurses believe that the best patients are those who are seen and not heard.' " The other nurses reluctantly agreed, and we began to explore ways that patients could be constructively brought into the health care process. Many considered this (believe it or not) to be a radical concept, but upon reflection it was clearly the way to go. With the help of the Ideal Team, the nurses concluded the day with 27 nursing-related changes to improve patient care. The workshop was a major success.

The Ideal Team is . . .

- A virtual team, consisting of only names on paper. As such, team members can be "hired" and "fired" as you find convenient.
- A small group (5 to 7 people or organizations).
- A known group—you have a clear concept about how team members would probably react to the challenges you're trying to overcome.

The Ideal Team is not . . .

- Role playing—your task is not to look at the world through team members' eyes but to listen to their voices.
- Only those who agree with you—bet your money on the fact that those who disagree with your perspectives will see more of your rules.

After years of helping organizations use the Ideal Team, I am convinced that role playing is, at best, not necessary and, at worst, counterproductive. If you are lucky, role playing will simply offer a nominal advantage over merely considering the perspective of the Ideal Team. More often, the working team member who assumes the role loses his or her identity as part of the working team. That is rarely a good trade-off.

Another critical consideration is how to make the Ideal Team members as three-dimensional and extreme in their perspectives as possible. It is difficult, for example, to consider how "a customer" might feel about the way you handle contracting but fairly easy to imagine what "Precision Products" might say. This is especially true if you imagine that your virtual contact at Precision Products is very upset with your firm.

Remember, the object is not to make things up, only to consider the extreme perspective. At a recent workshop, one of the groups was reporting on its customer service issues, several of which were raised using the Ideal Team. The group's vice president, visibly upset, interrupted the group's presentation. "This is simply not true," he said. I asked the participants whether they had ever heard anyone ever say things similar to what was being presented? The response was a sea of nodding heads. That, in fact, is the acid test when in doubt as to the validity of an Ideal Team observation. If we can imagine an extreme customer making a statement, and we have heard those kinds of statements before, you can assume the point is valid. To assist in the creation of the Ideal Team, let's examine some actual cases where the Ideal Team was applied. We'll look at how the working groups created the team, and later, how they applied the Ideal Team technique to solve problems. The first example, although a personal rather than organizational application, is still a remarkably clear demonstration of the Ideal Team's potential.

Teenage Turmoil

Tony was having problems with his 16-year-old daughter, Barbara. No, that's putting it too mildly. The Gaza Strip was peaceful compared to their home life. Both Tony and Barbara were absolutely certain everything would be fine, if only the other would be reasonable.

Clearly, Tony and Barbara could have benefited from family counseling, but Barbara refused to go. Tony decided to consider the possibility that maybe, just maybe, he could do something different. Although skeptical, he agreed to create his Ideal Team. "Not a problem," he sighed, "I'll just include those people in my nightmare last night."

Tony's initial Ideal Team included:

- Barbara (his daughter).
- His ex-wife.
- His aunt (who was close to the situation and had opinions on *everything*).

That was a good start, but then he dug deeper. Who else might have a very different way of looking at his parental problems? He added to his team:

- Dr. Spock.
- A friend whose daughter recently ran away.
- Himself as a teenager.

Tony later realized that he should drop Dr. Spock—not because he might not have an important perspective but because Tony actually didn't know how Dr. Spock would view his situation. Of course, he could have taken this opportunity to research Dr. Spock's (or another expert's) views on raising teenagers, but he chose to "fire" him from the team instead.

In the end, Tony did achieve a sort of breakthrough. Specifically, Barbara (who was at the mall at the time but participated on the Ideal Team in abstentia) observed that Tony's rules included "Dump on Barbara for everything." Thinking back to himself as a teenager, Tony admitted that he "rarely praises for the good things, but always points out the shortcomings." Finally, he remembered his friend saying that if he could do it all over again, he would "pick the fights much more carefully." Using the Ideal Team, Tony was able to accept that he contributed more to the fighting than did Barbara. Since then a fragile cease-fire has been declared.

A Yearbook to Remember

A publisher of yearbooks had experienced a steady decline in sales for almost a decade. The company pursued the market vigorously but was unable to reverse this trend. It invited me to conduct a workshop for them with the intent of reversing their situation. Five working groups were created. Each of these then composed its own individual Ideal Team.

One group's Ideal Team looked like this:

- principal
- student
- parent
- teacher
- competitor
- marketing manager
- yearbook adviser

Although the team was headed in the right direction, it was not complete. The yearbook adviser, for example, was crucial to the development of the yearbook design and content. What *kind* of adviser should be on the Ideal Team? This prompted a discussion about the traits of advisers the group members had worked with before.

There were advisers who followed recommendations to the letter. Others strove for maximum originality. Some were constantly calling, requesting more input from the yearbook company. Others were never heard from, serving their function as a source of extra income, working as little as possible to complete the job.

The working team all agreed that an omnipresent, vocal adviser would be a good addition to the Ideal Team. Since the adviser was so important to the success of the yearbook, however, I suggested that another kind, the minimum-work type, be "invited." Here team members protested, since this type of adviser was rarely heard from. The working team didn't think an invisible adviser fit the description of a vocal, in-your-face type that I normally suggest as Ideal Team material.

When I suggest that the Ideal Team member be vocal, I am not referring to the category he or she represents but to the characteristics of the imaginary person on the team. Even though the invisible adviser is not a vocal category, someone representing that category could be quite vocal. The person's refrain might be, "Don't bother me with details, I'm busy . . . just make my life easy and tackle the tough decision for me, OK? After all, you're the experts."

I also suggested that the working team change the Ideal Team student to a student on the *edge*, one who represents the increasingly difficult market with whom the company deals. Team members selected a minority student from an inner city, one who might not consider purchasing a yearbook.

The working team soon got the idea that the key to building a successful Ideal Team is to fill its ranks with three-dimensional, vocal, paradigm-diverse people and organizations. We will come back later to check on the progress of the yearbook company. For now, let's look at some other examples of how different businesses utilized the unique power of the Ideal Team to uncover exciting avenues of opportunity.

INVESTING IN CHANGE

In the late 1980s I worked with a medium-sized investment firm located in the Midwest. Business was good, but the CEO was concerned that the firm was becoming complacent. He wanted to be sure that the company could maintain its edge in a very competitive market. His goal was to challenge the way the firm ran its businesses (the company consisted of five distinct divisions, each representing an entirely unique business). The firm's specific target was aggressive; it wanted to double in size within the next five years.

Our working team began by questioning team members' views of the future, which was a critical first step. To this end each business unit broke off into teams consisting of managers from that specific business. I prefer to let groups organize themselves, but at this point I felt compelled to break in. "You people have about as much diversity as a loaf of white bread," I chided them. "Try shuffling the deck by mixing each of the company's divisions." This was an improvement, but not by much. They were, after all, from the same company, worked in the same building, and reported to the same man. Two of the group managers, in fact, had run one of the other divisions in the past. They still lacked diversity.

An Ideal Team has intrinsic value, but that value grows immeasurably when the actual working team shares a common perspective. Again, I stuck in my two cents. "I would like each business unit team to create an Ideal Team for the express purpose of better anticipating the selected target [double in size within the next five years]." What follows is the actual analysis of the commercial real estate group.

We began by creating a list of key stakeholders. Optimally, we would draw our workshop participants (working team) from that list, and the remaining names become candidates for the Ideal Team. Practically, the working team is often already selected, as it was in this case. The real estate group created its list of key stakeholders by asking the two questions: Who has significant influence *on* my target? and Who is significantly influenced *by* my target? A partial list of stakeholders included:

- Commercial developers.
- Competitors.
- Bankers.
- Federal government.
- Real estate investors.
- Other business divisions.

This list was a good start, but like most first attempts at an Ideal Team, it was far too general. Remember, our objective is to make the Ideal Team members as real as possible. Here are some of the thought processes behind the commercial real estate group's efforts to make the Ideal Team members more three-dimensional:

- **Federal government**—Everyone admitted, yes, this was a bit too broad. They settled on the President of the United States. This was an excellent choice, actually. Everyone knew the President's position on most issues and the group could visualize him taking those positions. Note: Famous personalities rarely make effective Ideal Team members because it is generally not known how those people would perceive our issues. This was an exception.
- **Bankers**—This was a good category, as bankers both influence and are influenced by commercial real estate investment. The group settled on two specific bankers, one representing the mainstream banking community (fully supportive of the real estate group's business) and one representing the margin (extremely conservative in real

estate investment). Note: Because some team members did not work in the real estate group, the other participants made a point of describing the bankers in sufficient detail so that everyone could understand how they might think.

- **Other business divisions**—Capital and other resources are always limited. This pits one division against another, effectively making them internal competitors for funds. They selected the largest capital user for the Ideal Team.
- **Competitors**—This was hard for them. Although group members could rattle off mind-numbing statistics about their mainstream competitors, they could not name even one competitor at the margin. They decided to investigate *edge* competitors at the conclusion of the workshop.

DESIGNING YOUR OWN IDEAL TEAM

Now it's time to create your Ideal Team. Remember not to restrict yourself while you are creating the team. After you've listed all the potential candidates, you can trim your list back to a more useful and more manageable size.

Who on your list will not participate? Who do *you* not want to participate? Cross those people or groups off your working team list, and record them on your Ideal Team list.

If your working team list consists of more than seven people, trim it down. You don't want to create a committee, just an intimate, targeted group. When I conduct workshops for organizations, we often work with groups of 35 or more but we always break the groups into teams of 5 or 7 people each.

If your Ideal Team has more than five people on it, also trim the list. Why only five? We want you to actively use your Ideal Team. If there are more than six or seven, there is a tendency to lose focus, to treat your Ideal Team as just names on a list, and to fail to use it as a representation of genuine perspectives. So keep your Ideal Team to five people/organizations, and once you add a Special Team Member (I'll discuss this concept later) or two, your final Ideal Team list will be about seven.

How do you know who to trim from your working team and Ideal Team? People you've listed all have an influence on, or are influenced by, your target, so that's no help. I don't suggest you use "degree of influence" either. Often those who have the greatest influence on us also share the greatest affiliation with the old beliefs, making them ineffective at revealing the very rules that we wish to expose.

Those who disagree most with the established ways of doing things make the best members of both the working team and Ideal Team. Try prioritizing all candidates using a score of 1, 2, or 3, using factors such as paradigm diversity (they either disagree with the established paradigm or don't work within it) and expressiveness. Also consider whether you know how an Ideal Team person might view the existing paradigms regarding how things are done today.

Finally, whenever possible, you want to make your Ideal Team members as detailed and specific as you can. It is far better to list a specific customer, for example, then just list the word *customer*.

Let's review some rules of creating *edge* teams:

- Keep working teams and Ideal Teams small, limited to 5 to 7 members. If you need to prioritize your candidates, then pick those with the most challenging perspectives.
- Always encourage honesty. This is best accomplished by selecting members who are vocal and convinced about the validity of their positions.
- Remember that every observation has some foundation in fact. Explore the facts; don't negate the observation.
- If you can't imagine how an Ideal Team Member would feel about the target you're exploring, you either have the wrong member or have not adequately described him/her.
- You should not try to describe what an Ideal Team Member *would* say about the target but what the member *might* say about the target.

The perfect working team member holds opinions very different from your own and has no problem expressing those differences. On your Ideal Team, you also want someone who holds different opinions, someone who pulls no punches. Finally, remember that the best Ideal Team member serves little purpose if you have no idea how he or she might consider your target and your practiced paradigms.

CREATIVE SOLUTIONS WITH YOUR IDEAL TEAM

Once you have created your Ideal Team, simply ask the question, What would this individual or group say about how we pursue our target? It may seem absurdly basic, but sometimes it really is just that simple.

Now that you have a better understanding of the mechanics of the Ideal Team, let's go back to the beleaguered yearbook company that I discussed earlier. The company complained that it wasn't coming up with anything new using its Ideal Team. This was a dead giveaway that the Ideal Team concept was not being used properly, because it *always* works. Sitting with the working team, I selected the minority student and asked team members to describe the student to me. There was no response.

I reminded them that every Ideal Team member must be fully three-dimensional if it is going to work and so began to ask specific questions of the group:

"Is the student a boy or a girl?"

"Boy," they responded.

"How old is he?"

"Fifteen."

"What does he look like?"

"He is an African American, 5 foot 10 inches, with average looks."

"Is he a good student or a struggling student?" I continued.

"He is a struggling student who skips a lot of classes and has little motivation to succeed."

"Fine," I said. "Now this 15-year-old African American fringe student with a chip on his shoulder is sitting in this chair [I pulled over an empty chair]. You have paid him $50 to come and tell you why he would never purchase one of your yearbooks. What does he say?"

After some silence one of the group members spoke up. "He would say that the yearbook is just some 'white-bread' product that has no relevance to him." Now we were making progress. "Hold it," said another member of the group, "that used to be the case, but now our yearbooks are the model of diversity. We have a good mix of races and ethnic backgrounds."

That last comment stopped the group cold again. "Wait a minute," I exclaimed, "this kid is still sitting in this chair. What do you think he might say to that?" Again a short silence, and then the person who objected spoke up. "He might say that all we did was take the white faces and color them in, replacing them with a different mix of kids." Suddenly the group stopped and stared at the empty chair. "I'll be damned," whispered the member who had objected, "that's exactly what we did. We never really changed the yearbook design at all."

This revelation opened up an entirely new way of looking at the company's target. Notice how difficult it was for the group to stay focused on the Ideal Team member, and how important it was to make that student as real and argumentative as possible. Naturally, if we had a real student with the desirable characteristics, those participating would most certainly have had even more value for their time.

When you create Ideal Team members, you are creating stereotypes and caricatures, since you are primarily interested in extreme positions. Out of 15 men (no women) working on this project, all were white. Certainly there were African American children who were good students, and white children who were failing, and anyone belonging to these groups might not purchase a yearbook. Our objective, however, was to stack the Ideal Team with three-dimensional images that struck a chord for the working team members. That these images are not necessarily representative of "reality" is not nearly as important as that they work.

Often it works well to be more specific when "asking" Ideal Team members for their input. An effective way to accomplish this is to consider the target from five perspectives, called facets:

1. Resource.
2. Influence.
3. Location.
4. Process.
5. Time.

Resource

Resource consists of those assets, tangible and intangible, that are associated with your target. For the yearbook company, resources included its sales kit, cars, the yearbook itself, the templates and guidelines they gave to the advisers to help in designing the yearbook, and the students who sold the yearbooks for the schools.

Influence

These are the people and groups who have an influence on or are influenced by your target. You will notice this is basically the same group from which you drew your Ideal Team. You may also see that the advisers and students we listed as resources are also influencers. It is not unusual for a group to appear more than once. There is no need to consider them twice, however, so after the first time they are listed, don't bother including them again.

Location

Location covers those places that are relevant to your target. Headquarters, regional offices, schools, and where the yearbooks are sold were all included by the yearbook company.

Process

Process reflects how things get done. For the yearbook business, this includes selling the yearbook contract to the school, working with the advisers to get student involvement, and producing the finished yearbook.

Time

Time is an integral and often neglected aspect of every business. Time includes not just the volume of time (how much time things take) but also sequence (what occurs first, second, third) and frequency (how many times per week, month, quarter, or year).

In every case, we consider an Ideal Team member and ask "What would this person say about . . . ," and then finish by considering one of the five perspectives. For example, we might ask what the student adviser would say about our attitudes regarding time. He or she might say, "You spend plenty of time giving me technical instruction but not much time on how to promote the yearbook."

Some people object to this technique, asking how we can be sure that the Ideal Team member is truly thinking the things we ascribe to him or her. For the purpose of this exercise, it truly does not matter. Can your group imagine the Ideal Team member saying something like that? If the answer is yes, then it is a valid comment. Remember that creating the Ideal Team is a strategy to help you articulate and question the rules and filters that you apply. Whether you have actually heard a customer say something you ascribe to him or her is not important, as long as it helps to highlight your filters.

I am not saying that your *edge* team should make up comments; the observation coming from the Ideal Team member is the kind of thing you would expect. Remember the nurse who, using the Ideal Team, speculated that the *edge* patient might say, "The best patients are those who are seen and not heard"? I said that the other nurses hesitantly agreed. That was true. What I failed to mention was their reaction immediately after the initial "seen and not heard" observation. When she made this comment, the other nurses shot her down. "We don't believe that," they exclaimed. I asked if they had ever heard any patients ever make comments like that? "Sure," they said, "but we don't *believe* it."

As long as they could imagine a patient on the *edge* making such a comment, or in this case, had actually heard patients making such remarks, the observation is valid.

USES FOR YOUR IDEAL TEAM

The Ideal Team is a simple and powerful technique for questioning some of your most implicitly held assumptions. A partial list of how some of my clients have used Ideal Teams includes the following.

Process Improvement

Early in the life cycle of a process, improvements come easy. There are so many new rules to be discovered and mined, the potential for enhancement seems limitless. As the process matures, however, every new enhancement seems to require much more than the enhancement it followed. When you get to the point of diminishing return (i.e., when you seem to put more into the effort than you get out of it), throw out the old rule book and begin writing the new.

One of the ways of determining which rules to cast off is to have both your *edge* team and Ideal Team help you examine your new direction (your target). The use of the five perspectives is especially helpful here. The five perspectives help your analysis from becoming too generalized and high level. Remember that your old rule book is not written in platitudes but particulars.

New Products and Services

In the same way the Ideal Team can help to dramatically improve processes, it can also provide an innovative shot in the arm to help search for product and service improvements as well. Although having a diverse *edge* team is always desirable, this is especially important when considering products and services.

A New Vision

Few changes are more fundamental than the movement toward a new vision. Adopting a new vision can affect the very essence of an organization, shaking it to its foundation. Not to worry, however, since most new vision efforts will result in only superficial change at best.

The Ideal Team can help your organization come to grips with just how extraordinary the task of adopting a new vision can be. The Team can help you to understand what must change and to anticipate and plan where and when the biggest changes should occur.

Be the Star of Your Next Meeting

The next time you are at a meeting, and someone makes a point, try this: Jot down two people or groups that have significant influence on that point, and two that are significantly influenced by it. Make sure that each one is a member of the *edge*. Next ask yourself what each would say about that point.

You will find, by using this impromptu Ideal Team, it is unbelievably easy to come up with perspectives no one at the meeting will have considered. Some of my clients tell me there is a serious downside to this idea, however. They say that their insights have given them a reputation, and now they are invited to meetings all the time.

Bulletproofing Your Presentations

I'm not sure, but I think senior executives attend training classes on how to shoot down presentations. During my time working in the automotive and chemical industries, I remember that I often felt, no matter how much I prepared, no matter how many angles I had considered, like a target in a firing range. The senior executive would sit back and casually (they must learn how to hide their glee) make statements like "Well, did you consider . . . ?" or "What happens if . . . ?" I would stagger out of the room, bloodied and bowed, determined to be better prepared next time. And next time would just be more of the same.

After you prepare for an important presentation, carefully create an Ideal Team, and let the Ideal Team take shots at your key points. They don't draw blood, and I guarantee that you will find yourself infinitely better prepared for the next target practice.

10

Working with Those on the Edge

PLUGGING YOUR INNOVATION LEAK: EMPLOYEES ON THE EDGE

Every year, every month, every week you open your doors to the people who hold your future . . . and push them out with both hands. But wait, it gets worse! In many companies, we actually interview these sources of valuable knowledge before casting them out. We ask superficial questions, or perhaps ask the right questions only to ignore the answers. I am speaking of the exit interview. Why is the exit interview so important? Because the employee on the *edge*, who is highly critical and often disenfranchised, always gets overshadowed by the mainstream. The farther out an employee is on the *edge*, the more difficult it is to hear him. Yet we know that people who live on the *edge* present the greatest potential to help us see tomorrow and change today. Unfortunately, the employee farthest out on the *edge* is probably the one who is on the way out.

Let's take a look at how you can capture the employee perspective. Do you survey your employees? Certainly the better companies do. A utilities firm brought me in to work with its employees. I was told that people were resisting the company's empowerment program, and they needed help in becoming more change oriented.

My meeting with the vice president of finance was . . . interesting. "We used to survey our employees," he said, "but we stopped. Every survey came back worse than the one before. I am convinced that when you ask for input, people take it as an opportunity to complain."

I asked whether the company had tracked survey results and was pleasantly surprised to hear that it did. When we looked at the results, it became clear that morale had started dipping about five years before. Coincidentally, that happened to be the same time the company began its "Our employees are #1" campaign. It seemed that the more it tried to "care" about the employees, the lower the surveyed morale dropped. The company's conclusion: stop the survey.

The problem with this utility was not its survey directly. By telling the employees that the company cared, and by touting its campaign, expectations were created that management was not prepared to meet. This is not all that unusual. The sound and the fury of enlightened management philosophy is much easier to emulate than to implement. This organization had the advantage of seeing the indications of low morale for several years before it became a full-blown problem. That was part of the value of the surveys; the sentiment of the *edge* was being heard. Because the company did not know to whom these sentiments should be attributed, however, they interpreted the results based on their own perspectives (transferability), and a valuable opportunity was lost.

By the time I was called in, the atmosphere of low morale was palpable. Everywhere I turned I faced cynicism and alienation. People talked about the company with an air of futility, mechanistically moving through their jobs. It was one of the most depressing environments I had ever seen, and the real sadness was, it was preventable. This was one of the few times in my career that I ever recommended that management stop their change program. It wasn't that the CEO and his staff weren't serious about change—they were. The problem was that they were delusional about what change required, and it was destroying the company.

Of course, surveys don't work unless they are anonymous. Not knowing who makes the comments, though, is a decided disadvantage if you want to understand the thought process behind the survey, but *all* answers should be gleaned for new perspectives. Since problems first reveal themselves through people on the *edge*, their viewpoints should be probed carefully. The *edge* is a minority that is perilous to ignore.

At first you may only see 5 percent of those surveyed who reflect any hint of a problem. The next year that number grows to 12 percent. By now you are concerned, so you conduct focus groups. Since the mainstream (the majority) does not see anything wrong, the *edge* voice, even if present, is rarely heard. The use of customer panels is even worse, since these are usually made up of volunteers—only the most committed mainstreamers. By the time the perception reaches critical mass, management goes into a reactive mode.

Those employees who disagree most with the existing rules, regulations, and processes respond in one of three ways: (1) they withdraw and merely go through the paces, (2) they become vocal critics (troublemakers), or (3) they leave. Certainly every employee who leaves is not a member of the *edge*, but those on the *edge* frequently do leave. We must recognize that the exit interview is one of the best methods of taking the pulse of the *edge*.

The Exit Interview

Does your company conduct exit interviews? Well over 90 percent of the firms that do query employees who leave treat the interview as an isolated event. The interview report may get sent to management; it may even hit the CEO's desk. But it rarely is tracked and reported along the constructive lines suggested in this book, so valuable information is lost. If five employees say that they did not feel trusted by management, then five different managers may receive a report to that effect. The data are scattered to the winds and become difficult to reassemble in a meaningful fashion. Kind of a corporate version of Humpty Dumpty.

In fact, the exit interview usually becomes a catch-22:

1. An employee identifies a major opportunity for improvement.

2. He or she points it out to management, who look to the mainstream for corroboration.

3. Seeing no evidence of a problem, no action is taken.

4. Frustrated by the lack of progress, the employee becomes more vocal.

5. The more vocal the employee becomes, the more he or she becomes labeled a "problem" employee.

6. Finally, the frustration builds to the point that the employee leaves.

7. In the exit interview, the employee "tells it like it is."

8. Management reads the complaints but dismisses them because they came from a "troublemaker."

9. As the problem becomes bigger, the more likely that "troublemakers" will leave.

10. The only trend that management sees is that an increasing number of troublemakers are bailing out. They say "good riddance" as the key to their future solvency walks out the door.

In Aesop's fable, Androcles represents management at its best. The general populace (the mainstream) only saw a raging lion. Androcles, however, recognized that the beast could be a tremendous asset and looked for the *cause* of its pain. By removing the thorn that made the lion howl, Androcles cultivated a lifelong ally. Essentially, Androcles tapped the power of the *edge*.

Remember Patrick Naughton, the Sun Microsystems engineer from Chapter 5? Frustrated by management's lack of receptivity to his ideas, he had accepted another position and had resigned. CEO McNealy, who persuaded him to continue at Sun, was rewarded with Java and a shot at market dominance.

How did Scott McNealy turn an *edge* defection into an innovation transfusion? He simply asked Naughton for his thoughts before he left. "Before you go," he asked, "write up what you think Sun is doing wrong. Tell me what you'd do if you were God."[1] As Naughton recalls with obvious relish, "It was an opportunity to point out that the emperor had no clothes."

Every maverick loves an audience, and Patrick Naughton was no exception. He threw himself into the task, E-mailing 12 screens of ideas to McNealy, who in turn distributed the memo to the rest of the management team. The following morning Naughton found his E-mail inbox was filled with comments like: "Many of us have recognized some of your observations, but just didn't speak up." A short time later, McNealy asked Naughton to stay at Sun and "Go do it!" By pulling the thorn out of the "roaring" Naughton, McNealy salvaged what otherwise would have been an invaluable loss to Sun.

Any company that strives to become a growing, dynamic, intelligent organization should learn its lessons first by listening to the *edge*. Using exit interviews for that instruction is not something we should strive for. The loss of the *edge* is a terrible price to pay for any knowledge. We will later consider much less painful ways of getting our *edge* lessons. Still, the exit interview will continue to be a rich source of organizational feedback. It is your mirror on the wall. You have only to ask.

HOW TO ATTRACT THE EDGE

Sometimes people resist the *edge* because they don't want to change. More often, the *edge* is resisted because the need for change is not perceived. This is a subtle but important distinction. In the movie *Butch Cassidy and the Sundance Kid*, the Kid could not swim. He was deathly afraid of water, and nothing (or so it seemed) could have persuaded him to jump into water above his waist. To any observer, he was vigorously resisting the water.

With a posse bent on killing him, and the realization that they were close behind, the Kid jumped off a cliff into deep and raging water. Once he saw the need, he acted. On one level he resisted the water, but on a very different level, he just had trouble perceiving the need.

When we resist the *edge*, we do so with religious fervor if we do not see the need for change. Because the *edge* sees a clear need, they become frustrated by our blindness. It was reputed that Chester Carlson, the inventor of the xerography process (xerox), would slump into his easy chair at the end of each day, gaze up at the ceiling and sigh, "They just don't see." He was right.

The *edge* does not merely want to be heard. They view that as condescension at best, duplicity at worst. How would you feel if you saw Clint Eastwood in your local grocery store, and you ran home to tell your wife and she responded, "Well, I'm sure you *thought* you saw Eastwood. It was probably someone who looked like him." The more you insisted, the more frustrated you became by the lack of validation.

Many enlightened managers believe that by listening to the *edge*, they are learning. They are not. When people on the *edge* take a position, it is because they see something to trigger that position. We do not have to agree with *edge* members, but we should recognize that they are seeing something real. Our objective should be more than hearing what those on the *edge say*; we need to understand those things people on the *edge see*.

MY MOST PAINFUL LESSON

How do you react when you hear things like "You don't care about your customers," or "You talk a good game, but don't really believe in empowerment"? Usually, because we "know" these things are not true, we either dismiss them or try to explain them away. Such reactions are understandable but never productive in attempting to learn from the *edge*.

Early in my career as a speaker and consultant, my wife would say, "You care more for your job than you do for our marriage." As a typical husband, I would respond, "Honey, that's silly. Of course you mean more to me." I would then count off all the things that I did that were evidence that my marriage was most important. It was true, I did not care more for my job than her; therefore, I was convinced that it was my husbandly duty to lend a sympathetic ear and then show my wife just how wrong she was.

Over the following few years, this became a recurring theme. I remember thinking, "What do I have to say to convince her?" Flowers no longer mollified her. Special greeting cards had no effect. She just wouldn't listen to reason, and I was clearly in deep trouble. I knew she was wrong. She knew she was right. This was not the stuff that harmony is made of.

Finally I stopped trying to deal with what she believed and asked myself instead what she saw that caused her to hold that belief. After much deliberation, I decided to try something radical, engaging in a frank discussion with her. It was most enlightening. I learned that my wife objected to my weekend travel. In giving a lot of Monday morning keynote talks, I was forced to leave on Sunday. Since our family life revolved around the weekend, she interpreted my actions as choosing work over our marriage.

Once I understood what my wife was seeing, we were able to come to a compromise. I curtailed weekend travel, and crisis was happily averted.

The reason we use *edge* people is because we want to hear things about ourselves that otherwise would not be heard. So we create a situation that encourages the expression of those comments. When we (inevitably) hear things that we do not like, however, we too often react in a way that negates what we are being told. We begin to use the dreaded *but* word: "I appreciated your comments, Bill, *but* . . ." Essentially we negate Bill's input.

No one appreciates feeling that his or her point of view is irrelevant. After complaining about the long, slow lines at the tellers' window of a major bank, a customer received a five-minute lecture on the complexity of staffing management. That customer was me, and I took my business elsewhere. A high school principal heard a student with special needs remark that no one cared about his problems, unless he caused trouble. The principal took on a pained look and, with great care, explained how deeply she cared about her student's problems, as did her staff. Eventually the student made the ultimate statement. He dropped out.

Sometimes we verbally attack a person who contradicts our beliefs (I've never seen a physical attack, but I guess it's only a matter of time). I have been present at sessions where a disgruntled customer was told that she was " . . . dead wrong, end of subject!" On another occasion, a salesperson who had recently resigned described the incredible burden of over 20 hours of paperwork that was required every week. The regional manager had shot back, "You never could sell. Now that you're gone, units [sold] should go up 10 percent!" How's that for a sympathetic ear for the *edge*?

When a customer says, "You don't give a damn about me," it is natural to want to point out why he or she is mistaken. You might even be able to convince that customer that, yes, you truly must care about his or her needs. By the next month, however, that customer will be overheard saying once again that you don't give a damn.

The issue is not whether you care about the customer, but rather what that particular customer is experiencing that causes him or her to have the belief. This is extremely important, because the *edge* always holds beliefs that contradict mainstream doctrines. The first step in learning from the *edge* is to accept a simple, immutable truth: *Every observation from the* edge *is based on fact.*

This does not mean that *edge* members are always right in what they say. But they are always right in what they see. Therefore, either you accept the premise that they are hallucinating, or you recognize that there is some reality behind their belief.

The value of the *edge* is not that they help us to understand our beliefs but that they help us to understand our practices. This point is the cornerstone of all progress. No growth occurs without a change in action. Alter belief, and you do not necessarily change. Alter action, and change is inevitable.

I was speaking to a gentleman who told me he had been dieting for two months. "Do you exercise as well?" I asked him. "Well, I used to think about exercising, but only rarely," he said. "Now I think about it a lot!" In his mind he was changing— unfortunately, the weight was not in his mind.

We can see this principle in every aspect of our lives. We believe in losing weight, but we continue to eat the same foods. We believe in spending more time with our families but continue our old work patterns. Frustrated by our lack of progress, we read, view, and listen to more philosophy. This bolsters our new beliefs but does nothing to alter our old patterns.

ALTERING PATTERNS

The *only* way we can change is to alter our patterns. But how can we alter what we cannot see? The irony is that we think the *edge* is challenging our beliefs, when in reality they are helping us to become the best of what we believe we should be. What they are challenging is our actions.

The mainstream is not the only group that sees belief in place of action. The *edge* suffers the same affliction. They think they understand what you believe but are often wrong. What they do understand, however, is how you act. It is from that action that they infer your belief. Progress is hard because the *edge* and the mainstream are viewing the world based on their beliefs, and each sees conflict.

We do not attract *edge* members by merely allowing them to express themselves. We attract them by acknowledging the "reality" behind their beliefs, and by working to identify and alter that reality. *Edge* members are attracted to us most when we, faced with their challenge to our beliefs, respond with "Why do you say that?" and persist until we get to the *rules* behind our beliefs.

Imagine you are an IBM sales rep. Your supervisor invites you to participate in a workshop intended to help IBM anticipate its ability to succeed in the personal computer market. You are on the *edge*, as evidenced by the fact that you have been repeatedly unsuccessful in making your PC quotas. In fact, you are known to be vocally critical of those quotas. You speak up: "I think that you don't really want us to be successful selling personal computers." A hush falls over the room. The manager conducting the workshop clears her throat nervously, looks at her watch, and says to the audience, "Any other comments"? You feel like the embodiment of the invisible man. The manager feels totally justified in her actions, however. After all, you have no credibility, especially compared with those who have been successful.

In this imaginary workshop, IBM does not stop by casually dismissing your comments. You are told during the break, in the nicest way possible, that IBM not only supports PC sales but recognizes that its entire future depends on success in that market. You are shown the millions of dollars in advertising spent by IBM in just one year alone. You are reminded of all the organizational changes specifically designed to maximize PC domination. By this time, unless you are incredibly tenacious, you have stopped talking completely. IBM has made its case.

Let me repeat that the preceding workshop never took place. I use IBM as an example because this scenario has taken place hundreds (or thousands) of times over the last five years, only under less formal circumstances. I believe IBM's problems in the personal computer market throughout the 1980s and early 1990s were certainly not because IBM didn't want PCs to succeed. The company very much wanted to establish a dominant position in personal computers. Why then did so many IBM sales reps believe otherwise? Because there was a dominant, unwritten rule that said: "Promote PCs, but *don't hurt the mainframe market.*"

BENIGN NEGLECT

There is one other way in which I've seen clients react after hearing from the *edge*. They thank *edge* members for their contribution, say they will "take it under advisement," and then query others as to their opinions. They are careful to ask representatives of the mainstream view. After clients are solicitously told that they are right and the *edge* is out of its mind, clients feel vindicated. They nod sagely and say that the *edge's* comments are "interesting but to be expected." In the end, they have unintentionally repeated the most deadly mistake of working with those on the *edge*—becoming overwhelmed by the sheer numbers of the mainstream.

In the case of IBM, its actions were in direct conflict with its beliefs when it came to cultivating the success of the company's position in the growing PC marketplace. This is not unusual. The principal who told the student with special needs that the principal and the faculty really do care was being completely honest. You could hook her up to a lie detector and it would register absolutely true. Yet the student *knew* that they did not care. He knew it because he had repeatedly seen evidence of this indifference. This is the difference between action and belief.

The student was really saying, "You act in a way that leads me to conclude you do not care." He was assuming that actions reflect belief. The principal was assuming her beliefs were reflected in her actions. They were both being completely honest, and completely wrong.

How we see the future is always a reflection of our beliefs. Those beliefs, however, have no real impact on the future. What does influence the future is our actions. If we want to anticipate the future, we must see it independent of our beliefs. By understanding the discrepancies between beliefs and actions, we can see the future in an entirely new way.

This is the value of using the *edge*. We gain incredible insight into the rules we practice, rather than the rules we believe in.

This is also the painful irony of dismissing *edge* comments that don't match our beliefs. I often see clients bring these people from the *edge* into a meeting because of their potential to contribute the margin's perspective and then negate them because their statements run contrary to mainstream beliefs.

The way to listen to the *edge* goes beyond merely keeping an open mind. We must recognize that we will hear things that range from the uncomfortable to the unthinkable. We must accept that every comment has some basis in reality.

PREDICTING RESISTANCE TO CHANGE

A marriage consists of two partners. So far we've looked exclusively at employees on the *edge*, but they represent only half of the equation. What about the mainstream employees? How do they react to their counterparts on the *edge*?

People can be quite threatened by the *edge*. Some of their most cherished beliefs are being challenged. Mainstream employees who resist the unsettling influence of the *edge* all share one or more of these characteristics: They hold *power*; they have *prestige*; and they have invested in *preparation*.

Power—Power goes far beyond the typical imagery of official, hierarchical power. It is far more subtle and tangible than that. If Sharon is placed in charge of the all-important Masterson account, for example, she wields a type of informal power, and she will enjoy all of the perks that accompany the responsibilities. If her project is attacked or questioned in any way, she will most likely resist vigorously.

Prestige—People associated with any past success hold a celebrity status within the organization and usually love to bask in their historic glories. Anything that might vilify that status will be deeply resented and resisted.

Preparation—Investment can be quite an anchor. If someone has spent a good deal of preparation with hopes that it will propel them through the ranks of the mainstream, you can expect their resistance to fundamental change will be great.

These three traits (the three Ps) don't only apply to dealing with the *edge*. They are excellent predictors of any change. When one of the three is present, expect resistance. Two of the three means you're in for a rough time. Three out of three, and you will have a revolution on your hands.

I was once asked during an interview, of all the different groups I work with, which were the most resistant to change? That was a question I had never been asked before, so I gave it considerable thought. And then it hit me. The three most change-resistant groups I encountered were surgeons, tenured university professors, and hospital pastors who tend to the spiritual needs of the sick and their families. How does this fit with the three Ps?

Everyone knows that it's the surgeons who hold the power in any hospital. They are the ones with the prestige, and they certainly have invested the most in preparation to get where they are. Three out of three.

Tenured university professors also fit this pattern. They hold the power, have the prestige, and are the most invested. Again, three out of three.

Pastors are the exception to the rule. I was invited to work with a professional organization responsible for delivering pastoral care within the health care system. Increasingly, the pastors were being asked to apply total quality measures and submit productivity reports. The organization's president told me that rather than submit to those requirements, many pastors were leaving pastoral care altogether. "I don't report to you," the pastors would say to the hospital administrators. "I report to God."

The pastors perceived no power in their job, nor did they feel it afforded them any prestige. Preparation, however, was a very different matter. What investment could be greater than dedicating one's life to a calling? Because this single factor among the three Ps was so great, it was equal in weight to having all three.

OK, you caught me. There are exceptions. Not all PPP people are completely change resistant. I have had the pleasure to work with wonderful people who led the charge for change, even though they were the ones with the most to lose.

I sat in on a budget meeting several years ago and saw one of these exceptions in action. Four department heads were vigorously defending the size of their staff. The fifth director just sat there, tapping his pen on his pad. Finally he spoke: "Look, no matter how you cut it, we can't continue with this 'business as usual' attitude. I figure that I can still do my job with a 30 percent cut in head count."

For most, however, the PPP rule still applies. The threat of pain and loss for these resisters is very real and can profoundly affect their ability to look objectively at anyone challenging the status quo. This can become a major stumbling block in your efforts to court the *edge*. It is unfortunate that the PPP employees are often in positions of authority over the *edge*, because they are unlikely to be open to the challenging insights that the *edge* will provide.

TAKE ME TO YOUR LEADER

When the *edge* knocks, the person on the other side of the door is likely to be a PPP. What can you do when the person the *edge* will call upon is also the most change resistant?

At the very least, every organization should take extra care to sensitize and educate management as to the importance of the *edge* and wide-angle vision. In addition, managers and executives need to understand how to use the *edge*. This is not easy, because they must learn to see in a totally new way. They also must be helped to recognize that *edge* members do not go away, they just go to someone else. If loss or pain seems to emanate from the *edge*, like the bad feeling you get when a trooper pulls you over to the side of the road, it is important to realize that the *edge* doesn't *cause* the pain or loss. The *edge* simply is the messenger telling you that something is wrong. Ultimately, it is for your own good.

Hewlett-Packard understands the need for self-inflicted pain. This is not some kind of masochistic, corporate initiation but a sound process for stimulating growth. HP regularly introduces a new product that is in direct competition with another product that HP already markets. When an item is at the height of its popularity, HP introduces its successor because the company understands that in a highly competitive environment, there are only two choices: Do it to yourself or have someone else do it to you. Open the door to the *edge* when it knocks, and we risk doing it to ourselves. Don't answer, and we are at the mercy of someone else's whim.

Naturally, not all managers and executives resist change. In fact, some senior executives have been among the most risk-oriented groups I have worked with. Often, however, a vice president of human resources will resist changes to the compensation plan while the vice president of sales will embrace it. Conversely, the vice president of sales will resist the idea of changing sales regions while that idea is championed by the vice president of finance.

In other words, the *edge* will most often present itself to those in positions of power because they are the ones who have the potential to bring about change. Unfortunately, they are also the very ones who are most likely to have the three Ps.

It is also recommended that every organization actively search out the *edge*. This serves two purposes. One, it is an excellent way to create a safety net, capturing the perspective that comes from wide-angle vision before it slips through the cracks of indifference and resistance. And two, it lowers the hurdles the *edge* must leap to get into your organization. With many hurdles, only the most motivated and persistent people on the *edge* will get through. Considering *edge* members' potential for reinvigorating the organization, the extra effort for lowering the hurdles will be well worth it.

11

Truly Delighting Your Customer

Competitive advantage is no longer maintained by merely satisfying the customer. Whether you operate a for-profit or not-for-profit business, you undoubtedly recognize that a highly competitive and turbulent environment requires that you be able to delight and pleasantly surprise the customer. You must discover how to deliver more to the customer than is expected.

According to a recent study by Bain & Company, lowering the defection rate of customers by merely 5 percent results in an *increase in profits of between 25 and 95 percent.* That is difficult to ignore. Further, it is generally recognized that over 50 percent of customers who leave say that they were satisfied by the product or service. They were unable to articulate what needs were not being met.

Any business that can satisfy its customers' needs *before* they are even expressed has a huge competitive advantage. Let's not, however, limit customers to only those whom you serve today. Other companies' customers are also fair game (unfortunately for them).

This philosophy of business was demonstrated by Princeton Review, a company that specializes in preparing students to take the SAT college entrance exams. Up until the early 1980s, the market was owned by Kaplan Educational Centers, the oldest, and for half a century, the uncontested leader in the field of test-coaching services. Kaplan was satisfying its customers; it was delivering a high-quality service and had statistics to back up its effectiveness.

Princeton Review was founded by John Katzman, who epitomizes the extreme, critical, and vocal individual who belongs on any *edge* team. Because of his diverse perspective, Katzman was able to see an enormous demand that Kaplan was not satisfying, despite its quality service. He set out to deliver what the market had never experienced: fun and exciting classes. In five short years, Princeton Review discovered the solution to the customer service paradox: *How can we deliver what the customer wants today, or will want tomorrow, but has not asked for?* By the mid 1980s Princeton Review had reportedly grabbed almost half of Kaplan's SAT business.

Most people would agree that delivering beyond the customer's expectations greatly increases the chance to maintain a sizable competitive advantage. How does one do it?

I recently experienced a wonderful example of listening to *edge* customers. While shooting a video out of town I needed the services of a doctor. One of the crew recommended a nearby physician. With extreme frustration I drove to her office, dreading the inevitable waiting room hell.

The receptionist informed me that the doctor was running about 20 minutes behind. To my amazement, she then asked if I wanted a beeper? The question took me completely by surprise, as must have been evident by my lack of response. The receptionist informed me that if I wished, she would beep me ten minutes prior to needing me in the examination room.

Intrigued, I asked if their patients had requested beepers. "No," she laughed, "not one." "Most of our patients just suffered in silence. But we knew that we had to do things differently if we were to keep our patients." She told me that she was instructed to ask every disgruntled *[edge]* patient what upset him or her most about coming to the office. "It was the wait," she said, "three to one." Needless to say, this customer was delighted!

To solve the customer service paradox, you need to learn how to both see beyond your current constraints and to anticipate trends *before* they achieve critical mass. Throughout this book we have examined the challenges of delighting the customer. This chapter is dedicated to learning those techniques.

WHY FOCUS GROUPS AND SURVEYS FAIL

How does your organization find out what customers *really* want? To those who would respond "We ask them," remember that no one ever asked Sony for a product like the Walkman. Compaq laptops came out when the standard of excellence was the portable. Hal Sperlich did not design the minivan in response to overwhelming customer requests. 3M couldn't point to one customer who had ever requested a product like Post-it. None of these fortune-building products were in response to customer demands.

The Princeton Review never conducted a formal market study to see whether students wanted small, more exciting classes. It was just as well; I doubt many students would have asked for such things. Yes, they wanted smaller and exciting classes, but like all customers, they were largely conditioned by the prevailing attitudes of that time. SAT preparation was supposed to be boring, so they never expected anything more.

By definition, even the best surveys and focus groups can only tell you what people say they want, and this is terribly limited by the vicious circle of mainstream reinforcement. As pointed out by Barry Diller, who pioneered Fox Broadcasting in the face of surveys that negated any need for a fourth network:

> We became slaves to demographics, to market research, to focus groups. We produce what the numbers tell us to produce. And gradually, in this dizzying chase, our senses lose feeling and our instincts dim, corroded with safe action.[1]

Even when focus groups and customer surveys accurately reflect what customers truly want, they are severely limited. They tell us what customers know they want but never what they want but are not aware of. Surveys are like taking the pulse of your customers. Remember, however, that the pulse does not anticipate the heart. It is a delayed response to the heart. In markets that are stable, a delayed reading of your customers can be a useful means of detecting subtle shifts. The only problem is, where exactly do you find a stable market today?

BE CAREFUL WHERE YOU WALK

Tom Peters popularized the phrase "manage by walking around." This was an excellent way of communicating to managers that they need to get out of their offices and get in contact with the people within the organization.

Peter Drucker later modified that phrase to be "manage by walking around . . . outside." Drucker correctly pointed out that many of the organizational problems experienced today find their roots in management seclusion. Peters identified that seclusion as being from employees, but Drucker saw the real villain as seclusion from customers, suppliers, and competitors.

Livio DeSimone, CEO of 3M, would agree with Peter Drucker. "The most interesting products," he observed, "are the ones that people need but can't articulate that they need."[2] To identify what cannot be articulated, he recommends that his salespeople interact frequently with the customer—look outside.

Despite DeSimone's recommendation, all customers are not created equal. If your objective is to delight the customer, it matters more that you interact with the *right* customer, not just any customer. It is difficult to delight the mainstream customer by talking to mainstream customers.

At the risk of destroying a good slogan, let me suggest that today the phrase should be "manage by walking around on the *edge.*" The mainstream will not see what they cannot see. Frequent interaction with mainstream customers, as laudable as it may be, will rarely provide the insights that Livio DeSimone expects.

Another troubling aspect of 3M's prescription is that salespeople, above all else, are expected to sell. Since the highest volume of sales come from the mainstream, exhorting your sales force to frequently interact with the customers will most often be executed as interaction with mainstream customers. Remember, all customers are not created equal.

Sure, there are occasions that an interaction with your customers will reveal what they want but cannot articulate. If you are lucky, that is. Further, if you work with enough customers, you will undoubtedly hit upon some customers on the *edge*. But wouldn't it be nice to stack the odds in your favor?

The first technique for delighting the customer, then, is to manage by walking around on the *edge*. We have to be very careful when applying this technique, however. It is a rare organization that would knowingly accept lower sales today in exchange for an increased chance of finding a new product or service.

Any firm that wants to discover products and services not yet conceived by the mainstream should create pioneering incentives for their sales force. One of my clients created "Wild Duck Awards" to those in sales who identified major shifts in customer requirements. They made sure that all in sales were sensitized to working with the *edge*. They then created a graduated set of awards.

For identifying at least two major shifts, the award consisted of peer recognition and dinner for two at an exclusive restaurant. The more shifts identified (which always included customer names), the greater the award. The company was careful to make the awards attractive, without distracting its salespeople from their primary responsibility of selling.

Walking around on the *edge* is not just a job for sales, however. Marketing, product development, and manufacturing (to name a few departments) all should be regularly exposed to the *edge*. We also need to be very careful to limit the amount of time we expect salespeople to spend on the *edge*. No organization should have to make a choice between revenue today and delighting the customer tomorrow.

Finally, one word of caution: Train your organization well in the skills of listening to the *edge*. Remember that some of what they will hear may fundamentally challenge popular gospel. Had Kaplan Educational Centers sent out salespeople to meet with the *edge*, they would have likely heard comments like "This is as boring as dirt" (John Katzman said that he heard that statement many times), "With class sizes this big, I might as well prep with my computer," and "It's as exciting as doing laundry."[3]

How do you think the Kaplan salespeople would have responded to such comments? Most likely they would have tried to "educate" the customers, explaining that SAT preparation is serious business, and that if they want high scores, they need to "feel the pain." They would have pointed out that large classes help to keep the cost of the program down and that the effectiveness of the program is not diminished by class size. In short, without an *edge*-educated sales force, valuable service and product input will be lost.

YOUR CUSTOMERS' CUSTOMERS

The customers of most manufacturers of bathroom tissue are not the shoppers in the supermarkets but the distributors that purchase their products in large quantities and distribute them to the retail outlets. The consumers are the ones who ultimately purchase the products.

During the 1980s, a small percentage of the distributors were requesting unique packaging. The standard-sized package at that time was 4 rolls per package, and these distributors were requesting as many as 12 rolls per package. Many of the manufacturers ignored these requests. My client was one of those who resisted the *edge*.

By 1990 the market for 12-roll packaging, which required a very different production system, had grown to 11 percent of the total bathroom tissue market. My client, and many of its competitors, still did not act. As the market for 12-roll continued to grow, the popular wisdom was that manufacturers could not make money with the larger package size. Finally, by 1995, the market for 12-roll packaging had increased to 22 percent. Manufacturers are now producing the larger packaging and both they and the distributors are making money doing it.

Distributors are no different than the rest of us—they tend to only see the mainstream. Because they don't recognize their *edge* customers, a change in what is required goes unseen until, reaching critical mass, it becomes a surprise. The distributors are unprepared for the "sudden" market shift, and "overnight" (in this case, over a few years), an entirely new buying pattern emerges.

Any organization that wants to minimize surprise must learn to watch the *edge*, not only of its customers, but of its customers' customers as well. If you sell to travel agencies, listen to travelers on the *edge*. If you sell to McDonald's, by all means listen to what it says it needs, but also seek out the fast-food patrons on the *edge*.

The chances are good that you are familiar with your customers' customers, at least to a limited degree. Do you know who their *edge* customers are? Are you familiar with their attitudes and problems? If they became the mainstream within the next three years, how would that influence your business? If you find that any of these questions cause you to feel exposed, recognize that they also represent enormous potential. If your competitors cannot answer those questions, imagine the potential for competitive advantage when you can.

THE *BLEEDING* EDGE

What are the limitations to listening to *edge* customers? If you are looking for ideas that will delight your mainstream customers, you will most likely get fewer than when you only listen to the mainstream. After all, much of what you will hear from the *edge* will be complaints. As we have discussed, even those complaints can be valuable in helping to redesign your company, but few of them will actually produce product and service ideas.

What an *edge* relationship lacks in quantity, however, it more than makes up in quality. An MIT study, years ago, concluded that 70 percent of all innovation is first requested by the customer ... 70 percent! That is a powerful motivation to partner with your customer. However, the study did not distinguish between mainstream and *edge* customers nor, unfortunately, did it evaluate which innovations were enhancements and which were breakthrough new offerings.

The mainstream is a valuable source of enhancement innovations. That is not a bad deal. By definition, most enhancements provide predictable return for limited risk and investment. Enhancement innovation, however, does not create breakthrough products and services; it is limited risk with limited reward. Enhancements rarely delight the customer.

The *edge* is far more failure prone than the mainstream. By failure, I do not mean to suggest that you will fail, rather that you can expect to have many conversations with the *edge* where you seem to walk away empty-handed. Still, the ideas that you

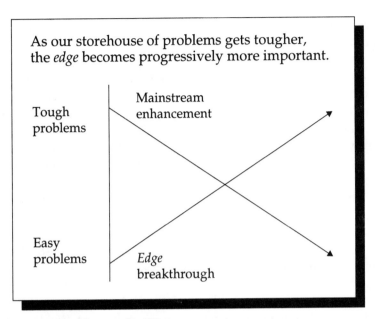

Figure 11-1. Storehouse of problems.

bring back from the *edge* will often enough result in product and service breakthroughs that make it clearly worth your while.

The answer is not to abandon the mainstream. Enhancement is usually a very good bargain. Nor is the answer to court the mainstream customers to the neglect of the *edge*. We have been trying that for decades and have only succeeded in delighting a never-before-heard-of competitor who walks away with our customers.

No organization can afford to abandon either customer. We need to strike a balance based on your product or service life cycle. As indicated in Figure 11-1, the earlier in the cycle, the more time we need to spend searching out the mainstream customer's perspectives. As products and services mature, however, more time needs to be spent actively seeking input from the customer on the *edge*.

I know of no hard and fast formula for striking the mainstream/*edge* balance. For most organizations, 100 percent of their listening time is spent with the mainstream. This continues until their product or service is so mature, it has fallen into crisis. By then the *edge* is easy to identify—mainstream companies merely have to look at the company to whom they are losing market share.

It would be great to see organizations dedicate 10 percent of their customer input resources working to establish wide-angle vision, even at the beginning of their product life cycle. This *edge* time should grow to as much as 70 percent by the time the product has reached the end of its useful life. In truth, I would be happy to hear of companies spending only half that much on the *edge*, which would still represent a major improvement over the condition that exists today.

Your customer on the *edge* presents a valuable opportunity to delight your mainstream customers with breakthrough innovations. To use oil exploration as an analogy, working with *edge* customers is like dropping a test hole. You have a reason to expect that there is oil in the area, but each hole is still very much a gamble.

There are a few methods that greatly increase your odds of getting a strike using some new aspects of the *edge*. We'll explore these in the next two chapters.

12

Breakthroughs for Your Toughest Problems

"The significant problems we face cannot be solved at the same level of thinking we were at when we created them."

Albert Einstein

Someone, somewhere today is either working on or has already solved your most difficult challenges. You may have been trying to solve these problems for years, or perhaps you have given up and consider the effort to be a waste of your resources. In spite of what you may read in your professional journals or hear from experts in the field, people are finding answers every day. Because they are on the *edge*, however, you will not hear about it.

THE ART OF THE IMPOSSIBLE

As communication and information retrieval improve, more and more of our easier problems begin to fall. In your industry alone, there are probably five or six publications dedicated to helping you solve problems. Every professional meeting and trade function promises a litany of solutions. Yet when the band goes home, you are still left with the really tough problems you brought to the dance.

The seeming permanence of impossible problems is exacerbated by the popularity of the quality movement. *Kaizen,* the

Japanese term for constantly improving the rules, is a fundamental tenet of total quality. Powerful and rewarding, it lends itself to solving the easier problems first. This makes sense. Few marathon runners would deliberately choose to run up a mountain if a downhill path was available. When striving for quality, as in business in general, the toughest problems remain on the shelf.

It is not that we truly believe these really tough problems are impossible. We are usually confident, at least on an intellectual basis, that they can be solved, given enough money, energy, and time. You will hear people say things like, "When technology gets good enough . . . " or "Over the next few years we will see. . . . " Our toughest problems may be difficult but are rarely *impossible*. We treat them as impossible, though, because, despite the plethora of information available to us and the years of chipping away, we still do not know how to solve them.

KNOWL-EDGE FOR THE ASKING

How far would you be willing to go if it meant meeting with someone who has solved your most vexing business problems? Would you go to New York or Washington or Europe? Of course you would! But would you be willing to travel to the *edge*? The road map is easy to follow once you have a sense of purpose and direction.

Saviors on the edge are different from the customers, employees, and competitors that we have been exploring. These three groups, though very different in their approaches, still have a vested interest in your problems. As we've seen, they often come to you with solutions. Saviors on the *edge* are unique because they have no interest at all in your problems and will rarely come to you. They are working to solve their own problems, and in doing so, inadvertently develop solutions that you can use.

Saviors on the *edge* are found outside your industry, outside your field. Biologists have a term that explains why these unlikely individuals hold your solutions. They call it *convergent evolution*. Convergent evolution means that two very different species develop features that are similar, not because they are related, but because they solve the same type of problems. This is the nature of saviors on the *edge*. They are related, not by industry or profession, but by a similarity of problems.

When I was conducting a seminar for the Frito-Lay research and development group, one of the group's scientists shared the following story:

> My brother works for Sony. I don't get to see him very often, but we were together for Thanksgiving. Over dinner, he explained his latest project. He said that for the past 15 months he was trying to increase the effective life of compact discs. CDs begin to degrade after about seven years, primarily due to oxidation. So far, he told me, he has had little progress.
>
> I told him that in the snack business, the thing that destroys the freshness of the chip is also oxidation. I then mentioned, in a matter-of-fact way, how we address the problem. Since this was common knowledge in our industry, I was certain he knew of it. He almost dropped his fork. He stared into space for a while, shook his head slowly and told me that, no, they had never thought of trying that approach.

The Frito-Lay scientist told me that his brother later reported that although Sony couldn't directly use Frito-Lay's technique, it had opened up an entirely new approach to the problem. The snack food and compact disc businesses could not be more different, yet they were closely connected by a similar problem.

The scientist from Sony attributed his breakthrough in reducing oxidation to dumb luck. He didn't know that there are other people, like his brother, who also have a great deal to contribute to his biggest problem. Most *edge* members will have unique contributions because, although they know your rules, they do not share them. Saviors on the *edge* aren't even *aware* of your rules and are not bound by any of your constraints.

With the exception of mavericks, most members of the *edge* are not experts. Saviors on the *edge*, however, are often experts, but in totally different fields. Because they are in different fields, they are very willing to share with you what they do and how they do it. They are in no sense competitors. Unfortunately, they may quite literally be in any industry and any profession. How can you find them?

Given enough time, you might hear about saviors on the *edge*. Eventually, someone (a competitor, perhaps?) will accidentally stumble on one of these breakthrough solutions and adopt it as his or her own. This is typically time-consuming because cross-industry transfer of knowledge is very slow and rare, especially in the early years. This slow transfer rate is not because the other industries don't want you to use their ideas, it is just that they quite honestly don't care. When you are outside an industry, you are out of sight and out of mind.

If the idea of someone unknown having already solved your most important problems doesn't frustrate you, consider this: Who bears the greatest risk, the greatest investment, and the most painful learning curve? Would you say it is the innovator or the person who learns from the innovator? In the majority of cases, the person who identifies an innovation early and acts on that idea gets one heck of a deal! That person can be you!

FINDING YOUR SAVIOR ON THE EDGE

To find your saviors on the *edge,* you need to ask yourself two deceptively simple questions:[1]

1. How can I describe my problem using *generic language?*

2. Who *outside my field* would be interested in solving that kind of problem?

What is meant by generic language? Most people will describe their problems by using the language of their industry and profession. This is, by definition, limiting. What if, for example, the Sony scientist had asked himself who outside his field would be interested in the oxidation of compact discs? The list would have been quite short—no one. We use generic language because it opens up new places for you to search.

For example, on a trip to London I was speaking to an extraordinary gentleman sitting across from me on the airplane. He was an astronomer who was about to address a symposium of scientists about his successes and failures in some obscure study that he was engaged in. Much of it went over my head, but he became so animated and passionate when he discussed his research that I quickly became infected with his enthusiasm. Later, over coffee, I described to him the work that I do. When I told him about the concept of finding a savior on the *edge*, his face lit up excitedly.

"Wayne," said the astronomer, "I love your premise. I'm not sure that it would apply with a technical problem such as the one that I face, but maybe we could give it a shot, OK?"

How could I refuse? I love a challenge. "Sure," I said, "tell me about it."

He said that he was conducting a study on the comparative structure and composition of meteorites. "The problem is that the meteorites don't actually hit Earth very often, and when they do, they are very difficult to find," he said. "This means that I have very few specimens to work with. Do you think that your saviors on the *edge* concept can do anything with that?" He threw down the gauntlet.

"I'm not sure," I told him, "but let's run through the process and see if anything useful comes up."

I asked him to restate his problem (finding meteorites) using generic language. I composed a list of key words and phrases that included:

- Trajectory.
- Falling objects.
- Things that hit the Earth.
- Things that shake the Earth's surface.

I asked him who would be interested in problems of trajectory. Who would be working on things that shake the Earth's surface? After ten minutes I showed him a list of eight professions, not one of which had he ever worked with. He was intrigued, but still a little skeptical, at the possibilities that he had never explored.

One of the professionals we identified was a seismologist. The next week I was pleasantly surprised when the astronomer phoned me at my home. "Wayne," he said, "my problem is solved. The seismologist told me that they have a worldwide array of sensing devices, all recording vibrations to the crust. They had been recording the impact of meteors for years but were throwing the data away!" he said. "Now I know exactly where to look for my specimens. The seismologists had disregarded this information because it was not related to earthquakes and considered to be dirty data. To me, it was pure gold!"

MORE DIAMONDS BENEATH YOUR FEET

If you are anxious to learn the details of how you can find your own saviors on the *edge,* help is on the way. The process is simple, rewarding, and even fun. First, however, I would like to share with you several examples of seemingly impossible problems that were solved by this unlikely group.

Hot Chips

Silicon wafers (the building blocks of computer chips) get thinner with every generation. As they approach the thickness of the wavelength of infrared radiation, slight variations in the film thickness cause the heat to shift randomly. This produces tiny hot and cold regions that can damage the wafer.

At Tufts University, the dean of engineering, Ioannis Miaoulis, and graduate student Bradley Heilman were frustrated that no one in their field had been able to come close to solving this problem. With a flash of insight, they decided to look for parallels in nature. Butterfly wings, they discovered, were constructed from microscopic films that allowed absorption of solar heat. These films were found in the scales that cover the wings.

Miaoulis and Heilman, propelled by this insight, are now investigating how the roughness of the scales helps to stabilize the temperature variations. They are actively working with lepidopterists (butterfly and moth researchers) and may be on the verge of a breakthrough in the science of chip fabrication. As Miaoulis observed, "We're operating in the crevices between fields."[2]

Movie Magic

Talk about frustration! Mark Lieberman wanted to be part of the emerging market to deliver movies on demand to cable TV subscribers. Unfortunately, incredibly fast computer servers are needed to dish out movies fast enough. That kind of mainframe horsepower is priced in the stratosphere.

With no adequate price/performance solutions from the established mainstream computer manufacturers, Lieberman went looking outside. In 1993 he saw a very impressive flight simulation demonstration while attending a conference. It was powered by a supercomputer designed to debug video circuitry for the David Sarnoff Research Center. The designers knew nothing about Lieberman's business; they just wanted to find an easier way to debug their electronic designs.

Now president of Sarnoff Real Time Corporation, Lieberman expects the price/performance of this revolutionary system to give the company better than a two to one price advantage over the competition—all because he walked outside his boundaries.[3]

Rock of Ages

With early detection, the ravages of osteoporosis can be minimized. Scientists have known for years that the fractal dimension of the bone can be used to predict a breakdown in the skeleton's structure. Using the accepted linear method to measure a bone's fractal dimensions, however, they have never been able to achieve acceptable accuracy. So spoke the industry experts.

Raj S. Acharya, an associate professor of electrical and computer engineering at the State University of New York achieved a breakthrough by creating nonlinear algorithms. His work was based on "mathematical morphology," a branch of image processing developed in France to study rocks.[4] Acharya's broad vision shed new light on a difficult problem. The solution had been there for years, but he was the first to step out of his established field and recognize its value.

FINDING NEEDLES IN HAYSTACKS

In each of the preceding examples, problems that stumped some of the world's top experts were overcome because they knew how to look outside their fields. How about you?

Using the following steps, write your problem. Make sure it is a very tough problem, and that its solution would make a big difference to you. The problem can be personal or professional. You can select your target as the problem to solve if you wish, but whatever you choose, it must be both very difficult and potentially quite important.

Step 1. Examine your problem statement for active verbs, such as *identify, detect, distribute, communicate, heat, filter, sort* and *combine*. Record any key verbs.

Step 2. Pick out action phrases, such as *hit a ball, heat a mixture, smooth a surface,* or *gain cooperation from competing parties.* Record these action phrases.

Step 3. Describe your problem as if you were speaking to someone who knows absolutely nothing about your field or your terminology. As you do, jot down the words and phrases you use. Record these as well.

You now have the rudiments of your problem, restated in generic language. Clean up your first attempt, and record your final words and phrases. By clean up, I mean be sure you have dropped all field-specific language. Only transfer those words and phrases that seem to capture the essence of your problem.

Now, look at your words and phrases and ask yourself who, outside your field, would be interested in that kind of problem? It is helpful to share your list with others, and ask them the same question. Remember, someone who helps you with your list does not need to be in your field. In fact, there is a decided advantage in showing your list to a spouse, neighbor, or friend who has nothing to do with your line of work.

In final preparation, list your potential saviors on the *edge*. Go speak to them. If you absolutely can't talk to them face-to-face (definitely preferable), then use the phone.

1. Briefly explain your field (so they know you are not a competitor).

2. Tell them that you are working on a problem relating to . . . (use the key words or phrases that led you to them).

3. Ask them how they approach that kind of problem.

Don't try to make sense of their answers immediately. Just listen or jot down their response, asking questions when you don't understand a point. Unless the connection between their response and your problem is obvious, thank them for their time, and leave. Remember that their response to you will be wrapped in their technical language. The value of this conversation will probably not be evident right away.

Don't worry if you find this difficult at first. Like any other skill, it takes some practice before it gets easy. But it *will* get easier. To give you the opportunity to become familiar with this powerful technique, I am going to share some real examples of employing saviors on the *edge*.

Cold Sore Conundrum

Cold sores are decidedly not fun. Patrick Beauchamp, a drilling fluids engineer for the oil industry, found that cold sore creams were just not very effective. "I realized that the biggest problem was that these medications were unable to penetrate into the skin," he said.[5] The pharmaceutical industry also recognized this problem but, even after decades, had not been able to solve it.

Now if you were a pharmaceutical scientist, how would you have described your problem in generic terms? What words would you have used? Beauchamp knew nothing about pharmaceuticals, but he understood the problem of penetrating beneath surfaces. This was, after all, a basic problem in the oil exploration business.

Using the same thought process, he created a gel in his hotel room that employed a solvent base common to the oil business. After seeing how effective it was on both himself and friends, he requested the help of J. A. Rogers, a professor of pharmacy at the University of Alberta.

If Rogers were like most scientists in pharmacology, he would have undoubtedly closed the door on Beauchamp. Everyone "knew" that solvents had no place in topical treatments. Rogers is not like most scientists. Displaying surprising openness, he was intrigued by something that promised even moderate success in treating what had been a virtually untreatable condition.

With Rogers's help, Beauchamp perfected the formula. Available in Canada under the name Libsorex, as well as Acsorex (acne cream medication), it has been tested as 62 percent more effective than leading products.[6]

As a pharmaceutical scientist, do you think you might have considered the oil industry as a source of your solutions? Let's look at another example of using saviors on the *edge*.

A Shot in the Dark

It is a simple matter for all but the deaf to hear a gunshot, but discovering *where* a shot originates is a much tougher problem. Imagine that you, a consultant to a law enforcement agency, are given the task of finding out where sporadic gunfire is coming from. A gunman has been taking potshots at random passersby, and someone could get killed. So far his aim has been poor, but things could get bad in a hurry if he is not found. But how? The shots have been clearly heard, but no one has a clue from where they originate. You frame your problem statement so that it is clear in your mind's eye: "Find out where a gunshot originates when it is heard within the city limits."

You understand that you must rid the problem statement of its field-specific language. For example, in this case you must drop the reference to gunshots. The statement that you are left with is "Find where a sound originates" or more generally, "Find the point of origination of an event." Both statements would make excellent starts.

Now describe the problem, keeping the generic language. Stop reading for a moment, and record as many words and phrases that capture the generic problem.

Here are some potential phrases:

Find something unseen.

Find sources of sound.

Track something back to its source.

Discover cause based on effect.

Who would you suggest your law enforcement client consult with? A diagnostician certainly tries to discover cause based upon effect. So does a fire marshall. Who tries to track things back to their source? Naturalists, who track migration patterns? What about seismologists, who try to determine the epicenter of an earthquake?

See if you can come up with any more. Remember that there is no right or wrong answer. Your objective is only to create a list of people whom you can discuss the problem with. You would expect that a diagnostician, a fire marshall, a seismologist, and a naturalist will all look at your client's problem from very different perspectives. That is what we are after. This process is not an intellectual exercise—it has very practical applications!

John Lahr worked with the U.S. Geological Survey in Menlo Park, California. When he began hearing gunshots around his home, he went to the police. They were not optimistic that they could help; hearing shots is one thing, finding their source is quite another. The next day another round of shots broke out, and Lahr decided that this had to come to an end. If the police could not find the source, he would have to find a way on his own. He just had to address the problem from a different perspective. Lahr knew that seismologists also had the problem of pinpointing the origin of noise (vibration) over large distances. He also knew that they had solved that problem.

Lahr placed four microphones at strategic points around his neighborhood, and one at his home. He then programmed his personal computer to regularly monitor for loud noises, using earthquake tracking techniques. He found he was able to triangulate many shots, including automatic weapons fire.[7] He turned this information over to the authorities, who were then able to begin surveillance of those specific sites.

THE CONSOLATION PRIZE

As effective as using saviors on the *edge* can be, you will not get a home run every time you go up to bat. In fact, you should expect that most conversations will result with no gain in insight at all. It is likely that you will "fail" a high percentage of the time. The good news is that your failures will cost you nothing more than a potentially fascinating conversation, and that every "failure" brings you closer to a hit.

Even when the conversation does not lead to a solution, most of my clients report that they develop a deep appreciation as to just how much saviors on the *edge* can contribute. Looking outside their field for answers cultivates a much broader view of problems and enhances the ability to spot solutions in exotic locations.

If your conversation does not result in an answer, does that really mean your time is wasted? Not at all. You will find that often one conversation with a savior on the *edge* leads you to a thought process you otherwise may have missed. A seeming failure today can pave the way for huge success tomorrow.

My friend and colleague Joel Barker has never restricted himself to mainstream solutions while addressing complex problems. Such was the case when he was working with a group of insurance executives. They were telling him about some of their toughest problems. One major problem that they grappled with regularly was the distribution of information to their thousands of worldwide agents. After years of effort, they had made little progress in improving the situation.

Joel zeroed in on the word *distribution,* and asked himself, "What organizations do I know that are trying to solve distribution problems?" Then it came to him. He suggested with a smile that the executives go to Sandia Labs, where they were working on splitting laser beams.

What do you imagine was the reaction of those executives? Sandia Labs? Laser beams?! "We are insurance executives," they probably thought, "not physicists." Instead, they just politely nodded their heads.

Joel explained that Sandia Labs was working on splitting a laser beam and, somewhere else on Earth, joining that beam—a very sophisticated *distribution* problem. "Try it," he said. "What do you have to lose?" A month went by, and they did nothing. Then the executives drew straws, and the loser went to Sandia Labs. He returned a few days later carrying reams of technical information about Sandia's operation.

"So, Max," his fellow executives asked, "did you find anything out that we can use?"

Max had a thoughtful look on his face. "Yes and no," he said. "We still don't have a clear-cut solution to our problem, but these people look at distribution from an entirely different perspective than we've been thinking about. They gave me some interesting ideas that I can't wait to try out." The insurance company began to track down each of these new concepts, some of which opened the doors to even more unique approaches to solving their problems.

As you have read about the saviors on the *edge* concept, I am sure that you have asked yourself the inevitable questions: Is it wise to pursue ideas that, at best, are less than sure things? Will

I be wasting my valuable resources, not the least of which is time?

These are good questions. Let's understand what is at stake. The problems that you select for wide-angle exploration should always be your most important and your toughest problems. Risk is not something to be avoided, but it should be managed. This means that you must decide when the risk is worth the gain, and then invest your resources accordingly. Go after the *edge* when none of your safer options are likely to pay off.

We also need to keep in mind the distinction between investigating the *edge* and actively investing in the *edge*. It costs very little to listen to the *edge*, to track it and consider its implications. This does not mandate that you develop new products, build facilities, or abandon established markets.

Investments in tracking and understanding the *edge* are among the best investments you can make.

SIMULATING SAVIORS

"Spiritual healer" is not written on my business card. Like a healer, however, people often turn to me only after they have tried more "traditional" approaches. This was the case when I was hired to work with the yearbook company described in Chapter 9. Implementing an Ideal Team had given management insights that they might have otherwise missed, but they felt that they needed more.

What they needed was a savior on the *edge*. Unfortunately, there were none in the vicinity. I explained to them how to use saviors on the *edge*, but that would not help us with our work session in progress. Just as the Ideal Team had been useful in simulating the *edge*, there is a way to simulate saviors on the *edge*. I call this remarkable person a "Special Team Member."

The Special Team Member is typically used as an addition to the Ideal Team. Like the Ideal Team, the Special Team Member is a simulation, just a name on a sheet of paper. Unlike the Ideal Team, the Special Team Member has no obvious relevance to your organization or your target.

To create the Special Team Member, you need to ask yourself the same two questions you asked when finding the saviors on the *edge:* How can I describe my problem using generic language? and Who outside my field would be interested in solving that kind of problem? Then, instead of finding and talking to a savior on the *edge,* you will create one on paper and give that person or organization a place on your Ideal Team.

Using the Special Team Member can result in some truly spectacular results. Try it yourself using your target, and be prepared for some exciting insights!

Like all the techniques introduced in this book, the more you practice, the better and easier it becomes. When the yearbook company was trying to reverse the trend of declining sales, it found itself stuck within the boundaries of its specific needs. In fact, the working team had so much trouble restating its problem using generic language that I tried a totally different approach. I asked members *why* yearbook sales were declining. Their response: "Because kids aren't buying them." OK, I guess I asked for that one. "Why," I persisted, "do you think kids aren't buying the yearbooks anymore?"

After an uncomfortable silence, the director of marketing spoke up. "Buying a yearbook used to be a tradition. Everybody who was anybody bought a yearbook. It's just not a tradition anymore, especially in the city schools." Now we had something to work with. "So the problem," I suggested, "is that something that once was a tradition had ceased continuing to be a tradition?" They shook their heads in agreement.

"OK," I said, "who outside the yearbook field would be interested in solving problems about bolstering interest when tradition is no longer enough?" Who would *you* come up with? Take a few minutes and jot down your thoughts.

Why didn't I let them use a more generic statement, such as "increasing sales"? Remember, our sole purpose is to identify people/groups who are interested in solving similar problems. While "increasing sales" does strictly qualify, it casts such a broad net, that there is no good way to limit it. Besides, the company's real problem was not just that sales were declining but that they no longer fostered tradition.

Who else would be interested in the problem of the loss of tradition? The working team came up with two groups: the Boy Scouts, and the church. Both groups, they reasoned, used to enjoy considerable popularity, but because attending church services and joining the Boy Scouts were no longer traditions, these organizations had to find new ways to appeal to the public whom they served.

Now team members had to consider how these Special Team Members might view the yearbook company's approach to the problem. One of the members of the team worked closely with her church and was particularly helpful in giving the church's perspective.

She said that her church had begun including popular music as part of the services. The sermons were geared more directly to the problems her community faced, and the parishioners were encouraged to become very active in community activities. Recently, she noted, they had begun to get the younger people more involved in directing their own programs. Interest was high, and church attendance was growing.

What followed was a one-hour discussion about how the yearbook company could learn from those ideas. Sometimes an idea was considered but quickly dismissed as not being relevant for the company. I saw that the group tended to especially dismiss the comments from the *edge* (simulated and real). This tendency should be resisted at all costs. *Any time* you find your group voicing the opinion that a Special Team Member's perspective is "interesting but irrelevant," challenge the group members. Often the perspective is not truly irrelevant but simply requires reexamining some fundamental beliefs. Much of a Special Team Member's value comes *after* challenging the belief that "such an idea just wouldn't work for us."

I have worked with computer programmers who "invited" Betty Crocker and a novelist to their work sessions, physicians who "took advice" from military strategists, and restaurant owners who "listened" to Japanese manufacturers. Each session was thoroughly enjoyable, lively, and produced valuable insight.

One final word on Special Team Members. Often your team will come up with individuals and groups who seem to be a good fit, but no one knows how they might think. Don't throw those names away. When your session is over, assign those names to members of your working team, and have them speak to those people at their earliest opportunity. A Special Team Member of today might become a savior on the *edge* tomorrow.

13

Why Organizational Change Is So Hard

Breakthrough ideas produce breakthrough change. Unfortunately, organizations like stability. The very mainstream that prevented you from anticipating the future and blocked you from seeing groundbreaking solutions also tends to perpetuate your organization's momentum. The problem is not that companies do not change but that they change too slowly.

Professors John Kotter and Jim Heskitt, from Harvard University, conducted a 16-year study on cultural issues within organizations. The study included 207 firms from 22 different industries. One of the researchers' most important conclusions was that an inability to change and adapt resulted in ineffective (and less profitable) companies.

Kotter and Heskitt found that adaptive firms outperformed the nonadaptive firms by a wide margin. Over an 11-year period comparing adaptive and nonadaptive companies, they found the adaptive companies enjoyed:

- Expanded workforces.
- Increased revenue.
- Improved net income.
- Growth in stock price.

Those are some pretty compelling reasons to change.

BEYOND LEADERSHIP

Why is it that more companies do not adapt quickly? A cynic might say that their leadership does not truly want to change, but I disagree. I have worked with many excellent organizational leaders who were extremely frustrated by their company's inability to change. I do not believe that Roger Smith, past CEO of General Motors, did not want GM to change. I have heard him complain, with frustration and passion: "Changing GM is like trying to turn an ocean liner. No matter what you do, it seems to continue on the old course."[1]

In 1992 I had the privilege of conducting a series of senior executive training programs for one of the most well-respected companies in the world. A Malcolm Baldridge award winner, it enjoys a well-earned reputation for top quality.

My first program with the company consisted of meeting with 14 of its top executives. I asked them to independently create a chart tracking their progress in quality. On the vertical axis we placed the percentage of their employees who had integrated total quality. While this is admittedly a very subjective measure, there was surprising agreement that 70 percent was the right number. On the horizontal axis, I asked them to place the year that they first "got serious" about quality, defining "serious" as a significant investment in training, backed by a consistent message from management. Again, most participants agreed that the year was 1982.

Next, I asked them to independently draw a line from 1982 to 1992. With amazing consistency, they each created curves similar to that in Figure 13-1.

When we finished comparing results, I asked the $50,000 question: Why, if they were serious about quality back in 1982, did it take almost five years before they began to see significant return on their efforts? They looked puzzled. No one had really thought about this before, and in the end, no one was really sure why it took so long. They knew their employees wanted to produce high quality. They knew they had provided the training and support necessary. The press had praised their leadership efforts in advancing high quality. Yet it still took almost five years before any progress was visible.

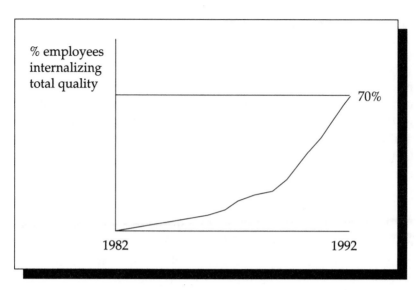

Figure 13-1. Progress in total quality.

To explain why organizational change is so difficult, I need to take you back to my first job after business school.

FORD FOLLIES

You can learn a lot about a company during an interview. For my first job, I was being considered for a position in Ford's controller's office. Although I didn't know what to expect, my friends were very impressed. They told me that the controller's group had a national reputation and assured me that I would learn a great deal about financial analysis at Ford. I had no doubt that there was a Ford in my future.

The controller's office was housed in Building #3 in Dearborn, Michigan. The building was actually a converted hangar in which World War II equipment was once constructed. The walls were gray, the carpet was gray, and the rows of metal desks were 25 years old . . . and gray.

As I walked from interview to interview, I could not help but notice that all 120 members of the group, wearing expensive three-piece suits, ties undone and sleeves rolled up, were running from room to room. That is, those who were on their feet were running. I saw legions of MBAs crawling on their hands and knees, collating reports with pages strewn around the floor. This was definitely not the executive image that my years at NYU had prepared me for.

My "host" was one of the supervisors from the controller's office. Like everyone else, he wore an expensive suit, tie undone, with sleeves rolled up. It wasn't until lunch that he finally filled me in on the facts of life. "This is a rotational program," he said. "Each job assignment lasts between four and six months. As soon as you begin to understand your current position, you are moved to another job. You do that until your two years are up."

I asked, "What happens after the two-year program?" "Don't worry about that," he assured me. "Most people don't make it to two years. But that's a mistake. The controller's office at Ford looks great on your resume, but you need to show the full two years." I was confused. "I'm still not sure," I persisted. "After the two years ... ?" "Listen, Wayne," he sighed, like he was explaining the most obvious of facts to a child. "Most people don't hang around after two years. Hell, I won't be around after my two-year hitch."

He must have seen the surprise in my eyes. "You were in the Marines," he said, recalling my resume. "Well, just think of this as a two-year boot camp." What could I say? I was so inspired by this picture of my future, I flew through the rest of the day and, six weeks later, found myself on my hands and knees with the best of them, working in Building #3.

There was no orientation for the Ford program. I was shown my desk, 1 in a row of 12. At the head of the row was the first-line supervisor. Every three rows was marked by a cubicle, which housed the second-line supervisor. There was one small office, where the manager managed, and a larger office for the controller. There was no mistaking his office, because it housed the much-coveted "jug of water," a golden chalice to Ford's rank and file.

On my desk sat a large, black three-ring binder, which contained the collected work of analysts who preceded me during the past three years. I was given a 15-minute overview of the job done by my predecessor and was left on my own. I quickly learned that Ford's philosophy was quite literally, drown in your job. As soon as you began to understand what was going on, you were moved again.

There were no written rules or guidelines. Well, that is not quite true. There was an entire case of procedure and policy manuals, but these were never opened and never referred to. The written rules were irrelevant; the unwritten rules, however, were everything. Here is a brief list of some of the unwritten rules in Building #3:

- Wear expensive suits (this showed you were successful).
- Treat your suits like rags (this showed you were very successful).
- As soon as you take off your suit coat in the morning, loosen your tie and roll up your sleeves (this showed you were a hard worker).
- Every other word out of your mouth should be of the four-letter variety (I think this reflected Ford's proud military style of organization).
- Every letter, memo, and report must be reviewed and modified by each link in the chain of command (this justified their value).
- Always run in the hallway (this showed you had important business).
- Eagerly work extensive overtime (this demonstrated commitment to the job).

Let me emphasize that no one ever discussed these rules, but because they were implied, they had that much more importance. We all knew that our performance review was determined in large part by how we fit the Ford mold. The formal evaluation criteria was nothing more than the template into which the informal standards were placed.

For example, every one of us eagerly worked extensive overtime. On average this amounted to 40 to 70 hours of overtime per week, most of which was uncompensated. Many days ended at 5:00 A.M. We would drive home, shower, change, and be back to work before 8:00 A.M.—no exaggeration. As you can imagine, turnover was quite high (all the sane among us bailed out first), averaging a 45 percent dropout rate per year.

After my first year in the training program, our controller called us into the cafeteria. He said, "For the first time, the automotive industry, and Ford in particular, are bleeding red ink. We can no longer afford 45 percent turnover each year. From now on, I want none of you to work more than ten hours of unpaid overtime per week." In retrospect, I am sure he thought that this proclamation from the heights of corporate heaven would be sufficient to reduce our overtime.

I remember walking out of that meeting talking about the financial troubles of the industry and speculating whether there would be layoffs. I don't recall anyone even giving a thought to his overtime restrictions. We just didn't take it seriously and continued working our usual overtime.

The next month he called us back into the cafeteria. "You're not listening to me," he bellowed. "I'm going to bring in the internal auditors with your names on clipboards. If they catch you working more than the approved overtime, you will be transferred to one of the factories [a fate worse than death]." We then understood that he was serious, so we took appropriate action . . . we hid from the auditors and continued working 100 hours per week.

What do you think is required for organizations to change? Top-level support? Motivation? Ability? We had all of those, but we still did not change.

THE SECRET TO ORGANIZATIONAL INERTIA

As you could see, Ford had a set of rules that, although unwritten and officially unsanctioned, determined how the game was played. Every one of us, from the first day we stepped into those gray halls, understood and accepted those rules as the necessary price for having the Ford controller's office appear on our resumes. We knew that performance reviews, rotational assignments, and promotions were closely linked to our being perceived as "real Ford employees." Real Ford employees play by the rules.

When the controller threatened to banish us to the factories, he was ignoring the very rules that had become our code. By merely adding a new penalty, the old rules remained. We knew that come performance reviews, our supervisors would still pull out the old rule book, regardless of the controller's demands.

> When you try to introduce a major change, and the old rules still exist, the old rules will outweigh the change 100 to 1 . . . you don't have a prayer.

The old rules do not go away. They have incredible staying power. Any new rule or new penalty will be ignored at best and create cynicism at worst. People are rational and behave rationally (usually). The old rules exist because, at least under one set of circumstances, they seemed to work. To expect rational people to abandon those tried and true rules is fantasy, because you are asking them to act in a way that is contrary to their best interests.

I use the example of Ford both because it is one that I relate to on a very personal level, and because it is such an extreme illustration of the longevity of rules. Ford is not the only institution to fall prey to rigid behavior.

One of my clients had tried for years to improve the safety performance of its plants, with very little to show for it. These plants had long histories, often having employed both the fathers and grandfathers of the current employees. Senior management was very serious about improving safety, and the plant workers were both motivated and capable of dramatically reducing accidents. Yet because of the culture (the unwritten rules) inside the plants, no amount of training, education, or propaganda was going to improve safety. The workers *knew* the way that things should be done, and that was that.

At IBM, everyone knew that the key to getting ahead was to get a reputation for making good presentations. People invested weeks preparing stacks of overhead transparencies (called foils) on the unlikely chance that one of them might be required. The presentation rules have been tracked back to Tom Watson Sr., who kept a roll of butcher paper near his desk for note taking.[2] If you dig deep enough, you can trace even the most absurd rules back to a very reasonable beginning.

TRAINING'S FATAL FLAW

Training will not create change. It *can* be a very important weapon; it can teach employees what to do and how to do it. It can excite and motivate them about what can be accomplished. Training, in fact, is a necessary component of change, but it is not sufficient to produce change.

Training is perceived as the new silver bullet. No challenge is so tough that it cannot be solved by a large training budget. We waste millions of dollars instructing employees to be more creative but do not improve the creativity of the organization itself. We waste untold years of our employees' time teaching them about customer service but do little to truly improve the service delivered to our customers. Training cannot create change because training does nothing about the old rules, standards, procedures, and policies that support the old patterns of action.

Training is extraordinarily important. Every dollar that we spend on training could be and should be a supremely valuable investment in our future. Unless the organization can actually act on that training, however, it is a wasted effort.

Not only is much of our training expenditure wasted, but in many cases it actually lowers the morale of the organization. We provide our employees with the motivation and skills to do the kind of job they naturally want to do, tell them how very important it is, and then keep the old restraining rules in place. There are some Greek tragedies with less pathos than that.

Imagine that your teenager has finally reached that dreaded stage of life when she wants you to teach her how to drive. You get behind the wheel and start the car. While you drive around, you explain the rules of the road, stopping distance, and other related information. Day after day you go driving with your teenager, but never hand over the keys. What do you imagine her attitude would be after one week? World War III.

The solution is not to cut back on training but to recognize its limitations. If we are serious about change, we must be willing to back up that conviction with more than just training. As long as the old rules are in place, few organizations will be able to shift direction. Those that do shift will do so only with an extraordinary investment in effort and time.

THE LIMITATION OF LEADERSHIP

If training has become today's silver bullet, leadership has become the gun. The decade of the nineties has become the decade of leadership. As with training, leaders have been dealt an unfair hand: Even the most sincere and charismatic leaders cannot be expected to bring about change when the old rules remain.

IBM policy was to revoke commissions of salespeople if their customers ever changed their order to another item. This was a functional, rational, and productive rule. It prevented the sales force from forcing products on customers who might then return them. It also motivated them not to let any competitors in the door (an IBM motto was always "control your account").

As personal computers became increasingly popular, IBM's leaders led the charge in support of selling PCs. They absolutely wanted to see their PC business succeed. But their policy of nonreplacement prevented the sales force from promoting new products such as minicomputers or PCs. "Who wanted to give up the commission on a $15 million mainframe in exchange for a commission on a $500,000 minicomputer or a dozen $5,000 PCs? Nobody."[3]

IBM could not possibly succeed in the PC business, because its old rules (protect the mainframe) and its new rules (support PCs) were diametrically opposed. The most effective leadership cannot hope to overcome the inertia of the old rules, any more than my controller was able to overcome it.

One of my clients is a midsized regional bank. Senior management clearly understood the importance of becoming more sales oriented. For more than two years they regularly conducted meetings, supported training, and gave impassioned and persuasive talks on the pressing need to actively sell the bank's services. The net result was more smiling tellers, brighter colors in their branch lobbies, and more money spent on training and marketing. Sales, however, remained anemic.

During my first meeting with the bank president, he made it clear that he accepted all blame. "I'm sure that if I was a more effective leader," he lamented, "we wouldn't be struggling the way we are today."

I suggested a test. Using the process described in Chapter 14, I worked with just one group. I chose the human resource folks. As they began to examine their rules, many of the unwritten policies began to surface. An important one was "Hire the best banker," which meant hire that person with the best financial skills.

The bank was hiring those candidates with strong number skills and then spending enormous sums of money trying to train these bankers to become better salespeople. "Why not place more emphasis on sales ability when recruiting your future employees?" I asked. "We'd love to," was the reply, "but we can't compromise our fiduciary standards."

The truth is that there are thousands of highly qualified banking candidates who would also be excellent and comfortable at selling. They may not, however, fit the mold of the "banker's banker" human resources was looking for. In this case, the bank's president was being far too hard on himself. As long as cultural anchors such as theirs exist, no leader could hope to be effective.

Effective leadership, like training, is extremely important to the change process, but it is not sufficient for change to occur. The old rules will not just go away.

14

Change—Fast and Efficient

Barriers to growth are less the result of external constraints than internal limits. Those self-imposed rules, regulations, policies, and procedures—both written and especially unwritten—inhibit a firm's evolution far more than competition, government regulation, or a poor economy. Like the Alcoholics Anonymous 12-step process, we need to recognize that we are the problem, as well as the solution.

The move toward any new direction depends on our ability to use the new rules of the game. Our ability to use the new rules depends not only on our learning of those rules but also on our ability to unlearn the old rules. As pointed out by Gary Tooker, CEO of Motorola, "With new processes and new technologies, you want to replace yourself instead of letting someone else do it. Success comes from a constant focus on renewal."[1]

Renewal is more than learning; it requires that we be able to unlearn as well. This concept is critical on all levels of organization. It is one of the primary reasons that Europe suffers from such an entrenched problem of low job growth. Europe's product market barriers, despite the new rules governing United Europe, are as evident as they ever were. These include new business license requirements, construction regulations, and severely limited retailing hours. More important than what can be legislated is what can be unlegislated; more important than what can be learned is what can be unlearned:

Nothing is harder than casting aside the thinking, strategies, and biases that propelled a business to its current success. Companies need to learn how to unlearn, to slough off yesterday's wisdom.
—Eckhard Pfeiffer, CEO Compaq Computer[2]

THE FORD SOLUTION

Ford never truly solved the overtime problem. After almost 20 years overtime has been reduced, but it still is quite evident within the rank and file. What could Ford have done to bring about a fast and efficient change?

Remember that the reason anyone adheres to rules is because they solve problems. For those of us in the controller's office, working extensive overtime resulted in favorable performance reviews and the chance of early promotion. The controller's new penalty (banishment to the factories) did nothing to solve the problem of how to stand out for the performance review. The controller, after all, did not fill out our reviews, our supervisors did.

Had the controller declared "If I catch you in here more than the approved time, I will send *your supervisors* to the factories," we would have been out the door in an instant. Rules, after all, have no intrinsic power. The rewards and penalties associated with those rules, however, have extraordinary power. Despite the controller's threats, he had little real authority over our actions. The supervisors who conducted our performance reviews had power in its truest sense.

If you want to effect change in your organization, the key is to first identify and then eradicate the old rules. They will not go away. Any firm that is not willing to dig up the old rules cannot expect the new rules to take root.

Much has been made in the press of the success of General Electric and, specifically, of the leadership of Jack Welsh. What CEO Welsh has done, in its essence, is to legitimize and support the overthrow of the old GE rules. That is what the much publicized "workout" program is all about. These next few chapters will give you the tools to accomplish a similar level of renewal, through the appropriate use of the *edge*.

And the Catch Is . . .

To change quickly and efficiently you need to eliminate the impediments to change. How can you eliminate what you cannot see? Had you asked those of us in the controller's office to list our rules, we could have come up with quite an impressive list. Some of our listed rules might have included:

- Use the word *present*, never the word *current*.
- Drive your supervisor's car to the car wash if requested.
- All memos need to be reviewed at every level.
- Do not use computers.

The reason that we could identify those rules so easily is that they were imposed on us, but we disagreed with them. We choked on them every day. The rules with which you disagree are very easy to see.

We would not have been able to articulate our overtime rules, our sleeve and tie procedure, the policy that we *should* run in the hall, or many of our other rituals. Because we saw these as serving our purpose, because they promised ultimate reward, we quickly grew to agree with those rules. For us they were invisible.

When my grandparents would come to our house for dinner, my grandmother would announce that she was on a diet (the perpetual diet) and that she had brought her own food. Sitting down to eat, she would unwrap a hard-boiled egg, a carrot, and a celery stalk. For the next half hour she would constantly eat off my grandfather's plate, "trying" a bit of this and a bit of that.

At the end of the meal my grandmother would look at her half-eaten egg and remnants of vegetables and remark, "Honestly, I don't know why I'm not losing weight. Look, I barely ate a thing and I'm already full." She would then berate my grandfather for snacking that evening, amazed that he should still be hungry. My grandmother never "unlearned" her old habits, and never lost weight. This vaudeville routine between my grandparents was obvious to all of us, yet continued every year.

Rules that are virtually invisible to the group who owns them are obvious to the *edge*. The *edge* can help us to become an "unlearning" corporation (apologies to Peter Senge), because it can help us to see what we otherwise cannot. It was, after all, this inability to see that caused the expert Soviet watchers to miss the single most important event in their professional lives: the collapse of the USSR.

> In the final analysis they [Sovietologists] seem to have taken notice only of those who attended their own conferences and seminars and contributed to their professional journals.[3]

TOP-DOWN OR BOTTOM-UP CHANGE

Should organizational change be led top-down or driven bottom-up? Both my executive audiences and nonexecutive audiences ask that question. What is amusing is that the executive groups ask that question expecting me to answer top-down, and the nonexecutive groups expect bottom-up. To both groups I throw caution to the wind and take my stand . . . both!

But management must always be ready to guide the rudders of corporate change. We are, after all, talking about striking out in brave new directions. It is up to the leadership of the organization to point out the new direction and also provide the resources to get there. The more turbulent the times, the more chaotic the circumstances, the more important leadership becomes.

Leadership has severe limitations, however. This was driven painfully home to me several years ago. I was conducting a one-day workshop in Phoenix with the human resources department of the globally recognized high-quality company I mentioned earlier. The target of the workshop was to find ways that would dramatically reduce the amount of time required to create training programs in quality, statistical control, and other areas.

Everyone felt the day was quite successful. The walls were covered with flip charts reflecting our accomplishments. By using some of the techniques you will learn in the next chapter, the working group was able to cut 60 percent off the department's training development requirements. In addition to the cycle time reduction, group members had also identified many systemic problems within the HR function. The group was pumped.

At the end of our session, the vice president of human resources was scheduled to make a presentation. She was flying in specifically for that purpose and did not arrive until 20 minutes before she was to "speak to the troops." No one knew the topic of her presentation.

She informed the 37 gathered there that the senior executive staff, along with a major consulting group, had been working for 18 months on a project to identify and initiate major changes within the HR function. Not one of the 37 had even heard about the study. She then outlined the Executive Committee Recommendations.

An eerie quiet followed her request for questions, a quiet before the storm. Suddenly the group was upon her. Everyone was speaking at once. They were clearly outraged.

"Look around you," one of them shouted, "do you see these flip charts? We spent one day and came up with probably 80 percent of what your committee took 18 months to discover!" There were questions concerning trust, others regarding a perceived executive conceit. "Do you think only the top executives are smart enough ... " You get the idea. Despite the success of that day, I was curiously never invited back by that vice president.

Organizational change must be led top-down but must be engineered bottom-up. As my Phoenix experience demonstrated, it is not that senior executives cannot create a new design, but it is much more difficult for them to do it without bottom-up input. The reverse is not true. The analysis and restructuring of a company can take place without direct senior management involvement, although I personally encourage top-level participation.

Senior management must be involved in business reorganization decisions. The analysis and recommendations, however, should be bottom-up. If I haven't convinced you yet of the importance of bottom-up reorganization, read on.

GOVERNMENT IN REVOLT

The U.S. Department of Foreign Service (USDFS) was in turmoil. Located in Washington, D.C., the department had been "reorganized" four times in as many years, and still the information systems group was at the throats of the USDFS community. Information systems wanted to move in one direction; the people it "supported" wanted to move in another.

As with the Phoenix group, I conducted a one-day workshop with the USDFS group to identify impediments to the department's ability to move forward. By the end of the day I was convinced that I was hired to give group members a common enemy . . . me. They were incensed over the issues that were identified. They wanted to know "Where do you get off saying that . . ." and "You're way off base making statements like . . ."

As the voices died down I took a much-needed drink of water and, pointing to their flip chart pages, said, "Wait a minute. Whose statements are these?" Staring at the sheets lining the walls, they slowly began to smile (all except the guy to my left—no way I was turning my back to him). "Oh," one of them muttered, "They're *our* rules." They hated what they had revealed, but it was *they* who had revealed it, not me.

Real change is about ownership. Until the USDFS employees accepted that *they* had to change, nothing would change. This is why psychiatrists don't tell you what your problem is. They know that it is human nature to reject (or "kill") the messenger, and the message along with it. Psychiatrists are facilitators who lead their patients to a point of self-discovery. This is the essence of organizational change as well.

15

Beyond Reengineering

Michael Hammer and James Champy, in their book *Reengineering the Corporation,*[1] popularized a powerful approach for redesigning business processes starting from scratch. Some organizations have attempted to follow their methods, with great success. Others have not found the pursuit of reengineering particularly rewarding. Still others are interested in the promise of reengineering but are unwilling or unable to commit the sizable resources required.

The *edge* can be a powerful and productive adjunct to any reengineering effort, both formal and informal. Those who subscribe to Hammer and Champy's process will find the *edge* a potent catalyst that both speeds and increases the effectiveness of their design efforts.

Hammer and Champy recognized the importance of employees on the *edge*. They suggested that reengineering teams include both employees who are mavericks and employees who are unhappy with the old processes. When you add customers on the *edge*, along with a highly effective Ideal Team simulation, the reengineering process sizzles.

For those who choose not to follow the Hammer/Champy approach, simplified techniques utilizing the *edge* (detailed in this chapter) can result in major improvements in your business processes. Many of my clients have reported impressive results with these techniques, which require just a fraction of the time and resources.

The critical part of any reengineering effort is to fundamentally reexamine a critical business process. Success is largely determined by your ability to separate the way things *should* be done from the way they have always been done. Appropriately chosen, the *edge* is never invested in the old process, which makes it the perfect catalyst to any reengineering project, if that is the direction in which you want to go.

Reengineering is about fundamental change. It is not about delayering, downsizing, rightsizing, or even reorganization. The reengineering effort may result in reduced head count, but that should never be its objective. Even when reengineering results in a more streamlined, efficient process, it does not necessarily follow that employees should be "made redundant" (a European term that shows that the United States does not have a monopoly on euphemisms). Employees who were worth hiring are usually worth retaining.

THE ILLUSION OF REENGINEERING

James Champy states in his book *Reengineering Management:* "I have also learned that half a revolution is not better than none."[2] Why does he believe there have been so many "half revolutions"? Champy says that dramatic change is only possible if managers can "organize, inspire, deploy, enable, measure, and reward the value-adding operational work."[3] He places much of the blame of reengineering's failure on management's doorstep. He is wrong.

I read recently about a man who walked into a Las Vegas hotel, having mortgaged, hocked, or sold every possession. He had emptied his savings account, and with literally every penny he had in this world, he placed the entire amount on black at the roulette table. The wheel came up black. Collecting his winnings, he left the hotel, headed for home.

Was that man heroic, someone to be emulated? Of course not! His was the act of a desperate man. Such men should not be emulated and should not be leading our companies. Yet that is what some practitioners of reengineering are asking of management.

We have all seen middle managers resist new ideas because they feared a loss of power or, worse yet, a loss of employment. We have also seen resistance to countless popular management philosophies that were later discredited. We must acknowledge that *not all resistance to change is wrong, because not all demands for change are right.*

To reengineer a corporation in the manner typically prescribed is to rip out the existing structure and build it up from scratch. Sometimes the results of a ground-up rebuild are truly remarkable. Sometimes the number of people required to process accounts payable will drop to a fraction of what was needed before. Sometimes the roulette wheel comes up black. How much of your company's life are you willing to bet?

It is noble to lay your life on the line for freedom. The doctors, nurses, and nuns who risked and forfeited their lives in Zaire fighting the Ebola virus were noble. Are managers and leaders being noble when they risk the livelihood of employees and the investment of the stockholders on the chance that what is rebuilt will work, and work better by a factor than what it replaced?

As you can tell, reengineering (as it is commonly practiced) scares the hell out of me. I have seen too many companies, mesmerized by the allure of big winnings, invest years of effort, spend millions of dollars, and disrupt production and service. For their efforts they have piles of charts and reports that few people understand. They have a small army of specialists who have created no value, produced no product, and serviced no customers. Blame it on management.

I cannot accept that explanation. It sounds too much like a fake faith healer who blames the sick for their lack of cure. If only they had more faith, they would be healed. I cannot speak for all management, but many I have had the privilege of working with have courage, faith, and inspiration. Their one "weakness" is they are not gamblers.

WHAT IS RIGHT WITH REENGINEERING?

Every process has the potential for dramatic improvement. This potential cannot be realized by small, incremental steps that build on existing rules. No organization can sustain itself by merely tinkering with what no longer works. Under these circumstances, the only option left to management is to throw out the old, dysfunctional rules and create new rules. Reengineering at its best allows you to create your own future.

As the speed of change increases, the half-life of our solutions decreases. Processes that worked for decades must now be reinvented. This goes beyond tossing out rules that no longer work. During times of turbulence, no business can afford to wait until it hears the final sputter of its 180,000-mile engine. Businesses must reexamine their processes and business philosophy based on an ever-shifting future. Businesses must *anticipate* the need for fundamental change.

It is healthy and necessary to constantly test the changing waters and to reconsider your strengths in the face of those changes. In this, Hammer and Champy are right: There are times when you must be willing to throw out old rules. But must you throw out *all* the old rules in doing so?

WHAT IS WRONG WITH REENGINEERING?

Eighty percent of the issues that reengineering addresses are healthy and necessary. It is the other 20 percent that are such a problem. These problematic issues fall into four categories:

1. Lack of divisibility.

2. Culture-shift confusion.

3. Process- versus outcome-driven change.

4. Poor direction.

Lack of Divisibility

Reengineering is typically applied to an entire process. Whether your business is manufacturing a product, educating a child, or delivering a service, the process you employ runs to the very heart of your organization. Certainly a dramatic improvement in any area critical to your business will result in a major payoff. But even if you are assured of success, biting off the entire process in one chunk is an incredibly difficult undertaking.

A business can lessen the pain of metamorphosis by initiating dramatic change incrementally. Many people have found themselves out of work due to the downsizing and reorganizations during this decade. Some have had to sell their homes, move their families, and start all over again in an entirely new line of work. Every month you can read or view a special interest story about one of these ex-employees who states, "It was very tough, but it was the best thing that ever happened to me."

Certainly total, cataclysmic change is necessary at times. It does not follow, however, that such a broad change should be your *goal*. For a family, a location change can be an incredibly unsettling shift. So is going back to school after working for 20 years. Changing careers can also be a wrenching change. Circumstances may dictate that all three shifts be undertaken at once, but anyone who is able to accomplish them in steps will find the change far less destabilizing and risky.

When television was first introduced, CBS did not abandon its radio investment while making the shift into TV. When American Airlines introduced its SABRE reservation system, it did not abandon all of its old reservation rules overnight. Shifting toward a new paradigm is not an all-or-nothing premise.

When a paradigm shifts, not every rule should change. After a decade of helping organizations to evolve, I have found that usually only 10 to 30 percent of their rules are truly dysfunctional. Is it always necessary to rip up the old book and start again from scratch?

Reengineering as it is currently practiced is quite correct— the more you are willing to throw out all the rules and start again, the greater the likelihood you will end up with a radical new design. By changing selectively, your new process may achieve only 80 percent of what it otherwise might have but will significantly reduce risk in the bargain. For many organizations, that is a pretty good deal.

Culture-Shift Confusion

Champy correctly points out that reengineering requires cultural change, and that cultural change is what management resists most. Without cultural change, there is "half a revolution." Clearly, cultural change is integral to reengineering.

But is reengineering integral to cultural change? Definitely not! An organization can implement work teams without formally reengineering its entire customer service process. Businesses can have an empowered workforce without formally reengineering. Many companies have made the move toward total quality, ultimately winning the Malcolm Baldridge award without reengineering their entire process. To resist reengineering does not necessarily mean that you are resisting change, any more than refusing to lay down your life savings on the spin of a wheel means that you are too cautious. You can change cultures and shift paradigms without necessarily engaging in a drastic reengineering process.

Before attempting reengineering, you must determine whether the expected benefits that result directly from reengineering outweigh the risks. Ask yourself the following questions:

- What are the costs associated with reengineering?
- What are the risks?
- What can we expect the benefits to be?
- How much of the benefit is attributed to cultural change alone?

What scares me about reengineering is that many consultants have difficulty in providing specifics about costs and risks. I become incensed at the inability of these consultants to segregate the benefits of reengineering from the benefits of cultural change. Placing reengineering in the same kettle as cultural change creates a volatile stew. Pause. When I was a teenager, I had to buy a car so that I could get a job as a delivery boy for the local pizzeria. If my boss had extolled car ownership as a valuable benefit of the job, I would have laughed out loud (and probably been out of work). Without changing the culture, there is no reengineering. It does not follow that one of the benefits of reengineering is cultural change.

Process- versus Outcome-Driven Change

I recently had an eye-opening conversation with one of the top reengineering consultants in the country. I asked him what he tells management to expect as a result of the reengineering effort?

"A thorough, ground-up redesign of their critical business processes," he responded.

"But what do you tell them they will get out of that redesign?" I asked.

"A whole new process," he said.

"OK, but what is the benefit? Forty percent faster response time, 60 percent lower costs, a doubling of customer satisfaction?" I could tell I was beginning to annoy him.

"Look, there's no way to know. All we can commit to is that we will give them a newly designed process."

The worse that your current process is, the greater the expected return from changing the rules. There is no way to know in advance how much you will benefit from reengineering, because there is no way to know just how much of your process is dysfunctional. Using similar companies as a guide is a poor comparison, because they do not share your culture.

Faith is a wonderful thing, but in business, it should always be tempered with pragmatism. It is one thing to invest several days or even several weeks on the chance that an internal process can be substantially improved. It is another to invest 12, 18, or even 24 months.

If you pioneer a radical change effort, it is very difficult to offer even an estimate of the expected return. The only people who can receive confident estimates are the ones who are late to the game. This is not an argument against taking risks or an argument against change. During these fast-paced, turbulent times, we have to take certain risks and be willing to change. Life has placed us all at the roulette wheel. The only question is how much of a bet are you willing to put down?

Poor Direction

We have all heard the expression "If you don't know where you are going, any direction will take you there." If you do not give proper direction to your reengineering effort, then roll the dice.

I am sure that you fully appreciate the importance of providing direction. Many reengineering efforts, however, either lack direction or provide direction that is too vague to ensure success. The irony is that the reengineering effort may be successful, but the patient still dies.

When a West Coast defense contractor began a ten-month reengineering effort to "improve customer service," it was confident that it was embracing the needs of its customers. The contractor's reengineering team delivered a new design, and the cultural transformation began. Departments were dissolved, work teams were established, and work flow was radically changed.

Less than six months later, the contractor made major revisions to lines of authority and product line responsibility. The newly reengineered design did not fit within the new product line orientation, and most of it had to be scrapped. The problem was not specifically attributed to the reengineering effort. Too many companies, however, believe that reengineering is about "customer service," or "quality." That is as much direction as the reengineering effort receives.

The reengineering effort must tie to the strategic direction of the organization and should be flexible enough to endure when that direction changes. Reengineering is not a finite process, and as such, I am extremely suspicious of efforts that strive to create the perfect process. Organizational strategy must remain flexible, and so should the reengineering efforts that support it.

Enhanced Reengineering

This chapter is not intended to convince you to abandon your reengineering plans. It is crucial, however, that you appreciate the risks and understand the options available to you. There are some very impressive success stories regarding reengineering, and it is possible that you too will share that success.

If you are either anticipating or have already begun the reengineering process, perhaps the single most powerful catalyst is the Ideal Team. Reengineering success largely depends on your ability to look at your business from a completely different perspective, to question things that have never been questioned before. The Ideal Team as described in Chapter 9 can be a great boost to those efforts.

Another significant enhancement to reengineering is the Special Team Member. The Ideal Team can help you discover what you need to change. The Special Team Member method, because it gives you breakthrough approaches to your problems, is a great way to create new and exciting answers to the problems that your reengineering team has discovered.

When you make the decision to tear up an existing process and start over again, you assume enormous risk. Through the use of both the Ideal Team and the Special Team Member, you can both reduce the risk and increase the likelihood of success. Both techniques require very little investment in time, and no extra resources at all. Don't attempt reengineering without them!

BLISTERING FAST REENGINEERING

In the following pages I describe a process called the Paradigm Prism. Joel Barker and I developed this process to help organizations quickly uncover the hidden rules, the hidden paradigms, the hidden barriers to change. It can be applied at multiple levels: problem solving, process redesign, even testing the fundamental premises of the business. Applying the Paradigm Prism helps to avoid some of the more troubling aspects of reengineering.

A POWERFUL ALTERNATIVE TO TRADITIONAL REENGINEERING

Reengineering using the Paradigm Prism requires a group of 15 to 25 people anywhere from two to five days. It is most effective when the first two days are contiguous. After that, the group can meet for as little as one day per week. Naturally, if you are working with a group that is geographically dispersed, you will want to consider conducting one long session rather than spreading it out.

The two major variables that determine the characteristics of your Prism workshop are the complexity of the process and the amount of detail that you want the session to produce. Some of my clients, for example, conduct a two-day workshop with the understanding that the redesign will be missing considerable detail. The advantage is that they get a pretty good idea of the magnitude and nature of the change, as well as the expected benefits, before the detail is flushed out. Armed with that information, they can decide how they want to proceed. Options they consider include:

- Proceed with the redesign as proposed.
- Proceed with only certain aspects of the redesign.
- Apply the redesigned process initially in a few select areas of the business.
- Do not proceed further.

Caveat

I do not agree with Champy when he says "half a revolution is not better than none." Half a revolution might be just about right. Sometimes the original business process is not sick enough to justify a complete revolution. Other times, due to any number of very real business conditions, you may not be able to afford a complete revolution, at least in the short term. Regardless of your situation, it is always preferable to give management as much information up front as possible before it commits itself to a complete revolution.

One note of caution: It is very easy for an organization to dismiss a very real need to change by rationalizing that they only need "half a revolution." The first half of this book was dedicated to showing you how to spot the signals that indicate when dramatic change is necessary. You should learn how to read the portents of change, rather than relying on your gut instincts. If the signals from the *edge* indicate that your rules are about to shift, you may have to embrace the full revolution. If people are en masse screwing around with your rules, if you have moved beyond the point of diminishing return, if your language begins to reflect the bankruptcy of the old rules, you may have to enter into revolution in its entirety.

THE SEVEN STEPS TO STREAMLINE REENGINEERING

1. Select the Process

Where are you going to start? The answer may not be as simple as you first might think. You may elect to begin with the process that will provide the greatest competitive advantage. Depending on your company, the criteria may be customer service, cost reduction, or some other criteria.

2. Prioritize Objectives

Every business would like to offer the greatest variety, fastest service, highest quality, lowest cost, and the most flexibility. Usually we can deliver two of the five, even three of the five. With hard work and insight, we might even deliver four of these items. Five out of five is as hard to achieve as the government being able to produce a balanced budget.

If you are in a fast-changing market, then flexibility to respond to those changes must be your highest priority. This is not a decision that can be left up to the reengineering team. The strategic direction of your business is a leadership issue. Too many reengineering efforts are launched without adequate guidance from the organization's leadership.

One of my clients is prominent in the field of telecommunications. During an executive retreat, the CEO acknowledged, "Our customers hate us. The only reason they do business with us is that we are the only ones who offer the technology they need." The goal of our meeting was to improve customer service, which desperately needed resuscitating. The CEO was acknowledging, however, that the strategic priority must be state-of-the-art technology and that everything else was second.

3. Design Your Teams

Based on the priorities of your business, the working teams (groups of five) and the Ideal Teams should be selected. Each team should contain one or two subject matter experts, people who understand the way the process currently works. Beyond that, the teams should draw as much as possible from the *edge*, as described earlier in this book.

Those members of the *edge* who cannot be part of the working team should become part of the Ideal Team. The working team and Ideal Team will be modified, based on the particular direction of the process. Making a preliminary determination gives you the lead time to juggle schedules and research potential Ideal Team members.

4. Break the Process into Its Primary Functions

These parts include the primary functions that support the process you want to reengineer. Hiring, training, accounting, information systems, purchasing, and marketing are all primary functions, at least as the process is defined today.

Certain primary functions that you have worked with for years may now be obsolete. This is a tough concept for many to accept. Remember, we said that reality is a set of rules we know and practice well. There is no absolute reality that we must produce—perhaps it is better to outsource. There is no absolute reality that we must include an accounting of an activity, given that the activity itself may no longer be required.

If you knew that a major competitor of yours was able to eliminate a function that you heavily relied on, would you be interested to know how they managed that feat? Of course you would! Bring this competitor into your Ideal Team and ask them how they did it. You might be astonished at the results you get. And pay particular attention to the input from your *edge* representatives. It often takes an outsider to see the possibilities.

One of my clients "knew" that it had to have training, but I insisted that the working team assume that a competitor eliminated all training. A member of the team said, "That's great for us if they drop all training. Long term, they won't remain competitive."

"Hold on," I said. "Our ground rules state that they do somehow manage to remain competitive. It is up to the group to decide how."

They decided to humor me (thank you very much) and then considered the possibility that some or all of the training could be outsourced. That was one answer. Then one of the group pointed out that she was never trained on using Windows. She just kept using the hypertext-based help system, and learned it as she went. A few eyebrows went up. Maybe it *was* possible that the company could eliminate training and still remain competitive (maybe even more competitive). The team decided not to include training as a primary function.

After the process is reengineered, your team can decide whether the nonprimary functions will be included in the new design, and in what form. Preceding the reengineering process by questioning primary functions avoids reengineering functions that may no longer be required.

5. Break Each Primary Function into Its Component Rules

The teams identify the visible and invisible rules that drive each function. This procedure relies heavily on the contributions of working team *edge* members as well as the Ideal Team, because they are instrumental in identifying the rules that are most important and least visible.

The more thorough the result required, the more detail you want. For example, a group I worked with at AT&T was instructed to design a brand-new, twenty-first-century division. This prototype was to become the standard for other divisions in the years to come. Management wanted detail down to job descriptions—needless to say, the rules had to reflect a similar level of detail.

6. Evaluate the Rules

How do you determine whether a rule should be retained? The standard is quite simple: If we continue with the rule, or even expand the parameters of that rule, will it move us closer to our desired future? Rules that no longer move us toward our goals are to be dropped like the bad habits that they have become. This is why a clear sense of direction and prioritization is so important. Otherwise, there is no valid way to determine what you must change. Those rules that you elect to retain are called *functional,* meaning they move you closer to your chosen strategic direction.

Many rules, policies, and procedures work well today. That is, they solve today's problems. When priorities and direction change, however, they may actually move us further from our desired state. These rules, policies, and procedures are called *dysfunctional.* Rather than throw out all the rules and start from scratch, evaluating the rules allows us to be selective. Further, it allows us to begin to prioritize those changes based on their expected impact on the organization.

7. *Assume Every Dysfunctional Rule Must Be Eliminated*

This step is both fun and frustrating for teams. Some rules are so universally resented, the teams almost feel like they are tossing effigies into the fire. That part is fun. Other rules are so culturally integrated, the pain is palpable as the team struggles with the thought of life without them.

A midwestern company that serviced mining equipment knew it had to change significantly if it was to survive the onslaught of new, low-cost competition. Each team included a subject matter expert, who was invariably one of the salesmen (they were never women) for this 110-year-old business. Many were third-generation employees, whose fathers and grandfathers sold in much the same way.

A typical sales call was a visit to the site foreman. They would go out for drinks, go fishing the next day, and sometimes hunting the day after that. Each sales call lasted between one and three days. This technique seemed to work well in the past, establishing a personal relationship with the buyer. The increased cost of mining began forcing the foremen to change their buying behavior, however, and the teams concluded that they had to change as well.

This kind of change may seem obvious and trivial to someone not in the business, but for this group, it was agony. That same type of pain has been experienced by those in pharmaceutical sales who were used to relationship selling with physicians. When HMOs and centralized purchasing shook up that pattern, pharmaceutical companies were left struggling to discover the new rules.

Those are the seven steps for fast, efficient, and lower-risk reengineering. The process is dependable and effective, but it is not a silver bullet. How much value your firm will glean from this process largely depends on its ability to both involve the *edge* and simulate the *edge* using the Ideal Team.

That does not mean, however, that the team's recommen-dations are always embraced. Dramatic change is always pain-ful. In fact, where there is no pain, significant change is rarely found. Anytime you introduce major change, expect resistance.

Now that you have learned the tools to uncover *what* must be changed, you must also learn the crucial techniques that will integrate change into your company's vision. Just as important, you will be shown how to stave off the frantic efforts of people in your organization who are drawn to the false sense of security offered by old and familiar ways. Whether you engage in formal reengineering or employ the Paradigm Prism, you are now in the change business. These are rules of the game we all need to master if we are to survive and prosper.

16

Dealing with Your Ever-Present Detractors

There are certain objections I regularly hear regarding the use of the *edge*. As you begin to introduce the *edge* into your organization, you also can expect to encounter these points. The major objections include:

- "There are a *lot* of crazy ideas out there."
- "We don't have enough resources or time."
- "We don't want our salespeople taking their eyes off the ball."

"THERE ARE A LOT OF CRAZY IDEAS OUT THERE"

Once you get sensitized to the *edge,* you can quickly become overwhelmed with ideas concerning change that is needed today and tomorrow. There is a practical limit to just how much you can process and still run a business. How do you decide what to listen to and what to ignore?

Having too many ideas is in many ways worse than having too few. If you only have a handful of ideas to consider, deciding which ones to prioritize is a relatively simple decision. Businesses that work regularly with the *edge* know that new ideas can flow fast and furious. You can't filter out those that seem "crazy," since quite often our criteria for crazy is defined by any idea that fundamentally violates our existing rules. That is often exactly what we want, not what we should avoid.

The challenge is knowing which ideas to listen to. Although the answer differs for each company, the following are some guidelines that make this decision much easier. The first step is to know thyself.

1. *What are your most difficult problems?* You should always give priority to ideas that, no matter how crazy, relate to the problems that you have repeatedly not been able to solve. The fact that you have been trying to solve them reflects that they are of value. The fact that you have not been able to solve them reflects that you need a different approach.

Identifying your most difficult problems is not always an easy task. If you have been unable to solve them despite Herculean efforts, eventually you are forced to put them on the back burner. It is not that you have necessarily given up on them, but you have given up on solving them *today*. Eventually, today becomes tomorrow, and they fall from your awareness.

Not surprising, most people, when trying to identify these problems, focus on the ones that are externally imposed: regulatory changes, policy changes, economic or competitive changes. In every case these problems represent someone or something changing the rules for us. These kinds of rules are definitely worth revisiting.

The U.S. Air Force Directorate for Civilian Personnel had one of these really tough problems. The USAFDCP employed many thousands of civilian workers, located across the United States. Although each area had a different cost of living (Alabama vs. New York), the federally mandated compensation schedule allowed for no variation in salary grades. Needless to say, this made it quite difficult to hire and retain good workers in high-cost-of-living locations.

When I was brought in, the organization quickly identified this to be one of their most difficult, yet important problems. They tried on three separate occasions to get the federal guidelines changed, each time to no avail. We talked about whether conditions had changed since then (there was a more supportive Congress). We explored options for getting people and governments to be more open to change.

USAFDCP ultimately did go back to Congress; this time management walked out with a new set of guidelines that were much more equitable. If they had not explicitly recalled and challenged a problem they had all but given up on, the breakthrough may have eluded them . . . they may not have even tried at all.

Another group that had problems with Congress (is there a pattern here?) was the National Association of Home Economists. The Association felt it needed and deserved an increase in funding to support the school programs for home economics, but the mood on the Hill was more conducive to cutting rather than spending. The group put together display booths for every state, depicting the practical education and training that was part of home economics. The Association desperately was trying to change people's image of home economics as simply sewing and cooking.

The display program was a success, and funding was eventually increased. When I spoke to members at their national convention, they were flying pretty high. I congratulated them, and then threw a wrench into the works. "You assume that the problem had been with Congress," I said (voicing what is usually a wholly reasonable assumption). "They are not, however, the only enemy to be vanquished." I reminded them of the comic strip *Pogo*, in which Pogo observed: "We have met the enemy, and it is us!"

There were nearly 700 home economists in attendance at the convention. I asked them to look around the room and see whether there was anything unusual. No one had an answer. Heads twisted this way and that while faces became perplexed. "Don't you find it interesting to note that out of 700 people, there is not one man—not *one?*" I have spoken to many "traditionally" women professions but have always seen some men. "Don't you find that a problem?" It was obvious from their expressions they did not.

I then suggested that the very name "home economists" might bear some of the blame for the Association's image problem and suggested that the group just might want to consider changing its name. You would have thought I was recommending banishing their firstborn. I backed away from the front of the stage, afraid to turn my back on the group. They were out for blood.

The national president was next on stage. She thanked me for my comments and then said: "Wayne, I am afraid, has stolen my thunder. I had already planned to announce that we have decided to change our name. Our curriculum will no longer be called Home Economics, but 'Life Science.' " It was now her turn to back off the stage. Hers was not a happy group.

Such externally imposed problems are definitely worth examining. Sometimes these challenges can be overcome, either with a change in approach or a change in circumstances. The type of problems that we are least likely to address, however, are those that are completely within our control. The home economists, for example, were able to easily articulate the funding restrictions that were imposed on them but were totally unprepared to face the restrictions they imposed on themselves.

It was easy for me to see the home economists' self-imposed constraints because I was an outsider. The fact that there were no men present would have quickly been seen by anyone not part of their profession. You can likewise benefit from an outsider's perspective when you use members of the *edge* to help in the identification of your most difficult problems. For you they just might be invisible.

2. *Restate your problems using generic language.* You have already learned how to use generic language to search for breakthrough solutions. This technique is just as useful in creating an idea filter. In Chapter 12 we were concerned with searching for solutions, but sometimes the solutions arrive at your doorstep with the morning's paper. When they do, it is a safe bet that they will not be clothed in your language.

An engineer from a major firm in Houston told me that one of his problems was how to best track and report the onslaught of product engineering changes. Product engineering changes track and report on the dozens, sometimes hundreds, of changes a product can go through in its useful lifetime, and he was responsible to sort through each item and evaluate their impact on his company. He had been working on this problem for years, with little success.

He and his wife (a physician) were getting ready to go to a party. While waiting, he began flipping through her copy of the *New England Journal of Medicine.* He suddenly stopped at an article written by the CDC (Centers for Disease Control) about how they track and report the changes of diseases and their treatments. "There on the pages in front of me," he said, shaking his head in amazement, "was the answer to the problem I had been working on for the better part of a decade."

If that engineer had not restated his problem, he would have just passed over that article as irrelevant. After all, it wasn't talking about products, but diseases. Only because he made his problem *generic* was he able to spot the problem when it appeared before him.

3. *Keep your list visible.* This is the third and the last step in creating a simple and effective filter for ideas. The engineer in the previous example was able to see the solution only because he was explicitly aware of the problem. Keep your list of problems where you can see them. Better yet, keep them where your colleagues can see them also.

There are a lot of "crazy" ideas out there, and the detractors are right—you can't possibly listen to every one. How do you know which to listen to? Based on the three steps we just reviewed, consider the following:

- If the idea or suggestion is one that could possibly influence your future, listen. The more you dislike what you hear, the greater the likelihood that the idea is rubbing against an ingrained belief. Those fingernails on the blackboard could be writing your future. If the idea relates in any way to your list of generic problems, listen. Even if you don't get *the* answer, you may get an entirely different perspective on the problem.
- It is good practice to have a separate list for the big problems of your key influencers: customers, competitors, suppliers, and employees. If an idea seems to fit one of their problems, listen. It might be more useful than would appear at first blush.

Finally, recognize that you can't listen to all solutions—there are too many of them out there. You may be turning away the next cellular phone, but if it doesn't have the potential to solve your big problems, let it go. You have created a "crazy idea" filter, so use it.

"WE DON'T HAVE ENOUGH RESOURCES OR TIME"

In business, profit or not-for-profit, time is scarce. There is hardly enough time to handle yesterday's problems without worrying about today and tomorrow. A typical group of detractors would probably say, "I would *love* to have the time to pursue all these wonderful ideas generated by the *edge*, but I live in the *real* world. Maybe when things slow down. . . ."

It is important to understand that there is a big difference between pursuing and investigating. You only pursue those ideas that both match your filter and seem workable, and this is a much smaller population to deal with. It makes little sense to invest in an idea that will not work.

Be very careful about the tendency to abandon ideas too early, however. The very reason that they have made it through your filter is because they might solve an important problem that has been nagging you for years. Those ideas will all likely contradict your sense of what works and what doesn't. After all, you have already tried the things you thought would work.

Schwinn has been through this process. After 97 years in business, the Schwinn Bicycle Company filed for Chapter 11 bankruptcy protection in 1992. Its sales dropped from a high of 1.5 million bikes in the mid-1970s to less than 500,000 in 1992. "What happened to General Motors is what happened to Schwinn," said Marc Sani, editor of *Bicycle Retailer & Industry News.* "They rested on their laurels, and you had really aggressive companies come on board."[1]

In the late 1970s lightweight racing and touring bikes started to become popular. Schwinn had years to adapt to these changes, but sadly for Schwinn, the company rejected the idea of racing bikes early on. The market for these expensive, top-of-the-line bikes went to companies such as Trek Bicycle Corporation. At the same time, firms like Huffy Bicycle Company attacked the lower end of the market, distributing through Kmart and Toys 'R' Us. These and a host of other competitors were effectively invisible to Schwinn.

The second blow came with the popularity of mountain bikes, those specialized high-strength and low-weight bikes that are designed for trails and other rough terrain. Incredibly, Schwinn again rejected this new and emerging market. Tom Stendahl, CEO of Scott, which ultimately purchased Schwinn, observed: "When they were asked who were their competition, they said 'We don't have competition. We're Schwinn.' "[2]

The racing bikes, touring bikes, and mountain bikes all were introduced by the *edge*. They were rejected by Schwinn. There is absolutely no evidence that Schwinn ever seriously investigated or considered adding to its existing product line.

Schwinn's reluctance to consider the new bicycle concepts did not stem from its resource concerns. I doubt the company would have seriously investigated innovations had it been handed the money and personnel on a silver platter. It would have taken few resources for Schwinn to have looked into the new bicycle concepts. Even if the company had investigated and then rejected the bikes, that investigation might have sufficiently motivated Schwinn to monitor the progress of the new markets.

"SALESPEOPLE SHOULD NOT TAKE THEIR EYES OFF THE BALL"

We have already seen the importance of salespeople in representing customers on the *edge*. The same customers who reject what they're being sold are the ones who are transmitting critical signals about your organization's future. I have no doubt that Schwinn's salespeople were reporting problems in competing with the new designs. Schwinn's flaw was it did not give the messages the importance they deserved.

When I speak to companies about the value of salespeople working with the *edge*, management, especially sales management, gets uncomfortable. They remind me that they do not pay sales to transmit signals, no matter how "theoretically" important. Especially, I am told, they do not want their people calling on "small, headache accounts when there are bigger fish to fry."

It is the job of salespeople to sell. No one with a semblance of sanity (that does not necessarily exclude me) would suggest that a sales force should deliberately ignore mainstream, profitable customers to court the *edge*. That is definitely not the recommendation of this book.

It is rare when salespeople find a need to court the *edge*. They encounter members of the *edge* daily. There will always be large, profitable customers who reject what you sell, and small, low-volume companies who want products and services that you do not offer. All that your sales force needs to do is recognize the potential value of this information and transmit it to a willing (hopefully) and receptive management group.

To encourage salespeople to be *edge* sensitive does not require them to "take their eyes off the ball." However, it is a very good idea to offer incentives for demonstrated *edge* sensitivity. These incentives can include:

- Recognition rewards for passing along *edge* information.
- "Black hole" awards for the group who transmits the least amount of information from the *edge*.
- Dinner awards.
- Movie or show tickets.

Incentives should not compete with the real job of selling. Their purpose is merely to provide a small inducement for the salesperson to take on that little extra work that is required. Try it—you'll like it.

17

Leading on the Edge

The role of every leader is to forge new directions for his or her organization. As you move up the corporate ladder, this responsibility grows proportionately. Without the benefit of *edge* influence, however, too many companies end up merely repeating old patterns.

FALLING THROUGH THE CRACKS

Winning on the *edge* demands, more than anything else, that leaders not only allow but *expect* their people to commit at least a small percentage of their time away from mainstream pursuits. This is not a trivial commitment. Whether we use the *edge* to challenge our established paradigms or to get a glimpse into the future, the present will suffer, to some degree.

One organization with a global reputation for innovation has always done an excellent job of investing in the *edge*. Its R&D is admired by all. When I asked a large group of this company's plant managers if they found their "*edge* time" rewarding, they guffawed. "Yeah, right! Are you kidding? We don't get time to breathe." They complained that only R&D is afforded the luxury to look beyond the mainstream. "Innovation and anticipation," they continued, "are just not part of our jobs."

When senior management was asked about the plant managers' observations, they confirmed it was true. Why only R&D? "Because it only works with R&D," was the response. "Have you ever tried it outside R&D?" "Of course not," they responded. "Why should we try something that we know won't work?"

This conversation occurred in 1989. It was not surprising to read in 1994 that this company, upon benchmarking its operating costs with other companies, found that these costs were excessively high. In some cases corporate overhead was more than 40 percent higher than the industry norm.

Any group that is not encouraged by leadership to explore the *edge* will have great difficulty innovating and anticipating. Those senior managers were wrong. Every plant, every function, and every department has the potential and the need to both innovate and anticipate. Changes in our external work environment must be responded to by changes in our internal work environment. Otherwise, we run the risk of becoming an anachronism.

Leadership, at its essence, is all about change. A good leader not only moves the organization in response to change but also is proactive. Effective leaders respond well to change. Excellent leaders anticipate change.

Leadership goes way beyond the top officer of an organization. Every person who promotes change is potentially a leader. This chapter is targeted for those leaders (including managers) who want to incorporate the power of the *edge* into their firms.

YOUR ORGANIZATION'S BUSINESS THEORY

Peter Drucker recently warned organizations about the dangers of allowing their "business theory" to go unchallenged:

> Every business, in fact every organization, operates on such a theory—that is, on a set of assumptions regarding the outside (customers, markets, distributive channels, competition) and a set of assumptions regarding the inside (core competencies, technology, products, processes). These assumptions are usually taken as holy writ by the company and its executives.[1]

It is very difficult for an organization to challenge its own established business theory. Like water to fish, even the most fundamental boundaries can be invisible. Fortunately, a company's business theory is not taken as "holy writ" by the *edge*. Just as kings used to allow the court jester to question their decisions when no one else dared, organizations can use the *edge* to challenge their most profoundly held beliefs.

Tropicana, for example, is the most successful and profitable producer of juice products in the world. Their mission statement (holy writ) is on every container: "Fresh, not frozen." Showing great courage they applied the *edge* mentality, challenging their very own century-old business philosophy. Tropicana's leadership had to acknowledge that the technology for freezing has improved greatly. Although management ultimately concluded that fresh is still superior to frozen, their willingness to examine their most fundamental business philosophy was an inspiration. Tropicana recognized that any business philosophy that goes unchallenged runs the risk of becoming an epitaph.

DISASTER PLUCKED FROM THE JAWS OF SUCCESS

Several years ago I conducted a two-day intensive executive retreat for a consumer packaging company. The participants determined that the company's survival depended on increasing its gross margin from its current 2 percent to 5 percent over the next five years. By the end of the second day, each of the vice presidents reported the gains they thought they could realistically achieve. When totaled, they concluded that they could potentially increase gross margin, not by 5 percent, but up to 22 percent within five years!

Needless to say, the CEO was thrilled. "Terrific," he beamed, "now who is going to volunteer to implement these changes?" Silence. Faces reddened, and one vice president turned to another and said, "Tom, that's a good one for you." Tom, in turn, turned to Bill and said, "Bill, you should pick up that one." No one was willing to accept the consequences that come from challenging a basic philosophy of business. Neither the CEO nor any of his staff had the courage to risk the company's entrenched belief system, regardless of the potential.

Few things are more difficult for an organization than to question its business philosophy. Practicing wide-angle vision can be a powerful aid in this regard. An effective way to examine your business philosophy is to:

- Identify your business philosophy.
- Gather an *edge* team whose sole purpose is to test that philosophy.
- Assume that your business philosophy is no longer useful—that is, its continued use *has caused failure.*
- Ask your team (working team and Ideal Team):
  —what are the external factors (competitive changes, customer shifts, economic/political changes, demographic shifts) that caused the failure?
  —what are the internal factors (employee attitudes, business structural changes, labor challenges) that have caused the failure?
- Consider whether you or your team think any of those events (customer shifts, economic/political changes, etc.) may become possible.
- Determine whether any of those conditions are in evidence today.

If you conduct this exercise and conclude that none of the events are possible, you should be very concerned. Cray Computer concluded that parallel processing was impossible, and they went out of business. Remember that *every* business philosophy has a limited life. It is up to the leaders to acknowledge and anticipate limits; few things are more deserving of a leader's time and attention.

PLANNING: BACK TO THE FUTURE

We can't really predict the future at all. All we can do is invent it.
  —Dennis Gabor

Sometimes I don't know when to keep my big mouth shut. I was sitting in the executive dining room with the executive team of a large east coast brokerage firm. Over salad, the head of one of the business groups mentioned that they had just completed a 14-month strategic plan. He informed me that my role was to help the organization prepare for the changes inherent in that plan.

Not satisfied to leave well enough alone, I mentioned that I could probably describe their plan to them. With his best poker face, the vice president raised both hands, palms up, and invited me to give it a try. With all the good sense of a fullback with no helmet, I spent the next five minutes detailing what I thought the firm's plan might be. My host, through gritted teeth, told me that I was right on the money.

With all the good sense of a fullback *after* playing with no helmet, I then proceeded to describe three likely scenarios, any one of which would render the plan impotent. The firm's management later informed me that their "grand plan" had not only taken 14 months to prepare but that it also required a small army of internal experts and outside consultants. Yet they had considered only one of the three scenarios I outlined.

It has been said that organizations don't plan to fail, they just fail to plan. That is not so. Most organizations build their plans with the detail and certainty found only in people who know the future. What they "know," however, is not the future but their unspoken assumptions regarding the future. They do not plan to fail; they plan as if their assumptions are reality.

Your assumptions regarding the future, as well as your organization's response to that future, is based on the mainstream. When (not if) the mainstream is challenged by the *edge*, we are confronted with the conviction that the problem was not with our elegant plan, but with uncontrollable and unforeseeable events. Quite the contrary. As Shakespeare penned: "The fault, dear Brutus, is not in our stars, but in ourselves."

HOW I DESTROYED TWO COMPANIES

Over a decade ago, *Business Week* ran a lead article entitled "The Failure of Strategic Planning." This article included a long list of businesses with fatally flawed strategic plans and a small handful of companies that had top-notch plans. I had personally participated in the strategic plan development of two of the touted companies . . . and watched helplessly as the plans destroyed the companies (this fact has managed to escape mention in my resume until now).

One of those plans was an "affiliation" between American Motors and Renault. The other reflected Uniroyal Chemical's diversification from a rubber chemical company to a specialty chemicals company. Both plans were elegant and well thought out. They received the stamp of approval from a top business publication; but they were destined to become the equivalent of a hemlock cocktail for each company.

I can't begin to express just how profoundly that article affected me. I had rationalized away my culpability in the two disasters, but I was not as easily able to shake away the shock at seeing the two plans praised. Why, I asked myself, did these plans in particular, and most plans in general, fail?

A Self-Diagnostic for Planning

Plans fail for many reasons, and you should have no illusions that they will all be covered here. What I do want to explore with you, however, is how I was able to easily "guess" the brokerage firm's plan and how you can use the same technique to improve your own planning.

Ask yourself (or better yet, ask an employee on the *edge*) the following questions regarding your strategic plan:

1. Do your assumptions about the future require you to leverage your existing investment (financial, infrastructure, training, culture)?

2. Do any of your assumptions about the future require disinvestment (erode your financial, infrastructure, training, or cultural investment)?

3. Does your plan anticipate possible dramatic changes, either regulatory, competitive, or customer-based?

4. Are any discontinuous (nonincremental) changes reflected in your plan, changes that will require you to alter how you conduct business in a fundamental way?

5. Does your plan reflect an improvement from year to year?

6. Will you be significantly better off at the end of your plan than you are today?

A typical company would probably provide the following answers:

Question 1: yes.

Question 2: no.

Question 3: no.

Question 4: no.

Question 5: yes.

Question 6: yes.

If your answers are compatible with those shown, then your plan is in big trouble.

Am I telling you that a good plan should show you worse off than the year before? Obviously, that is absurd. But let's put "plan making" in perspective. Your advertising and public relations departments are designed to show investors how well your company can thrive within all economic environments. Their job is to highlight your strengths, and possibly even to downplay your weaknesses. A business plan that is based on the same premise is going to rob your firm of valuable opportunities. The great majority of plans are constructed upon an assumption of divine intervention—God is on our side. The economy, demographics, tastes, competition, and technology (to name a few) do not conspire to help you out. As Joel Barker says, "Shift happens!"

No senior executive or manager really believes that God is on his or her side, but many behave as though this were the case. This is why most plans consider the future to be benign. We create a strategy that seems appropriate (brilliant and blessed by the angels), and then construct a scenario that supports that strategy.

It should be no surprise that in 1977, when Xerox was experiencing its companywide identity crisis, a critical self-examination by its planning department revealed:

The [Xerox Long Range Plan] is a desired outcome; rather than a probable outcome based upon an objective assessment of an achievable plan. . . . Our strategic approach tends to be too introspective.[2]

This Xerox phenomenon is an affliction that has overcome no less than 95 percent of all organizations.

Organizations that conduct a "risk assessment" of their plan will usually create a series of potential problems and then shoot them down. "The economy could turn down, but . . ." "Raw material prices might rise, but . . ." We rarely expect to encounter new competition or any serious challenges to our strategy.

At Uniroyal Chemical we conducted exhaustive computer simulations that reflected a large number of scenarios. This produced an impressive analysis of the risk/reward exposure of multiple options. In the end, the CEO made the decision based on which scenario he believed. Although he did not select the most optimistic, he believed in a view of the future that supported rather than contradicted the desired strategy.

So, how did I know the brokerage firm's plan? I understood where its biggest investment was (its extensive network of branch offices) and realized that its plan would call for leveraging those branch offices into greater success. The firm's view of technology, demographics, client demand, and legislative action all would conspire to exalt those branches.

Unfortunately, I cannot outline the details of the plan, out of professional obligations to the client. Although the firm was upset that its brilliant plan was in fact transparent (and vulnerable), I was more concerned with the money, effort, and time that went into something that was little more than a well-documented fantasy.

Planning's Harsh Realities

Before we examine some alternatives to traditional Western planning, let's review some of the realities of strategic planning:

Reality #1: *The future will just as easily shaft you as shield you.* At the end of 1994, a survey of CD-ROM publishers showed that the great majority of them had plans that reflected *no probable drop in prices.* In 1994 the average computer CD was $45. 1995 saw prices fall to under $40. Over the next several years, prices are projected to drop to less than $30.

Not every CD-ROM publisher, however, was so naive. Bobby Kotick, CEO of Activision, noted: "There's an assumption that the industry will increase the volume and at the same time maintain the current retail price levels. History would indicate that this is not the way it works."[3]

History is a succession of events whereby the mainstream is overturned by the *edge*. No matter how carefully we plan, the *edge* will find a way. It will be heard. Plans are natural reflections of the mainstream. Remember, ignore the *edge* at your own peril.

Reality #2: *It is not possible, even in theory, to forecast the future.* Someday, this may change, but for the foreseeable future, we should accept that we will be flying blind. This is a very radical departure from most planning today. We assume that if we just have enough time, data, and computer power, we will be able to create "accurate forecasts." *Accurate forecast* is an oxymoron.

> *If you can't do better than 80 percent accuracy, you have no business forecasting. If you can do better than 80 percent, you probably have no business.*

Paleontologist Stephen Jay Gould wrote about the randomness of events, applying this concept to evolution. He pointed out that: "Little quirks at the outset, occurring for no particular reason, unleashed cascades of consequences that make a particular future seem inevitable in retrospect."[4] Gould's point was that no matter how massive your database of knowledge, no matter how powerful your computer, you would not have been able to predict which different anatomical types disappeared during the Cambrian period. The survival of some species over others was not based on the properties of the organisms themselves. It was based on the cascade of consequences.[5]

Three 1994 Nobel Prize winners for economics (Reinhard Selten, John Harsanyi, and John Nash) won the coveted prize based on their study of "game theory." They proposed that virtually every game (social, economic, and business) has many outcomes, called *multiple equilibria*. In other words, every event has an enormous range of possible outcomes. Each of these possibilities represent stable outcomes.

The very act of creating "a plan" is to declare a single stable outcome. Think of how absurd this is in the face of hundreds, or even thousands, of possible outcomes. The goal of creating accurate forecasts is far more difficult to reach than we ever realized.

Reality #3: *Accuracy is undesirable.* Frederik Pohl, a science fiction writer, said: "The more complete and accurate a prediction is, the less use it is."[6] By this he meant that if we know *absolutely* what lies ahead, what could we do with that information? Because our future is certain, we have no options. An accurate prediction is like an accurate historical statistic. It might be interesting, but what can you *do* about it?

Does the reverse apply? Does the value of a prediction increase as its accuracy declines? Are poor predictions of greater use? Strangely enough, the answer is *yes*—not because the prediction is poor, but because we *know* it is poor. With that knowledge we can stop thinking in terms of *the* future and start thinking of multiple possible futures. This provides us options, freedom, and hope.

Reality #4: *Culture beats strategy every time.* Think of a competitor that is roughly your size. Assume that your competitor copies your strategic plan exactly and implements it precisely as you do. Would you expect the competitor to achieve exactly what you would achieve?

Every company has a culture that is defined by its personality and habits. Each organization is unique. Your firm has strengths and weaknesses that either impede or accelerate your ability to achieve your strategic plan, and these characteristics are different from every other firm. Does your plan accommodate those strengths and weaknesses?

I once worked with a national retail chain that was having trouble implementing its strategic plan. It called for centralizing many administrative functions, an idea that had received unanimous support from the executive strategy committee. After two years, however, it had made little progress.

It quickly became evident that the culprit was the company's attitude toward information systems. Because IS had two major fiascoes in the past, it was not popular at this firm. Since the new plan depended on heavy IS involvement, every corner of the company resisted it.

The plan failed because it did not reflect the culture of the company. Those things that made the company unique, both positive and negative, were ignored in planning, but could not be overlooked in the implementation. Without taking adequate account of the culture, any plan is doomed.

PLANNING ON THE EDGE

During times of peace, the military produces forecasts. During war, it produces plans. Turbulence, be it environmental, economic, competitive, or educational, is effectively equivalent to war. The *edge* does not create turbulence (a faster and more furious flow of information can be blamed for that). The *edge* simply feeds on and contributes to that information flow. For better or worse, we must forever separate the fiction of forecasting from the very real challenge of planning.

The first step in planning on the *edge* is to recognize that the future will always surprise us. In most cases we can eliminate crisis, and we can certainly reduce surprise, but surprise will always be a part of your future. Using the techniques described in this book, however, you will be able to anticipate most of the curve balls that the future will toss your way.

Before You Start

Concentrate on your strategic vulnerabilities. What are those things that would cause you to fail? Be sure to include the events that directly contradict what you now believe to be your greatest strengths.

Caterpillar Tractor had a strategy of "grow or die." During the late 1970s and early 1980s, the company added state-of-the-art facilities designed to produce top-notch products and increase capacity. Since Cat "knew" that its business was energy related, management thought that profits would continue their upward climb. After all, they reasoned, construction goes hand-in-hand with energy production. In 1981, for example, Caterpillar spent $836 million on capital projects, a record for the industry at that time.

Caterpillar management never considered events that contradicted their expansive approach, because they never entertained the possibility of softening of the oil market or an excess capacity in the industry. Had they been really sharp, they may have even expected the appearance of a new competitor. Any of these events would have devastated (and did) their grow-or-die strategy.

After you have isolated what events might precipitate failure, ask yourself, and especially ask the *edge*, whether any of those events are *possible* over the next three to five years. Are there any indications of those events today? If the answer is no (even from the *edge*), you can breathe a sigh of relief. Continue to watch for the onset of those events, but exclude them from your plan. If the answer is yes, they must become components of your plan—regardless of explanations, rationalizations, or rebuttals.

For Caterpillar Tractor, not one but *both* of its "unthinkable" events occurred, virtually simultaneously. Oil prices began to decline and industry capacity increased. The company's trouble was compounded by increased competition from Japan's Komatsu. Both a weak yen and Komatsu's high efficiency contributed to its becoming a formidable adversary. With events set in a downward spiral, the results were inevitable. During the period from 1982 to 1984, Caterpillar was awash in losses, amassing $92 million of red ink in the third quarter of 1984 alone.[7]

Finally, identify those potential positive events that might occur but would surprise you. This is an important but often overlooked step. IBM lost market share to Compaq because the demand for its home personal computer, Aptiva, far exceeded its expectations. After IBM ran out of inventory, Compaq virtually owned the market. The painful lesson was that planning for success can be just as important as planning for disaster.

Creating the Plan

On the surface, it might seem appropriate to make your plan flexible through the use of scenario planning. That is not true, at least not in the traditional sense. With traditional scenario planning, you examine various possibilities and then select the one that appears most likely. That is a sucker's bet. That which is expected will rarely, if ever, happen. If you doubt that statement, reread the section on forecasting in Chapter 6. Aspects of the most likely scenario may occur, but don't lay your money down on any one single scenario.

The problem that is inherent with scenario planning manifests itself after you select the most likely event—because then you are plunged right back into steady state forecasting. The answer is not to pretend that there is a steady state but to create a plan that accommodates a turbulent, chaotic, constant flux environment. The roller coaster ride is not going to stop, so you had better learn to conduct business while the wheels are moving.

CORE COMPETENCY OR CORE DEFICIENCY

Core competency[8] (concentrating on your strengths) is a powerful force in management philosophy today. Based on the collective learning in the organization, it has challenged companies to refocus lines of business and to leverage their investment in people. For many, applying core competency has transformed a strength into a powerhouse.

The term *core competency* was introduced by C. K. Prahalad and Gary Hamel and first appeared in the *Harvard Business Review* in 1990:

> Core competencies are the collective learning in the organization, especially how to coordinate diverse production skills and integrate multiple streams of technologies.[9]

It is a very useful and powerful concept that says, in effect, that management must give its attention to those bundles of skills and technologies that are most critical to long-term competitive success. More recently, Prahalad and Hamel extended their definition of core competency to include:

- Customer value—contributes significantly to the customer's perception of value.
- Competitor differentiation—distinguishes the core company from the rest of the industry.

- Extendability—offers growth beyond the markets of today.[10]

How does an organization develop core competence? As it develops skills, its competencies increase. A competency that forms the core of its success, its strength, is called a core competency. The collective learning behind the core competency is usually based solely on an organizatic.n's experience with the mainstream. The greater its success in dealing with the mainstream, the more the organization celebrates its core competency.

As long as that experience goes unchallenged, the core remains competent. This accounted for five decades of success at IBM. When circumstances change and the mainstream is assaulted, however, the core can quickly become deficient in dealing with the new realities.

Dramatic environmental changes can herald the fall of a core competency. As we've seen, the *edge* is an excellent early warning system for such changes, for no company's core competency is eternal. Some, like IBM's, may last half a century or more. Others, like People Express's, may come and go in a matter of years.

Nothing in business is impervious to the *edge*. Core competency is no exception. It is a concern that, although many companies are aware of their core competency, they are wholly unaware of the changing tides that challenge that core.

How do you know which competency is core? This question may be considered in many ways, but they all revolve around the criteria of success. Companies with core competencies have all been very successful in applying their particular skills. The greater the strength and uniqueness, the greater the success, and the more powerful the core competency.

Dr. Jekyll and Mr. Hyde

Walt Disney is an extraordinary company. It was founded on a set of sacred principles and has successfully maintained them for more than half a century. Until recently, Disney's core competency was neatly wrapped in the packaging of "family entertainment." Its core competency was killing it.

As you have seen, success is always defined by the mainstream. Acceptance by the *edge*, although a good indicator of future success, does not in itself constitute critical mass. Therefore core competency is always a reflection of the mainstream. How did Disney know that its core competency was family entertainment? The company had to look no further than its bottom line every year.

Family entertainment meets the three criteria to be considered a core competency. It certainly has contributed to perceived customer value, it has differentiated Disney from the rest of the industry, and it has the potential to evolve with tomorrow's markets.

As the world began to change, Disney tenaciously hung onto its core competency and everything that derived from it. In the early 1980s, the company conducted intensive training programs for all employees, instilling in them a sense of the strength of Walt Disney. Just a few of the derived principles included:

- All employees must be clean-cut (no long hair, please).
- No alcoholic beverages in theme parks.
- Only produce films with a "G" rating.
- Target kids; include parents when possible.
- Childless couples and singles can spend their money elsewhere.
- Make hotel rooms very large so entire families can stay there.

The core competency of family entertainment obviously worked quite well for Disney, but if management had watched the *edge*, they would have perceived fundamental shifts in the tastes and sophistication of their market, and the world at large. Had they listened to the *edge*, they might have reexamined their core competency. Instead, Disney dismissed the *edge*, and by 1984 it held a mere 4 percent of the film market.

There was no doubt that Disney had lost its leadership position. According to *Fortune* magazine, "The studio's resident producers ground out a thin stream of formulaic pictures fewer and fewer people would pay to see. A similar low-horsepower approach to television production led to CBS's cancellation of the hour-long 'Wonderful World of Disney,' leaving the company without a regular network show for the first time in 29 years."[11]

What was once a core competency for Disney had become a core deficiency. Happily, the story didn't end there. Michael Eisner took over and began to challenge the established beliefs regarding their core competency. Alcohol was permitted on theme park grounds, and Disney launched Touchstone Pictures, so it could release movies such as *Good Morning, Vietnam* without offending its traditional family market. Within a handful of years, profits had quadrupled, and Disney's market share skyrocketed to 14 percent.

The challenge of managing your business using core competency is to anticipate and recognize when it will no longer be core. Prahalad and Hamel recognize this risk:

> What was a core competence in one decade may become a mere capability in another. . . . Over long periods of time, what was once a core competence may become a baseline capability. Quality, rapid time to market, and quick-response customer service—once genuine differentiators—are becoming routine advantages in many industries.[12]

Let me make this point even stronger: What was once a core competency can become a *core deficiency*. This goes far beyond mere "baseline capability"—it can destroy you. This transformation can occur on two fronts.

First, anyone who fails to recognize that their core competency has ceased will continue to plow resources, people, and attention into what is no longer a prized set of skills. This can actually put that company at a competitive disadvantage relative to firms that never followed the core competency doctrine at all.

Second, and more perverse, sometimes a set of skills that is highly valued by one customer can be as welcome as a plague by another. This is what happened to IBM and its vertically organized, IS-oriented skill base. In a dramatically changing market, the value of these skills did not just slip by degree. It was a transformation every bit as radical as that experienced by Dr. Jekyll. Do you have a Mr. Hyde camouflaged as core competency? It is easier than you may think to make the transformation from competency to deficiency without even recognizing that the ground has shifted.

Defense Insecurity

After the military's first round of downsizing, defense contractors saw that they had a major challenge on their hands. They needed to change, and change fast. Every major defense contractor realized that it had to shift its emphasis from the government to the commercial sector. The management at one of these contractors asked me to help them navigate this unparalleled journey.

During the course of a one-day workshop, I learned just how obsessive the security was throughout the organization. Later in the day I had a closed-door meeting with the head of the company to discuss the situation. "I think you will find this to be an important issue," I said in muted tones to the CEO. I assumed that he didn't appreciate the degree to which security had a stranglehold on his company. A sampling of their security-based rules included:

- Only hire citizens born in the United States (everyone else is a security risk).
- Only give employees just enough to do their jobs—not a scrap of data more.
- Never talk to the people around you about your job.
- Never let customers inside your business.

He looked at me quizzically. "What exactly do you see as the problem?" he asked. "Of course security is pervasive. It is our core competency." This last remark really threw me, and the stupid expression on my face must have reflected that. "Look," he said patiently, using the same tone that I use when speaking to my young son, "private industry is very competitive, isn't it?" "Of course," I said, unsure of his point. He went on, "Well, you need to keep your secrets from competitors. The better your security, the better you keep your secrets, and the more competitive you can become. It's simple."

I nodded my head sagely and said, "Ron, maybe it isn't really quite that simple." Ron's eyebrows shot up, surprised. For the next 45 minutes I explained to him the realities of the new world that he was venturing into, laying all the cards on the table.

First we discussed the need for open information exchange. "The commercial market is different in many ways," I said, "and security can never take precedence over flexibility, openness to outsiders, and innovation." I didn't pull any punches with him. I know our conversation must have made a real impact, because that client never again called. The defense industry has always been regulation sensitive and cost insensitive. In such an environment, security can certainly be considered a core competency. By comparison, the commercial world is regulation insensitive and cost sensitive. What was once a competency does not just disappear, it becomes literally poison.

How do you keep from making the transformation from competency to deficiency? As we have seen in the previous examples, perception is extremely selective, and such limited vision can be as dangerous to your company as Mr. Magoo's attempts to navigate a highway. To merely "be aware" of the risk is not enough. Although Eisner has been effective in helping Disney move from "family entertainment" to general entertainment, the company still has a long way to go. I recently read that Disney is going to introduce "adult learning vacations" in Orlando, called the Disney Institute. These vacations, I read, will offer classes in cooking, gardening, music, and other hobby interests. Professionally, I was impressed by the change that Disney had effected. Personally, I was intrigued with the thought of surprising my wife with a one-week trip to indulge her passion of cooking.

Upon further investigation, I was told that these vacations were designed for the family. The children would have their activities, and the parents (plural) would have theirs. This was not appropriate, I was assured, for a single adult, despite what the literature described. Disney has made great strides, but inside that Mickey Mouse costume still lurks . . . Mickey Mouse!

Companies that prevent their core competency from becoming a core deficiency do so by regularly challenging the very things that contributed to their success. The *edge* can be particularly helpful here. The ability to wrestle with core competency is not just a function of your good intentions. If you don't feel the pain of honest self-examination, the chances are good that your core competency is getting off easy. This takes great courage, since core competency often dictates how investment is directed. Although challenging core competency demands a willingness to turn your back on past investment and culture, you should find it a most valuable exercise in creative destruction.

EXAMINING BUSINESS THEORY

We saw that the *edge* can be a valuable tool in challenging core competency. This can be difficult enough. Even more ingrained, though, is an organization's business theory. Not surprising, it is also the most difficult concept to challenge.

Every network executive (and much of the developed world) understands the first rule of television: Ratings produce profits. The better the ratings, the better the profits. This philosophy has spawned an incredible array of network norms, such as "major sports programming at almost any price," "shoot for the blockbuster hits," and "revenue is more important than costs."

In the early 1990s, ABC challenged the established rule. The recession had reduced advertising spending, and with it the size of the revenue pie to be divided up between NBC, CBS, and ABC. With both NBC and CBS fighting it out for the top Nielson ratings, ABC took a gamble. They stacked their schedule with shows that were cheaper to produce and started cutting costs in an industry hardly known for austerity.

ABC's performance was hardly stellar, showing only $120 million profits on revenues of $2.6 billion. But during this time, the other networks lost millions. During an up market, ABC's strategy may not have worked. They demonstrated, however, that even a decades-old philosophy, under the proper conditions, will have a limited life. Courage is not measured by what you change. It is a reflection of what you are willing to question.

EXECUTIVE INFORMATION DELIVERY

Ignorance is not bliss if you are responsible for leading your company into new and unchartered territory. Information on the *edge*, perhaps the most critical information to a decision maker, rarely makes it across any executive's desk. The problem is certainly not a lack of information but a lack of the right kind of information.

Most of the information an executive receives is mass-produced, historical (reflects past events), and inwardly focused, thus giving the executive a limited perspective. Sometimes, some of the most valuable information is systematically excluded from the executive's purview. The popular solution to this nearsightedness is to produce so many reports, from so many different perspectives, that the required information must be found somewhere.

Data Everywhere, and Not a Drop to Drink

When Abraham Lincoln was a young man he took a sack of grain to be ground at the mill. The owner had the reputation for being the slowest and laziest miller in Illinois. After watching him for a while, Lincoln said, "You know, I could eat that grain as fast as you are grinding it." "But how long could you keep it up?" the miller replied ungraciously. "Until I starve to death," the future president retorted.[13]

It seems that no matter how fast our computers, no matter how many reports we produce, the real information we need to run our businesses seems to grind out with frustrating sparsity. At this rate we will all starve to death.

The 1960s and early 1970s were marked by a notable lack of data. As the end user computing revolution took hold in the early 1980s, we were already drowning in data. We began praying for information—data with perspective—what is commonly known as "the report."

Fueled by the personal computer, the data generated in the eighties became the answer to our prayers. But like the sorcerer's apprentice, once the reports started flowing we didn't know how to turn them off. As one analyst remarked, "I don't know what they [executive management] want, so I give them everything and let them decide." Management became inundated with reports when what we needed all along was not data with perspective, but reports with perspective. Whose perspective? *Your* perspective.

Executive information systems are the solution to the problem of how to customize information delivery.[14] Essentially, these systems allow executives to select and format information that is critical for making tough decisions. But that is only half the story.

You cannot select and format that which does not exist, and for most information systems, the *edge* is nonexistent. Behind every report that crosses your desk, the *edge* lurks, unseen, unheard, until it surprises you, seemingly out of nowhere. Considering its importance to your organization, this fact should make you very uncomfortable.

Most executives, even those who are computer literate, are passive consumers of information. The blame for this cannot be dropped on the doorstep of information systems, because every executive has the responsibility to actively demand the information that he or she requires to successively navigate the future. This cannot be done with old and aggregate data.

Executive information systems are far more than just the electronic delivery of reports and graphs. If the technology appears trivial, it is because it has all too often been implemented as trivial. The emphasis needs to be shifted away from the computer and toward business issues, both *edge* and mainstream, that every executive is struggling to address.

The unknown is scary, and the *edge* represents the unknown. No matter how much we try to anticipate the future, much of what we face is new territory. This is why leadership is so important, because a leader doesn't just tell you where you need to go. A leader shows the direction by going in advance of the rest of the organization.

The *edge* is a great asset to leadership, because it both points to new directions and provides a road map that shows how to get there. That is the first part of the battle for success. Persuading others to hear about the new land with open minds is the next part of the battle that we will explore.

18

Surefire Ways to Reduce Resistance

PREDICTING RESISTANCE

Japan's banks are in trouble. After more than half a decade, its top 21 banks still carry over $550 billion worth of bad loans or restructured loans, and these are conservative estimates. Despite bleak assessments by Moody's Investors Service, as well as other financial experts, little substantive action has been taken.

The Ministry of Finance (MOF) has tinkered with the system for years but has steadfastly refused to consider the fundamental deregulation generally believed to be the necessary fix. To embrace deregulation would mean an end of the power, prestige, and preparation that the MOF has enjoyed for decades. Without overwhelming "encouragement," it is unlikely the MOF will do anything more than apply window dressing at the fringes of the Japanese financial system.

Power, prestige, and preparation are all driven by the dominant paradigm, a concept introduced in Chapter 1. The dominant paradigm is so central to the culture of an organization, so systemic, that it becomes the last thing that any firm is willing to give up when times get really tough. It is also an excellent predictor of resistance.

This is why savvy analysts were not surprised that the personal computer was a flop at Xerox, where finance ruled as king. Jim O'Neill, who headed Xerox's information technology group, had come from Ford, where the dominant paradigm was "control through numbers." This was hardly conducive to an innovative environment. Bob Potter, head of the office systems group, noted:

> I had to get through O'Neill and his financial ratios, to stand the test of return on investment, and of marketing and business plans. Not just gut feel. The pressure on me was to make money.[1]

Subsumed by this cultural imperative, Potter himself became one of the primary resisters of word processing and the personal computer. "Moving to the office of the future cannot be a social revolution. It has to be an evolution."[2]

Xerox's resistance to the personal computer, and, more fundamentally, to risk taking, was predictable. The knowledge of such resistance is very dangerous in the hands of your competitor and very powerful when you have such knowledge of a competitor. It is also vital for anyone considering introducing change.

TIME: THE DOUBLE-EDGED SWORD

As the decade of the 1970s began to melt into the heated competition of the 1980s, there was little doubt from anyone at Xerox that the company was in trouble. The Japanese were selling copiers in the United States at a price that was less than Xerox could manufacture similar machines. To compound its problems, Xerox's personal computer efforts were floundering.

> "In 1979, morale was really getting low," said Eddie Miller, a management consultant who worked with Xerox at that time. "There were already people taking wagers on Kearns [Xerox president] not lasting the course. And a little bit of pain was beginning to show up because it was getting harder and harder to manage the numbers by selling off the lease base. . . . We kept talking to David [Kearns] periodically about how he really had to change the company. Then sometime in early 1980, he called us in for a frank discussion about change."[3]

Despite the performance problems, competition challenges, low morale, and groundswell requests for change, Xerox was still not *ready* for change. Kearns had already spent three years trying to create a new Xerox, with little to show for it. It wasn't until the end of 1980 that he declared his complete readiness to try anything new that would help Xerox. "It was clear that he'd crossed some kind of Rubicon. He said he'd decided he wanted to change the company and wanted our help."[4] Now Xerox was ready.

Change is ready for you far earlier than you are ready for it. This is the dilemma that comes from trying to time the introduction of change. The need for change arises long before a crisis situation develops, and exists even longer than it takes for the crisis to be recognized. The good news is that the *edge* can become your secret weapon in recognizing early the emergence of a crisis. The bad news is that, once recognized, most of your organization may act like Kearns in 1980—possibly aware that things are not great but not ready to change the dominant paradigm.

The *easiest* time to introduce dramatic change is during a crisis. People are eager for change because they have given up on the existing rules. The *best* time to introduce dramatic change is at the earliest recognition of that crisis, when it is still a twinkle in the eye of tomorrow. This is also, not surprisingly, the most difficult time. The more you learn from and act on the *edge*, the greater the resistance you can expect.

During a retreat in Phoenix, a vice president pulled me aside. He placed his hand on my shoulder and said in a confidential voice, "Wayne, I like your approach, so I am going to share with you the secret that I've developed to introduce successful change within my company." "I'm all ears," I said, honestly intrigued by this revelation. "What I do," he said, his whisper now barely audible, "is *create* a crisis. That way, people are eager for change!" He stood there, expectant smile on his face, waiting for me to be appropriately impressed. Fortunately, his boss diverted my attention before I had the opportunity to say what was on my mind.

Creating a crisis will definitely work. People will be far more open to your change ideas, and quite eager to act on them . . . once. By the second or third crisis, you have shot your credibility and placed your entire organization at great peril. Everyone will wonder whether the next crisis is real or whether you are crying wolf. Creating a crisis is not a recommended strategy—it is a desperate solution of last resort.

Throughout this chapter you will learn several safe and effective ways of reducing resistance. One fact is quite true, however; crisis is the best catalyst to initiate change. It is also the worst time to change. The key is learning to use *anticipated* crisis.

BECOMING SUPERMAN

George Bernard Shaw, in his play *Man and Superman*, portrays most of humanity as living for today, worried only about procreation and nourishment, money and pleasure. He likens humans to dinosaurs who, unable to anticipate the cliff, are just as likely to run right over the precipice. For Man, crisis is always a surprise. Motivation to change does little good as the ground comes rushing toward you.

Superman, according to Shaw, moves life forward by exploring, provoking and by anticipating what lies around the corner. Superman creates crisis, not by fabrication, but by anticipation. My conspiratorial vice president got it half right—crisis is a powerful motivator—but he will never join the ranks of Supermen. To become one of their elite, you must learn to anticipate and be able to communicate that vision in a compelling manner.

How do you persuade people to follow you based on an anticipated crisis? This can be a frustrating experience. With so much terrorism internationally, and experts and nonexperts alike agreeing it was "just a matter of time" before it hit the United States, you might think that the White House would have acted to fortify its defenses. Yet it took three direct attacks, as well as the Oklahoma City bombing, before the government took direct precautions.

Of course, an anticipatory politician is somewhat of an oxymoron, so no surprise here. The FBI, however, showing impressive anticipation, recognized that terrorists might just well use the type of "fertilizer" bomb employed in Oklahoma City. They experimented with that kind of material, exploded sample bombs, and were prepared. When the federal building was attacked, the FBI knew exactly what to look for and was able to respond with incredible speed.

Several techniques can work quite well in prompting action based on anticipated crises: benchmarking, stories, learning from others, and executive information systems (described in Chapter 17).

Benchmarking

I recently participated in a management meeting for one of the top consumer goods companies. I displayed a graph showing how well it had done during the previous year; the graph painted a picture of record sales and profits. I then superimposed a second graph and the room grew still. This graph reflected the recent performance of the company's three major competitors. The competitors' rate of growth substantially exceeded the company's and was projected to overtake it within 18 months.

An excellent way to get an organization, especially a successful organization, to anticipate crisis is to help it see beyond itself, and beyond today. Benchmarking forces organizations to confront and challenge their own insular optimism. It can lift laggard companies to a new level of performance and can prevent the best from slipping behind the pack.

If you are a peak performer in a particular area, look to other industries and other countries for companies against whom you can benchmark. People will complain "Oh, sure, *they* can perform that well, because . . . but for us, it's different." Every organization is different from the rest. There will always be reasons (excuses) why one can do it and another cannot. Under scrutiny, these reasons fall like a house of cards.

This is what ultimately saved Xerox. Most of the company was mired in the Ford-like process of phased program planning. Under this approach, every level and every function had to sign off on programs and their changes. Cycle time dragged, and excellence was dragged down to the lowest common denominator. Fuji-Xerox, however, was able to produce copiers of much higher quality and lower cost by delegating tasks and holding each small group accountable for its actions. Fuji-Xerox's accomplishments inspired CEO David Kearns to finally launch a major change initiative.

Xerox was fortunate to have a friendly relative (Fuji-Xerox) as a role model. Had that not been the case, the company most certainly would have suffered many more years before waking up to its crisis.

Benchmarking increases people's willingness to act on an anticipated crisis in direct relation to the degree of its visibility. The more vividly people see the benchmark, and the more frequently they see it, the more powerful the effect.

An executive information system is highly effective for this purpose. Regularly updated, the facts make it almost impossible for an organization to insulate itself. It is especially effective because it provides information in a manner that is meaningful to the viewer.

Stories

At the turn of the century, most people were aware of the cruel working conditions endured by many workers in the industrialized cities. Still the country was not moved to action. Upton Sinclair's *The Jungle* changed all of that. Following its publication, detailing the abject conditions under which employees of the meatpacking industry worked and lived, there was a public uproar. People began to act.

For a crisis to move people to action, it must be felt viscerally, not intellectually. Stories are powerful because they can transport us to a possible future and let us experience a crisis in a virtual sense. In 1995 the news services carried daily reports of a "killer" virus in Africa. It took the fictionalized movie *Outbreak*, and scarier still, the nonfiction novel *The Hot Zone*, by Richard Preston, before anyone appreciated just how serious the threat from the Ebola virus and other such contagions might become.

The use of the story to communicate anticipated crises does not demand the talents of a professional writer. Perhaps you will want to call it a "scenario," rather than a story. The term *scenario* is business jargon for boring story. Yours need not be boring, however. It can be a powerful way to communicate the urgent need for change. Simply follow a few simple steps, include them in a memo, and you are on your way. The steps are:

1. The tragic end—this is a brief but descriptive picture of the possible sad conclusion of events if the crisis is ignored.

2. Brief summary of events that have led up to today.

3. Conditions and characters that are in force today.

4. What conditions are either emerging today or may emerge tomorrow that will adversely affect us.

5. How the emerging events (#4) may combine with today's situation (#5) to create a crisis.

When using a story (scenario) to communicate an anticipated crisis, *always write that story as if it has already happened*. Never use the words *possibly* or *may* or *perhaps*. It is the fiction that it has already occurred that makes it powerful.

The following is a brief, sanitized version of a story I included in a memo to an organization some years back. In truth, it was only semisuccessful. Although it triggered serious discussions on issues that the company was unwilling to consider previously, including the competitive nature of each branch office, management decided that they had things under control and ignored the recommendations.

In 1995 Sunenco has suffered through two straight years of losses. It has been "right sized" three times, and morale is desperately low for both shareholders and employees. Once the market leader, it now drags behind products that are more functional, easier to use, and are less expensive but with higher quality. Sunenco's costs per sale are the highest in the industry; it is suspected that it actually loses money on each sale—the joke going around is that they will make it up with volume. There is no savior product in the foreseeable future.

Comment: As part of the history, I touched on some hot buttons at Sunenco, such as its products' complexity, and the high cost of sales.

Sunenco stumbled upon a niche just as its market began to take off, which was generally embraced as overwhelming market acceptance. Sunenco was approached by many innovative companies looking for joint ventures and marketing relationships. Quite a number of agreements were reached by corporate, but the branch offices' attitude was, at best, benign neglect. No one wanted to share customers and, potentially, share commissions.

Ultimately, the suitors tired of doing battle with the branches, and they either joined with new competitors or developed competing products themselves. The initial market enthusiasm, it turned out, was in reality from early adopters who had limited choices and unlimited funds. Once the cream had been skimmed, Sunenco was faced with a price-sensitive market that was extremely competitive.

Some of the new competitors employed state-of-the-art technology and applications far superior to that of Sunenco. Now the shoe was on the other foot. Sunenco courted others to join forces, but again, the branches would not cooperate. Corporate would make the relationship, and the branches would break it. No amount of pep talks and threats would budge the branch offices, as long as their compensation was pegged to the old "winner takes all" sales philosophy.

Without strategic alliances, and facing increased competition, the sales cycle continued to lengthen. Without the added value of alliances, aggravated by high competition, pricing also began to fall. In the end, sales, revenue, and profits all declined, while the cost of sales increased unabated.

OK, after reading this story, I am sure that you are thinking that I should keep my day job. Fortunately, rich character development and intricate plots are not important. The story/scenario will allow you to quickly relate, in a visceral way, a major problem that might be developing. This is infinitely more memorable than a mere memo or report could ever hope to be.

One word of warning—be careful where you post your story. One of my clients created a crisis scenario and posted it on the company electronic bulletin board. There it was passed from employee to employee, each adding his or her own twist. After ten days, it grew into marvelously biting characterization of the company's culture. It focused attention on much more than the one potential crisis, spawning a minirevolution within the company. The original author had more than a bit of explaining to do to the division's vice president.

Learning from Others

Nothing focuses the mind like failure—if not your failure, then the failure of someone so similar that it cannot be ignored. This is why learning from others is so effective. When done properly, the message is clear: "Ask not for whom the bell tolls. It tolls for thee."

The key to transforming another's real crisis into your anticipated crisis is accomplished through the application of consistent organizational pressure points. For example, if you worked at Sunenco, you would want to draw attention to the fact that internal competition was running head-on with the corporate intent. And don't stop with internal competition! List all the other areas of strategic vulnerability that you can think of (the mutated story off the previously mentioned bulletin board was filled with them).

Next, create a list of companies that seem to have walked through the fires of crisis *because* of your strategic vulnerability (internal competition). These are to be called your "reference companies." For each company, identify as many of its areas of strategic vulnerability as you can. This may take some research for you to find these firms, but your efforts will be immensely rewarded.

You have probably guessed that the next step is to select the reference companies that most closely match your own areas of strategic vulnerability. There is rarely a perfect match because there are usually multiple areas that play against each other.

For example, IBM suffered from internal competition between its mainframe and PC products but also lacked a customer-based orientation, was arrogant due to decades of success, and on top of it all, was enormously bureaucratic. These are qualities that would seem to be better suited to the IRS than to an international company designed to serve the public. However, the more of these areas of strategic vulnerability that you can match to your own pressure points, the better reference company it would become.

Try to select at least three reference companies, if possible. People may try to dismiss your "history lesson" because they easily spot all the reasons why "they" are different from "us." With three reference companies, the similarities (all centered around your primary areas of strategic vulnerability) acquire more weight than the differences—the pattern becomes clear.

It is not important for reference companies to be part of your industry. In fact, it may not even be advisable. Because of your organization's intimate knowledge of the competition, people can become overwhelmed with the detailed (but often superficial) differences. Selected from other industries, reference companies can easily accomplish your objective.

Finally, concerning your objective, remember that the use of reference companies is *not* to prove that you will inevitably share the same fate. Like a biblical prophet of old, your role is to point to a *possible* crisis that can be avoided entirely by taking appropriate action. At the very least you should be able to initiate important dialogue and help your organization to become more proactive. All in all, not a bad deal.

PROACTION AND REACTION

Not all anticipated crises will actually occur. Sometimes your actions (or should I say proactions) prevent the crisis. Chalk one up to anticipation. Other times, however, despite our best intentions, we are just flat-out wrong, and the crisis never materializes. Can we just shrug our shoulders and say, "Oh well, no harm done"?

Unless we are careful, promoting an anticipated crisis can render extraordinary harm. Company assets may be reallocated to stave off the crisis, robbing valuable resources from other programs. Perhaps more costly but difficult to measure is the loss of credibility every time we holler "crisis" and nothing materializes.

A case in point is the ozone "catastrophe." Those who communicated this anticipated crisis did everything right. With the help of the media, they vividly depicted the vision of what might (this soon became *would*) be. The Environmental Protection Agency (EPA) projected that ozone depletion would result in three million deaths by 2075. Proponents enlisted credible(?) sponsors such as Vice President Al Gore, who told the U.S. Senate that this was the "greatest crisis humanity has ever faced." Globally, nations rallied around the specter of this cataclysmic event. Such is the power of an anticipated crisis.

As a member in good standing of this planet, I was also concerned about the validity of these claims. I was troubled by the fact, however, that many of these proponents seemed to have too much to gain: The media was collecting viewers and readers, politicians were collecting media attention and voters, and the scientists were collecting vast sums of government funds to aid in their research.

The fact that those pointing to the crisis have a vested interest in it should not by itself dissuade anyone from becoming interested in those events. It should, however, give people cause to pause before jumping in with both feet. Our actions in response to an anticipated crisis should be in proportion to the certainty in which we hold that event. When it comes to the future, there ain't no such thing as a sure bet.

Investing funds to certify an anticipated crisis was appropriate. Creating early warning systems to track its progress was desirable. Establishing contingency plans, such as the first chlorofluorocarbon (CFC) phaseout, was probably prudent, given the enormity of the projected consequences and the lead time for action required. Each of these proactive events spoke to the importance of being reasonably prepared.

Somewhere between "20–20" and "Nightline" we lost the standard of reasonableness. Well-reputed scientists began cautioning that the link between CFC and the ozone was spurious. Others were questioning whether the ozone was truly shrinking. These dissenting voices were ignored. Rather than monitoring for confirmation, we began a global countdown until the inevitable event. Then, hyped by Vice President Gore's speech, the Senate voted 96 to 0 to move up the CFC ban by five years.[5]

S. Fred Singer, inventor of the satellite ozone monitor, wrote that the accelerated CFC ban was "based mainly on panicky reactions to press releases . . . rather than on published work that has withstood the scrutiny of scientific peers."[6] Top experts have maintained that the band of ultraviolet light that would penetrate a thinner ozone does not cause melanoma. Other experts have challenged virtually every aspect of the CFC crisis—and still we are poised to wreak havoc on industrialized production.

If it is found that the CFC and global warming crises are nonevents, we will have paid a terrible price. The real cost will ultimately not be the money and energy wasted, although that is certainly substantial enough. The true price of promoting an anticipated crisis as a real crisis is the loss of faith and credibility in our media and leaders. How many times do we think we can cry wolf?

THE CHANGE AGENT'S FATAL FLAW

Imagine that you were walking along a beach and found an ancient-looking bottle. Of course, you'd have to pick it up and examine it closely. It might be a valuable antique, or perhaps even . . . So, you remove the cork and look inside. Amazingly, a mist starts to swirl around, and before your astonished eyes a genie appears. Not your ordinary garden-variety genie, mind you. This turbaned genie is dressed in an Armani suit and is sporting a solid gold Rolex on his wrist. You have discovered the long lost business genie. "You have but one wish," the genie tells you, "and be quick about it—I am late for a meeting."

What do you ask for? Health? World peace? "No good," says the business genie, "for I am a specialist. Your wish must be cost effective, and therefore impact the bottom line of your organization." He looks at you impatiently.

"Well," you splutter, "I'd like you to endow me with a character trait that will help me to introduce change within my company."

"A good choice, my corporeal friend!" booms the genie. "But you get just one trait. What's it going to be?"

Your face lights up and you yell decisively, "*Passion!* If I have passion, the power of my convictions will sway all doubters. No, wait! Make that *expertise.* If I possess expertise, then I'll be able to answer all of their questions with authority, and change will be certain . . . I think."

The business genie smiles mischievously and says, "I am feeling generous today, mortal. I will bestow upon you both of these qualities."

You chortle with joy while the genie thinks, "Foolish mortal, because of your wish, this proposal for change will surely fail!" And the genie was quite right. Let's see why.

Passion

In 1847 Dr. Ignaz Philipp Semmelweis observed that 8.3 percent of women admitted to the maternity service died of puerperal sepsis, also known as childbed fever. He began to suspect that puerperal fever was being transmitted by medical students as they moved from the dissecting room to treating patients. Following the death of his close friend under similar circumstances, he took action.

Semmelweis had his students wash their hands, but after no improvement, he instructed them to wash in a solution of chlorinated lime. Mortality rates dropped to 2.3 percent, but resistance was widespread. "Wash our hands? Scrub our nails? We are residents and physicians, not schoolchildren!" They found the process humiliating and refused to do it. Semmelweis's peers found any number of reasons to explain away his success, and even more ways of rationalizing their own failures (they referred to them as "reality").

Semmelweis shared his results with anyone who would listen, and many who would not. He was driven, a nonconformist who did not "suffer fools gladly." When the director of his clinic would not support this new procedure, Semmelweis left for the University of Pest (in what is now Budapest, Hungary).

In his new post, mortality from puerperal sepsis dropped to an amazing 0.85 percent. He continued to rage at the "stupidity" of the medical community for not embracing such an "obviously important idea." Semmelweis became despondent. He claimed through the press that his colleagues were participating in a "massacre." In 1863, after pushing for 13 years, he wrote, "I find the amount of progress has not been made which is necessary for the welfare of mankind." Unable to free himself from the belief that thousands had died because of his failure to convince the medical community to adopt his findings, his depression deepened. In 1865 he was admitted to an insane asylum. He died six weeks later.

Semmelweis had passion—so much passion that in the end, it killed him. Yet that passion was not an asset but his fatal liability. Every week I meet people like Semmelweis—passionate, fiery, and absolutely convinced that those who resist are at best stupid and, at worst, self-serving and hypocritical. I admire the passion, but true believers make poor salespeople. Promoting change is all about sales.

The worst salesperson/change agent I have ever met is John Saxon, the test pilot turned math teacher turned publisher (see

Chapter 4). Invited to present his teaching method to a high school staff, he arrives all fire and brimstone. John has been known to literally jump onto a cafeteria table, point his finger at the group, and berate, shame, and insult the gathering. He has described contemporary teaching methods as "stupid, meaningless wastes of time," and, upon encountering resistance, has suggested that those who oppose his ideas are self-aggrandizing and care little for the students' best interests.

As you can tell from this description of Saxon's method, I admire and applaud both his ideas and his passion. He is not, however, the type of person you would willingly select as a change agent. As with most of the overzealous converted, his enthusiasm, in the final analysis, works against his cause.

Passion will attract those who are already converted and may sway a few sitting on the fence. Those who are inclined to defend the status quo, however, will not hear a word the zealots utter. Worse, it may actually turn them into enemies. Since the biggest defenders of the status quo are often (but not always) those in positions of power, passionate members of the *edge* offend the very decision makers that they are relying on to adopt the change. The greater the proposed change, the less effective passion becomes.

Expertise

A friend of mine has colitis and is plagued by periodic bouts of pain and discomfort. This is a disease that can be controlled by long treatments of medication, but there is no known cure. He told me that he found a book about curing colitis with diet and was going to give it a try. "Anything is better than what I've been going through," he explained.

A week later I asked him how the diet was going? "Actually, I stopped it yesterday," he admitted. "It was just too confusing. Many of the foods my doctor told me to meticulously avoid, the author says are permissible. Many other foods the doctor told me that I can eat, the author doesn't allow. I figured that I should only eat those foods allowed by both my doctor and the author, but there's just not much left." My friend then pointed out that this is a two-year, very restrictive diet. It was all too much for him to "swallow."

He lent me the book, and I read it from cover to cover. It is a perfect example of a brilliant expert's inability to sell a change. The book is called *Breaking the Vicious Cycle*.[7] It targets those suffering from serious digestive disorders, virtually all of whom would be receiving traditional medical treatment. The author, Elaine Gottschall, is an obviously knowledgeable expert in her field, holding a master's degree in nutrition and specializing in bowel problems. She does not, however, hold a medical degree.

The lack of a medical degree is not in and of itself a problem. As you know from reading this book, breakthroughs often come from those outside the traditional field. Lacking appropriate credentials, however, does tend to diminish your credibility with the mainstream. I read her book because I was interested in how she "sold" her ideas to the reader.

The book is 155 pages, broken down as follows:

- 84 pages of recipes.
- 46 pages explaining the theory behind the diet.
- 10 pages of references.
- 7 pages describing the diet.
- 6 pages proving "scientific evidence," which consists of two studies.
- 2 lines pointing out that the diet has helped her daughter and "Many students, friends, and others . . ."[8]

There was not one chapter, one page, even a single line that addressed existing popular medical treatments or the generally accepted diets. Gottschall's mistake is the same one committed by most experts; she is so taken with her own vision of what should be that she cannot understand why most people, like my friend, will not immediately turn their backs on the past, throw their arms in the air, and scream "Hallelujah!"

Gottschall's diet may well have merit. Further, I am sure that her book would be quite sufficient to persuade members of the *edge* (those who have or are ready to give up on the mainstream treatment) to give it a try. To convince the mainstream, however, requires more than just expertise—you need to be able to sell.

The downside to an expert presenting change ideas to the mainstream is identical to that of the passionate—they cannot see the concept through anyone's eyes but their own. Although their styles may differ (unless you are dealing with a passionate expert, in which case run for cover), they both are unlikely to present an idea from any perspective other than their own.

Even more problematic, the experts (especially *the* expert) are the ones who helped create the idea. This moves them from the role of change agent to that of parent. Make no mistake, these parents protect their young with vigor. I have yet to meet the inventor of any idea who, after having their "baby" attacked, could pause momentarily and say, "Good question!" Defensiveness is not an effective sales tactic.

Were I advising Elaine Gottschall, for example, I would recommend that she add the following to her book:

- Why the medical community has missed the compelling truth of her diet.
- Why the medical establishment prescribes the diet it does, and what is wrong with that diet.
- Why foods specifically not permitted by most physicians are acceptable on her diet.
- Statistical evidence that her diet is effective.
- Without statistical evidence, more anecdotal evidence to illustrate its effectiveness.

Of course, if her program had not required such a prolonged commitment (two years), or such a radical departure from the standard diet, the need for additional justification and explanation would have been less. The greater the pain and/or risk of the proposed change, however, the greater the need to explain, justify, and add credibility.

The following is an insightful passage from the book *The Cry and the Covenant*,[9] a historically based novel covering Semmelweis's attempts to change the medical mainstream. Semmelweis had just completed presenting his case on how to prevent childbed fever to a medical review commission in Prague:

> He sat down. For a moment there was silence. . . . "I make this motion, that Dr. Semmelweis be asked to elaborate on his theory at the next meeting."
> More? he thought to himself. All right, I will tell them more. I will tell them the same thing all over again if necessary. Hebra

carried him off to dine at his house. "Now," he said jubilantly, "you must work out an elaboration."

"You know, it troubles me, I don't see how to elaborate, really. What more is there to say?"

"Oh, there's always a lot of loose ends, little things. Bring up the matter of prophylaxis in surgery, for instance . . . elaborate on that. And next time hit back at Scanzoni, Seyfert, and Braun. You said nothing about why their attempts with chlorine washing didn't work."

"Answer Zipfel too?"

"Answer everybody. Every fool in Europe, if necessary."

In one line, Morton Thompson captured the reason that, after 14 years, Semmelweis was unable to convince the medical mainstream. "I don't see how to elaborate, really. What more is there to say?" Semmelweis was a passionate expert, and he didn't see, he couldn't see, the world from any perspective other than his own.

THE PERFECT CHANGE AGENT

Both experts and the passionate see the need and rationale for their ideas as being self-evident. It is not that they are unwilling to explain; they honestly don't see how their points could be any more obvious. As a result, it is the rare invested change agent who can explain without some trace of irritation and frustration in his or her voice.

Who, then, should propose change? The ideal candidate should have credibility in the eyes of those you wish to persuade. The more believable the candidate, the easier your job of selling the idea.

Albert Einstein is an excellent example of a perfect change agent. In 1939, in collaboration with several other renowned physicists, he wrote a letter to President Roosevelt. In it, he described the possibility of making an atomic bomb and expressed his opinion that a similar development by the Germans was likely. The letter was signed by only Albert Einstein.

Einstein was well known to be a pacifist—he was one of the last people who would be expected to support the bomb. Further, he had unquestioned credibility. Most historians credit that letter with swaying Roosevelt to support the bomb's development. Einstein the change agent altered the balance of the war.

The candidate should also have knowledge about, but not be overly invested in, the new idea. Those with considerable investment (time, money, emotion) will have a difficult time escaping the passion and expertise trap. Further, those you wish to persuade will tend to be suspicious of anyone they know to be invested.

Beyond those two criteria, you want the candidate to be a good communicator, someone who can listen and respond well to both questions and assaults. Introducing change has no place for defensiveness or evasiveness. You must try for an atmosphere of open and honest communication.

Some people tell me that they bring in consultants to play the role of change agent. That approach does have some compelling logic. Consultants are not typically invested in the change, so they avoid both the passion and expert trap. They are often experienced communicators, and that makes for constructive meetings.

On the downside, consultants typically lack two key attributes, and this disqualifies most from becoming change agents for hire. First, they lack believability. No, I am not saying that you cannot believe consultants. As change agents, however, they are paid for this purpose, and everyone knows it.

The second reason that consultants usually are not good change agents is because they are perceived as lacking commitment—of not being connected emotionally or intellectually to the idea. Too much emotional connection, and you fall into the passion trap. Too little, and people are left cold. If you don't care about the idea, why should they?

BREAKING DOWN THE WALLS

The *edge*, as well as people who present ideas from the *edge*, face a significant challenge. The people they need to sway are the decision makers, people who possess one or more of the three Ps: power, prestige, and preparation. They often owe their success to the status quo and are less than thrilled at anything perceived as an attack on the established order.

To further complicate matters, the *edge* and its promoters typically lack credibility. In fact, much of the *edge* actually has negative credibility. How can you get the people who count to listen?

Benefit versus Advantage

When a major accounting firm enlisted my aid last year, it was desperate. The firm had developed a breakthrough product, and it couldn't give it away. The software package it designed had initially been intended for in-house use exclusively, but it soon became clear that the company had a revolutionary item on its hands that could automate accounting, billing, and inventory in one fell swoop. After almost 18 months of marketing attempts, management was getting discouraged.

They decided to conduct a public seminar to show people what they were missing, and they spared no expense in the attempt. Invitations were sent, and a buffet lunch was promised. When a full house showed up, they were jubilant. I sat in the back of the room to watch the proceedings.

Their presentation consisted of a thorough description of the product, and a well-thought-out, seemingly impressive set of advantages. Six members of the team took turns fielding questions from the audience, but from my vantage point, more people were eyeing the buffet table than the products being touted by my clients. A handful of orders were written up, but business could hardly be called brisk. When the presentation was over, I tucked my badge into my pocket and circulated in the atrium as the audience descended on the promised feast.

"Neat product," one banker said to the other, helping himself to the roast beef. "Yeah," said the other, "it doesn't fit with our business, but it's impressive." Pouring some coffee, a woman from a large retail chain was talking to her boss. "The demonstration gave me some great ideas," she enthused. "The way they handle inventory reminds me of another package that I heard about. Marlene loves it!" Her boss suggested that she get some information on it. "On their product?" she asked, pointing to the presentation room. "No, the inventory thing you mentioned. Marlene knows her stuff, so it must be good. I know we're having a problem. . . . "

During the debrief, I mentioned the conversations I overheard. The group was incensed. "We do those things," one of the presenters complained, "and much more, too! How could they have missed it?" After some more hand-wringing and general griping, the product manager turned to me and asked, "How do you get people to listen when they don't want to change?"

The question was a good one. How *do* you make people listen to your ideas?

This group of programmers and accountants were very skilled at presenting the compelling advantages they offered. They in essence were saying: "Here are the top ten reasons that you can't live without this product." With such an array of pluses, how could anyone resist?

An *advantage* is an outcome that is desirable, and that is a good start. A *benefit* is a desirable outcome that accrues to a specific person or group. To put it bluntly, a benefit is the answer to the inevitable question: What is in it for me?

Put yourself in the position of the banker sitting in on the seminar. He doesn't want to change. He probably doesn't see any pressing need to change. He has survived very nicely up to this point, thank you very much. He listens to the first stated advantage . . . and doesn't relate. He thinks about the second advantage . . . still no connection. Anything beyond that is noise.

When people believe they are in crisis, they want to change and will be desperate for every idea. They will look at any reasonable suggestion and try to figure out how it might benefit them. They will struggle to find connections even where they may not exist. Most people who you will deal with, however, are not nearly so motivated. They don't actively want to change. If the value of the idea does not jump right out at them, they just turn off. Every benefit is an advantage, but many advantages produce no benefits.

Sony and Philips have a lot to learn about the difference between advantage and benefit. Working together, they promoted their videodisc system to Hollywood. "Revolutionary," they said. "It will herald a new era." In particular they chose to emphasize its future recording potential. To Hollywood, where paranoia over copyright infringement is rampant, this was hardly a benefit!

Just one year before its Hollywood debacle, Sony was promoting the DAT (digital audiotape) format for tapes to the music industry. Although it offered CD-like quality using tapes, it was also a recordable media. The music industry, like Hollywood, was so distrustful of copyright infringement that most recording companies refused to support DAT. At least Sony is consistent.

To Sony, the recordability of the videodisc was an advantage. To the music industry, it was no benefit. To produce a benefit, you must know something about the critical needs of the customer for your idea. The advantage must be something that customers can relate to; otherwise, your potential customers will quickly tire of your harangues.

Associated Believability

Steve Wozniak was not believable when he suggested the personal computer to Hewlett-Packard. He was a "lowly" technician. Semmelweis was unpublished. Patrick Beauchamp, the drilling fluids engineer, had never even taken a single course in pharmaceuticals. None of these people were believable. They were all members of the *edge*.

This is the *edge*'s dilemma: The people who are most likely to have breakthrough ideas often have the lowest believability factor. They are typically greeted with the time-honored salutation: "Who the hell are you?!" As a group, the *edge*:

- Lacks credentials.
- Is unpublished.
- Lacks a track record of success.
- Knows little or nothing about your field.
- Is not part of upper management.

On those rare occasions when the *edge* does have some level of professional respectability, they are perceived as mavericks— "Oh, you know Mary . . . she's always coming up with off-the-wall ideas." Regardless of how compelling the change may be, when considering the source, it is too easy to dismiss an idea based solely on the person presenting it.

A simple and powerful solution to a low believability factor is to acquire what is referred to as *associated believability*."[10] Consider who you are trying to sell the idea to, and discover who he or she holds as believable. Then find a way to associate your idea with that person or group.

For example, let's assume you are advising Elaine Gottschall, the author of the colitis diet book. You might have the following conversation:

"Elaine, who are you trying to sell your ideas to?"—She responds that she has multiple targets: physicians, people with gastric diseases, and nutritionists. This is quite usual. Change agents normally have multiple targets. Part of your role as an adviser is to help her understand that they are very different targets, each with different benefits and criteria for believability.

"Of your three major targets, let's start by selecting one."— Elaine decides to select her biggest target, people with diseases. That is progress. You can only successfully sell to one group at a time.

"What people, groups, or companies do longtime sufferers of gastric diseases hold as credible?"—Elaine doesn't like to admit it, but despite only mediocre success in curing these illnesses, people still have quite a bit of faith in physicians. They also place a lot of stock in others who have been through similar experiences.

You would then suggest to Elaine that she try to get endorsements from some of the top medical schools. If she can't, you might suggest that she research what some of the top experts have published, and find a way to associate their remarks with her findings.

When you read her book, you are pleased to find that she does refer to two physicians, which would be great, except that they both practiced at the turn of the century. Strike one. You also note that she includes a handful of patient endorsements, but these lack any substantial description of their cases. Without those descriptions, it is difficult to relate to them. If you can't relate, no believability. Strike two. Struggling to help, your optimism perks up when you find that she includes reference to two studies . . . until you read that the studies consisted of less than 30 people. Strike three!

In business, associated believability is actually quite easy. Use the same process I described with Gottschall.

1. *Select your target individuals or groups,* based on both desired benefits and believability requirements.

2. *Discover who they hold as credible.* If you cannot, ask secretaries and employees. If you still are not sure, quoting the top gurus (e.g., Peter Drucker) and publications (e.g., *Wall Street Journal* or *Harvard Business Review*) is usually safe. In the last decade, Japan has also been useful—"In Japan, they handle team decision making like this. . . ." General Electric, Motorola, and Hewlett-Packard also are regularly referenced in this way.

3. *Find a way to associate your proposal* with the believable individuals, groups, companies, or nations. Never before has information access been so easy. This step is by far the easiest.

THE INSULT OF CHANGE

After years of working in the field of change, and even more years of observing the human condition, I have come to an epiphany—don't call the people whose support you seek stupid. I am sure you are curious as to how I arrived at this subtle psychological principle. Amazingly, I see it violated regularly.

Consider this recent event that fairly typifies the finesse some people demonstrate while introducing change. Michael managed a small group called the New Venture Support Group (NVSG). This group was responsible for investigating proposed high capital projects and exploring ways to make them successful. One of NVSG's more successful ventures involved providing the components to construct high-pressure pipes. This business was launched by one of Michael's predecessors almost ten years ago.

The research department of the company had recently made a breakthrough in the formulation of coating material. Michael's NVSG believed that with this material, it could construct the entire pipe and not sell merely a component. The group worked for two weeks on the following proposal, and Michael was prepared to make his case before the review committee. To the best of my recollection, this was the exchange:

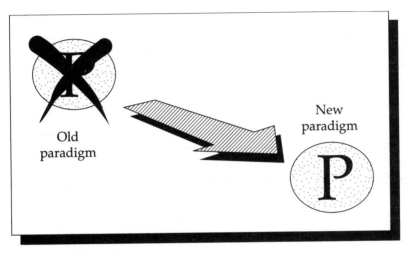

Figure 18-1. Old versus new paradigm.

Michael: This process will revolutionize our involvement in the industry! *(Interpretation: This can rock the boat of an already successful business.)*

Michael: The old components business is a dinosaur by comparison. This new approach will stave off its imminent demise. *(Interpretation: The old components business [which by the way, many of you fine people were responsible for] is a stupid business. I am much hotter stuff than you ever were.)*

Committee member: Michael, the existing components business is doing very well. It is consistently profitable and is an integral part of our strategic plan.

Michael: That strategic plan is two years out of step. We need to become a global player, and this is the only way to get there. We've got to let go of the old paradigms. *(Interpretation: You are stupid, out of touch, and throwbacks to an era gone by.)*

Anyone want to take odds on Michael's tenure with the firm?

No matter how you look at it, what Michael had just told those people—that they are useless appendages—is not a good way to win friends and influence people. Yet this is what we do every day. By presenting our new ideas as superior replacements for the status quo (Figure 18-1), we insult every person connected with the status quo.

What is the solution? Recognize that people personally associate themselves with the ideas that they helped create. Attack those ideas, and you attack the person. The key is to present your new idea in a way that does not confront the previous one.

Let's revisit the presentation Michael made to the review committee, this time using a more constructive approach:

Michael: The components business was one of the best new ventures to come along in a long time. It provided strategic connections we lacked and has produced cash at a time when it was badly needed. *(Interpretation: This is what Joel Barker calls "honoring the innovator." Michael recognizes that any action taken in the past was for the best interests of the organization, and he should acknowledge it.)*

Michael: In the past decade, while the components business continues to enjoy record sales, we have seen a major shift in circumstances. Increased globalization has brought with it increased competition, and with that, a constantly shrinking margin. To remain competitive in components will require a major investment in new facilities. *(Interpretation: While continuing to honor the innovator Michael draws attention to the change in conditions. Notice that he can still make a powerful case for change without attacking the original idea.)*

Michael: Although the simpler aspects of pipe production have moved downstream, there are still only a few players who have the know-how and facilities capable of producing the entire pipe. This area of the business has retained its profitability. Further, as components production becomes more of a commodity business, the potential for strategic linkages has been seriously diminished. *(Interpretation: Michael must still make a strong case for the new conditions, since they become the foundation for his proposal.)*

Michael: Because conditions have changed so much, we need to consider expanding the strategic linkage approach that was so successfully used these past years. We can leverage our experience and success into a new set of opportunities. *(Interpretation: Rather than describe his program as "revolutionary," Michael positions it as an enhancement of what has come before. At this point he is swept off his feet and rides off on the shoulders of the review committee.)*

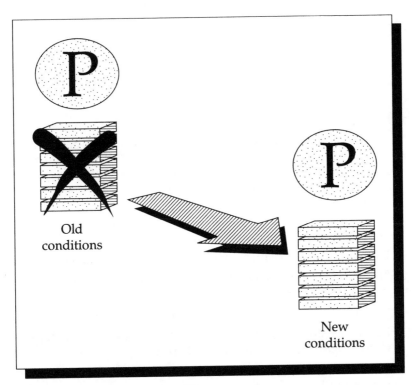

Figure 18-2. Old versus new conditions.

Naturally, there is no guarantee that the review committee will accept the proposition that the old conditions have changed (Figure 18-2). They may not even agree that new conditions are compatible with Michael's new proposal. This is not snake oil selling. You still must make a compelling case for change.

What this process does accomplish is to transform the change proposal from one of personal confrontation to one of personal communication. If people disagree, they are more apt to disagree on intellectual, rather than purely emotional, grounds. You can suggest change to people who do not think they are in crisis and still get them to listen . . . just don't call them stupid.

Notes

Chapter 1

1. Throughout this book I use IBM as an example of an organization that has consistently lacked wide-angle vision. I have enormous respect for IBM. With a few notable exceptions, however, it has repeatedly disappointed me by its inability to see the *edge*. While drawing on many other companies, I also often refer to IBM because I believe much of the analysis of their challenges (such as arrogance) have been overly simplistic.

2. From an interview with an ex-Clark executive, November 2, 1995.

3. "How U.S. Forklift Makers Dropped the Goods," *Business Week*, June 15, 1992, p. 106.

4. "Boeing: Sleepy in Seattle," *Fortune*, August 7, 1995, p. 96.

5. Kathy Rebello, "What If Apple Held a Software Sale and Nobody Came?" *Business Week*, July 19, 1993, p. 23.

6. Kathy Rebello, "Anybody Wanna Clone a Mac?" *Business Week*, September 26, 1994, p. 64.

Chapter 2

1. Joel Barker called this inability to see the "Paradigm Effect." He observed the first two forms (invisibility and impossibility). I later added the third form, transferability.

2. Editors of Horizon Books, *The French Revolution* (New York: American Heritage, 1965).

3. Lieutenant Kermit Tyler, quoted from Walter Lord, *Day of Infamy* (New York: Henry Holt, 1957), p. 48.

4. Lee Smith, "Rubbermaid Goes Thump," *Fortune*, October 2, 1995, p. 100.

5. Walter Laqueur, *The Dream That Failed: Reflections on the Soviet Union* (New York: Oxford Press, 1995).

6. Dean Phypers, quoted in Paul Carroll's *Big Blues* (New York: Crown Publishers, 1993), p. 60.

7. Dana Tanyeri, "Getting Clubbed," *ID: The Voice of Foodservice Distribution*, June 1995, p. 65.

8 Ibid., p. 66.

9 Paul Carroll, *Big Blues* (New York: Crown Publishers, 1993), p. 134.

10 David Owen, "Copies in Seconds," *The Atlantic Monthly*, February 1986, p. 70.

11 Marc Levinson, "Dismal Science Grabs a Couch," *Newsweek*, April 10, 1995, p. 42.

12 Ken Olsen, quoted by David H. Ahl, *The Experts Speak* (New York: Pantheon Books, 1984), p. 209.

Chapter 3

1 Based on discussions with Jacob Miles, November 28, 1995.

2 From interviews with a senior manager at Hewlett-Packard, October 19, 1995.

3 Based on a conversation with John Saxon, March 9, 1995.

4 Anne Faircloth, "The World Takes on the USPS," *Fortune*, July 24, 1995, p. 28.

5 The real company behind Kranton and Company withheld permission to use its real name. This is quite common with companies about whom you have few positive things to say. It is also common with those firms who believe their work on the *edge* gives them a competitive advantage. Kranton and Company, for whom I have much respect, shared none of these motivations. Their culture is one of remaining low-key. Although the company showed itself quite capable of challenging and changing culture in some areas, clearly there are some lines it will not cross.

6 Greg Gleason, Abbie Griffin, Rich Preiss, and Dave Shevenaugh, "Best Practice for Customer Satisfaction in Manufacturing Firms," *Sloan Management Review*, Winter 1995, p. 87.

7 The following discussion is based on several interviews with Bruce Grench and Lisa Messmer, September 11, 1995.

Chapter 4

1 "Smith Corona to Mexico," *Television Digest*, July 27, 1992, p. 16.

2 Ibid.

3 Author's interview with John Saxon, March 1994.

4 "Math Angles & Saxon," *National Review*, November 25, 1988, p. 30.

5 As reported by teachers at North Dallas High School.

6 Based on interviews with Gordon Peters December 14, 1995.

7 From an interview with Dr. Francis Barnes, M.D., October 11, 1995.

8 "Renegade Surgeon Seeks to Compete with Hospitals," *Business First—Columbus*, January 30, 1995, p. 3.

Chapter 5

1 I worked with Surtak in the fall of 1994. All quotes are from conversations during our meetings.

2 From discussions with Jacob Miles November 28, 1995.

3 Based on conversations with Patrick Naughton March 7, 1996.

Chapter 6

1 Paul Carroll, *Big Blues* (New York: Crown Publishers, 1993), p. 3.

2 "Pick a Number, Any Number," *Worth*, April 1995, p. 82.

3 Peter M. Senge, *The Fifth Discipline* (New York: Doubleday/Currency, 1990).

4 "A Snail's Take on Climate Change," *Science News*, March 4, 1995, p. 143.

5 From interviews with a Secret Service agent who asked not to be identified, June 1995.

6 I worked at Uniroyal Chemical Company during this time. The events are based on my experiences while there.

7 Rai Acharya, "An Early-Warning System for Bone Loss," *Business Week*, February 20, 1995, p. 55.

Chapter 7

1 From discussions with a manager who works at Rubbermaid, April 7, 1995.

2 George Will, "The Excuse Industry," *Newsweek*, December 11, 1989.

3 Douglas K. Smith and Robert C. Alexander, *Fumbling the Future: How Xerox Invented, Then Ignored, the First Personal Computer* (New York: William Morrow and Company, 1988), p. 121.

4 George Will, "The Excuse Industry," *Newsweek*, December 11, 1989.

5 Kathleen Kerwin, "Vapor Lock at GM," *Business Week*, November 7, 1994, p. 28.

Chapter 8

1 B. Bower, "Brain Clues to Energy-Efficient Learning," *Science News*, April 4, 1992, p. 215.

2 Ibid.

3 Paul Carroll, *Big Blues* (New York: Crown Publishers, 1993), p. 64.

4 Unfortunately, this story was related to me on a plane. I lost the woman's business card, and so, regrettably, I cannot give her credit.

Chapter 9

1 This is changing. It is more common now to court regulatory involvement as early as possible, although it is still doubtful the FAA would agree to a role in an *edge* team.

Chapter 10

1 Based on conversations with Patrick Naughton March 7, 1996.

Chapter 11

1 Justin Martin, "Ignore Your Customer," *Fortune,* May 1, 1995, p. 121.

2 Thomas J. Martin, "Ten Commandments for Managing Creative People," *Fortune,* January 16, 1995, p. 135.

3 I hold no personal grudge against Kaplan Educational Centers. In fact, they have done an excellent job of reinventing themselves, prompted largely by the Princeton Review competition. To their credit, they avoided becoming another Schwinn. While they could and should have responded sooner, they did not wait until their position was unsalvageable. Today, Kaplan offers preparation classes competitive with those provided by Princeton.

Chapter 12

1 This technique was first shown to me by Joel Barker in 1987. Although I have enhanced its application over the years, Joel deserves full credit for its invention.

2 "The Lab Where Madame Butterfly Meets Mr. Chips," *Business Week,* January 30, 1995, p. 75.

3 Lisa Sanders, "From H-Bombs to Video," *Forbes,* March 27, 1995, p. 120.

4 "An Early-Warning System for Bone Loss," *Business Week,* February 20, 1995, p. 91.

5 George Schmidt, "I've Got You Under My Skin," *Omni,* June 1992, p. 31.

6 Based on three independent clinical tests.

7 "A Shot at Gumshoe Seismology," *Science News,* May 29, 1992, p. 351.

Chapter 13

1 During a conversation with Roger Smith at an automotive industry conference in 1987.

2 Paul Carroll, *Big Blues* (New York: Crown Publishers, 1993), p. 62.

3 Ibid, p. 63.

Chapter 14

1 Rahul Jacob, "Corporate Reputations," *Fortune*, March 6, 1995, p. 56.

2 Peter Lee, "It Doesn't Have to Be American," *Euromoney Magazine*, April 1995, p. 45.

3 Walter Laqueur, *The Dream That Failed: Reflections on the Soviet Union* (New York: Oxford Press, 1995), p. 114.

Chapter 15

1 Michael Hammer and James Champy, *Reenginering the Corporation* (New York: HarperCollins, 1993).

2 James Champy, *Reengineering Management* (New York: Harper-Business, 1995).

3 Ibid.

Chapter 16

1 Farrell Kramer, "Foreign Rivals Can't Be Blamed for Schwinn's Fall," *Business Week*, August 23, 1993, p. 79.

2 Ibid.

Chapter 17

1 Peter F. Drucker, "The New Business Game," *The Wall Street Journal*, 2 February 1993, 14.

2 Douglas K. Smith and Robert C. Alexander, *Fumbling the Future: How Xerox Invented, Then Ignored, the First Personal Computer* (New York: William Morrow and Company, 1988), p. 189.

3 Stephanie Losee, *Fortune*, October 3, 1994, p. 17.

4 Stephen Jay Gould, *Wonderful Life: The Burgess Shale and the Nature of History* (New York: Norton, 1989), pp. 320–321.

5 Ibid., pp. 47–68, pp. 232–238.

6 Frederik Pohl, "The Uses of the Future," *The Futurist*, March–April, 1993. p. 9.

7 Ibid.

8 C. K. Prahalad.

9 C. K. Prahalad and Gary Hamel, "The Core Competence of the Corporation," *Harvard Business Review*, May–June 1990, p. 82.

10 C. K. Prahalad and Gary Hamel, *Competing for the Future* (Boston: Harvard Business School Press, 1994), pp. 204–206.

11 Myron Magnet, "No More Mickey Mouse at Disney," *Fortune*, December 10, 1984, p. 58.

12 Prahalad and Hamel, *Competing for the Future*, p. 211.

13 Peter Hay, *The Book of Business Anecdotes* (New Jersey: Wings Books, 1993), p. 91.

14 For more information on executive information systems, including a detailed description of conducting executive interviews, you may want to read *Executive Information Systems: From Proposal Through Implementation* by Wayne C. Burkan (New York: Van Nostrand Reinhold, 1991).

Chapter 18

1 Douglas K. Smith and Robert C. Alexander, *Fumbling the Future: How Xerox Invented, Then Ignored, the First Personal Computer* (New York: William Morrow and Company, 1988), p. 169.

2 "The Office of the Future," *Business Week*, June 30, 1975.

3 Smith and Alexander, *Fumbling the Future*, p. 220.

4 Ibid., p. 223.

5 For an excellent article on this crisis overhype, see Paul Craig Roberts's "Quietly, Now, Let's Rethink the Ozone Apocalypse," *Business Week*, June 19, 1995.

6 *Technology*: Journal of the Franklin Institute, 1995.

7 Elaine Gottschall, *Breaking the Vicious Cycle* (Kirkton, Ontario: The Kirkton Press, 1994).

8 Ibid., p. 1.

9 Morton Thompson, *The Cry and the Covenant* (New York: Doubleday & Company, 1954), p. 327.

10 This concept was first introduced by Everett Rogers, *Diffusion of Innovations* (New York: The Free Press, 1983).

Index